A Guide to
the Selected Poems of
T. S. ELIOT

A Guide to
the Selected Poems of
T. S. ELIOT

Sixth Edition

B. C. Southam

A HARVEST ORIGINAL
HARCOURT BRACE & COMPANY
San Diego   New York   London

Library of Congress Cataloging-in-Publication Data
Southam, B. C.
[Guide to the selected poems of T. S. Eliot]
A guide to the selected poems
of T. S. Eliot/B. C. Southam.—6th ed.
p.   cm.
Originally published: London: Faber and Faber, 1994.
"A Harvest original."
Includes bibliographical references.
ISBN 0-15-600261-2
1. Eliot, T. S. (Thomas Stearns), 1888–1965—
Criticism and interpretation—Handbooks, manuals, etc.
I. Title.
PS3509.L43Z869   1996
821'.912—dc20   96-4007

Printed in the United States of America
First U.S. edition 1996
C E F D

Contents

Acknowledgements

I would like, first, to thank Mrs Valerie Eliot for her interest and advice in the preparation of this book. I am most grateful for the suggestions and corrections which she has so kindly and patiently advanced. My second, and more general debt, is to the long line of scholars and critics who have written on the poetry of Eliot. I have drawn upon hundreds of books and articles, and consulted thousands of notes, so many that a full list of acknowledgements would be pages long. At the risk of discourtesy, I would like to excuse myself from such a listing, mentioning instead only the key works, from which I have learnt much in my general approach to Eliot and in the treatment of specific details. These works are listed on pages 265–7; and of these I must acknowledge my prime debt to the one indispensable guide to Eliot's sources and references – *T. S. Eliot's Poetry and Plays* by Professor Grover Smith.

I am grateful for this opportunity to express my thanks to a number of colleagues and friends who have been kind enough to let me make use of their judgement and scholarship: Philip Gaskell; Rebecca Mead; Lyndall Gordon; John Haffenden; Miss Lesley Brown of Routledge and Kegan Paul; the late F. W. Bateson, Corpus Christi College, Oxford; Martin Dodsworth, University of London; the late Professor J. C. Maxwell, Balliol College, Oxford; Hyam Maccoby, Dr Roger Gard, Canon Frank Colquhoun; Antony Woolf, who helped me in fact-finding; Stephen Erskine-Hill, whose discussions with me of the *Selected Poems* called this book into being.

I also have to thank Michael Herbert of St Andrews University for his valuable list of suggestions and corrections to the Third Edition.

For their help in this Sixth Edition, I would like to thank Gordon Williams of the University of Wales, Dr Heather Bryant Jordan of Harvard, Andrew Wiffin, M. Pierre Leyris, Michael Hastings, Dr G. C. Faulkes (Institute of Zoology, London), Dr R. W. Bushaway (University of Birmingham), Colin Bruce (Imperial War Museum), Professor Andrew Roberts (University of London), Dr Kevin Ray (Washington University Library), Dr Ione Martin, Dr John Mack (The Museum of Mankind), Christopher Ricks, Kenneth Blackwell and Noel Stock.

Preface

'The more we know of Eliot, the better.'

Ezra Pound, 1969

'And I am accustomed to more documentation; I like to know where writers get their ideas from.'

Charles Augustus Conybeare (alias 'Old Possum' Eliot), in the correspondence columns of *The Egoist*, December 1917

This *Guide* must open with a word of explanation. People are rightly suspicious of notes – and this book is made up of little else. Worse still, they are notes that seem to load the reading of poetry with a burden of fact and speculation. But in compiling this *Guide* my one aim has been to help the reader towards his own understanding of Eliot's poetry in the volume of *Selected Poems*. Basically, this *Guide* is an aid, to be used like any dictionary or work of reference, to be consulted and then put aside.

It was my original intention to keep the notes quite free of interpretation. But in some cases our recognition of a source, an allusion or some other kind of 'fact' is dependent upon interpretation. So, in the event, it has proved impossible to exclude this speculative element from notes which are primarily factual.

A second intention I have kept to: that is to avoid any direct critical discussion of Eliot's poetic methods. Clearly, this would touch upon questions of organization and unity in poetry which involves a good deal of quotation and external reference. These are questions which arise with every poem. Our view of Eliot's achievement cannot remain unaffected by our knowledge of his areas of reference and allusion, and by our understanding of the uses to which this material is put. These matters are left for the reader to judge for himself.

In attending so closely to Eliot's sources, we do so with the knowledge that they were important to the poet himself. On a copy of *Ara Vos Prec* (his third collection, published in 1920), Eliot privately pencilled in some of these references for an old friend. On the other hand, he could be possum-like (Pound's description) when questioned and I have recorded his response to other people's speculations about the sources and meaning of his work. This is somewhat in the spirit of the second quotation at the head of this Preface. Eliot was a joker and it is useful to sense this trap (for very often it is a deceptive trap) in his writing and to understand the layers of concealment that Old Possum so ingeniously devised for himself.

There was no such irony, however, to Eliot's admission at the opening of his 'Dante' essay:

> In my own experience of the appreciation of poetry I have always found that the less I knew about the poet and his work, before I began to read it, the better. A quotation, a critical remark, an enthusiastic essay, may well be the accident that sets one to reading a particular author ...

In that case, Eliot found 'an elaborate preparation of historical and biographical knowledge' to be 'a barrier'.

This *Guide* is organized – simply and straightforwardly – in the same spirit, trusting to Eliot's maxim 'that genuine poetry can communicate before it is understood'.

Preface to the Sixth Edition

Over the twenty years of its existence this *Guide* has been updated in each of the six successive editions, in an attempt to keep abreast of the quantity of new material which has come to light. In 1968, the long-lost manuscript of *The Waste Land* was discovered together with the manuscripts of some of the most important of the early *Selected Poems* (including 'Preludes', 'Prufrock', 'Portrait of a Lady', 'Rhapsody on a Windy Night' and 'Mr Eliot's Sunday Morning Service'). Three years later appeared Mrs Eliot's edition of *The Waste Land* manuscript; in 1977, Lyndall Gordon's *Eliot's Early Years*; in 1978, Helen Gardner's *The Composition of Four Quartets*. Most recently have appeared the first volume of the collected letters, up to 1922, and Lyndall Gordon's *Eliot's New Life* (1988). All these books contain important information about the poet's life and works and I have drawn upon them freely in the revision of this *Guide*.

The availability of the manuscript materials has stimulated critical attention to the genesis of Eliot's poetry and to the relationship between his poetry and his life. This has a direct bearing upon this Sixth Edition of the *Guide*, since we are now able to confirm the extent of Eliot's serious engagement with the literature of anthropology, from his student years at Harvard on into the 1920s, an interest which emerges in his poetry, both before and after *The Waste Land*. There has been similar recent attention to the major classics of the Hindu and Buddhist traditions, which Eliot also studied at Harvard. He confirmed that the Upanishads and *Bhagavadgita* were the prime Eastern texts which influenced his poetry and said that when he wrote *The Waste Land* he had been on the verge of becoming a Buddhist.

I have also drawn attention to the influence of Bergson in the Paris poems, up to 1913, and added some guarded speculations of my own, including the suggestion that Eliot used his knowledge of music halls in the final version of *The Waste Land*; and I have mentioned some of the tantalizing puzzles which remain in the poetry, private references meant only for his circle of friends or details even more obscure, whose solution lies in parts of Eliot's life so far hidden from view.

If any readers have notes to add, or to correct, could they please write to me care of Harcourt Brace.

Biographical Table

In this table are set out the main facts of Eliot's life and the chronology of his writing career.

26 September 1888	Thomas Stearns Eliot born in St Louis, Missouri; seventh and youngest child of Henry Ware Eliot and Charlotte Champe Stearns. The Eliot family is of English origin, the American line descending from Andrew Eliot who came to Massachusetts from East Coker, Somerset, in the mid-seventeenth century.
1905	Early poetry and prose is published in the *Smith Academy Record*, the school magazine of Smith Academy, St Louis.
1906	Enters Harvard University, to which he belongs as student, post-graduate and Assistant in philosophy, until 1914.
1907–10	Early poetry appears in *The Harvard Advocate*, a student literary magazine of which he was an editor.
1909–11	The period during which were written the earliest pieces in *Selected Poems*: 'Preludes' (1910–11, published July 1915), 'Portrait of a Lady' (1910–11, published September 1915), 'The Love Song of J. Alfred Prufrock' (1910–11, published June 1915), 'Rhapsody on a Windy Night' (1911, published July 1915).
1910–11	To Paris, autumn 1910. Stops in London *en route*. Studies French literature, and philosophy, at the Sorbonne. Attends Henri Bergson's

weekly philosophical lectures at the Collège de France. At his *pension*, meets Jean Verdenal, to whom *Prufrock and Other Observations* is dedicated. So completely does he identify himself with the French that he writes poems in the language and seriously contemplates settling in France. Visits London, April 1911. Visits Munich and Northern Italy, July–August 1911. Returns to Harvard, October.

1914   Arrives in Europe, June; summer study at University of Marburg stopped by threat of war; August, returns to England; September, meets Ezra Pound; October, to Merton College, Oxford, to complete his thesis on the philosophy of F. H. Bradley, published in 1964 as *Knowledge and Experience in the Philosophy of F. H. Bradley.*

1915   June, marries Vivien Haigh-Wood; teaches autumn term at High Wycombe Grammar School.

1916   Teaches for four terms at the Junior department of Highgate School.

1917   March, joins the Colonial and Foreign Department of Lloyds Bank in the City of London, remaining there for eight years. *Prufrock and Other Observations*, his first volume of poetry, is published in London. Becomes assistant editor of *The Egoist* (a London literary magazine) until 1919.

1919   *Poems*, his second collection, published privately. Four of the seven poems in this volume are included in the *Selected Poems* under the head 'Poems 1920'.

1920   *Ara Vos Prec*, his third collection, published in London (in New York as *Poems*): contains all the twelve poems included in the *Selected Poems* before *The Waste Land.*

1922	*The Waste Land* published, in London in the October issue of *The Criterion* (the literary magazine Eliot founded, and edited until 1939) and in New York in the November issue of *The Dial* (published around 20 October). First book edition published by Boni and Liveright, New York, December 1922, 1,000 copies. Reprinted early 1923, 1,000 copies.
1923	First UK book edition, The Hogarth Press, Richmond, September, about 460 copies.
1925	Becomes a director of the publishing house now known as Faber and Faber. *Poems 1909–1925* published in London and New York.
1927	June, baptized into the Church of England.
1930	*Ash-Wednesday* published in London and New York.
1932	September, to Harvard as Charles Eliot Norton Professor (lectures published in 1933 as *The Use of Poetry and the Use of Criticism*).
1933	July, returns to London. Separates from Vivien.
1934	*The Rock* published.
1935	*Murder in the Cathedral* published.
1939	*The Family Reunion* and *Old Possum's Book of Practical Cats* published.
1943	*Four Quartets* published in New York, in 1943, London, 1944. The four poems appeared separately as follows: *Burnt Norton* 1936; *East Coker* 1940; *The Dry Salvages* 1941; *Little Gidding* 1942.
1948	Awarded the Nobel Prize for Literature; received Order of Merit.
1950	*The Cocktail Party* published.
1954	*The Confidential Clerk* published.
1957	Marries Valerie Fletcher.
1959	*The Elder Statesman* published.
4 January 1965	Death in London.

A Guide to
the Selected Poems of
T. S. ELIOT

Introduction

'A large part of any poet's "inspiration" must come from his reading and from his knowledge of history.'

T. S. Eliot, *To-Day*, September 1918

'The historical sense compels a man to write not merely with his own generation in his bones, but with a feeling that the whole of the literature of Europe from Homer and within it the whole of the literature of his own country has a simultaneous existence and composes a simultaneous order.'

'Tradition and the Individual Talent', 1919

I

No one, however learned, has ever claimed that Eliot's poetry makes easy reading. This book is designed to elucidate one particular kind of difficulty – the special problems of meaning which face the reader immediately, on the very surface of the poems, in Eliot's use of quotations and allusions, his reference to many languages and literatures, and his implication of a wide range of fact and learning. Sometimes quotation and allusion become the very language of the poetry, as we see at the end of *The Waste Land*, whose closing lines are a mosaic of literary fragments; and the body of the poem involves a 'concentration' of learning 'resulting from a framework of mythology and theology and philosophy' (to quote Eliot's comment on the poetry of Dante). Sometimes the learning seems to raise a barrier, a literal barrier, as it becomes at the head of 'Burbank', whose epigraph is a maze of scrambled quotations to be penetrated before ever the poem comes into sight.

It is no surprise then that Eliot has been accused of obscurity and pretentiousness. This is the cost of writing difficult poetry, of being judged by readers who have not attempted to test the poet's meaning or analyse his technique. Even some of those who would describe themselves as Eliot admirers are not always prepared to face the demands of sheer knowledge that his poetry makes. On many occasions we are called upon to translate words, lines and passages before we can even begin to tackle the questions of meaning and the larger issues of interpretation. And beyond this we face a wilful, or playful obscurity on Eliot's part, sometimes by way of private jokes and allusions, sometimes in what Hugh Kenner has called his 'besetting vice, a never wholly penetrable ambiguity about what is supposed to be happening' – to be distinguished from what Helen Gardner has described as 'a deep ambiguity which it is not the critic's business to remove'; to be distinguished again from elements in the poetry which are not incomprehensible but inexplicable, as Pound judged the 'three white leopards' and the 'juniper-tree' in *Ash-Wednesday*. Protesting mildly, Virginia Woolf saw it, in 1924, as an historical issue: the difference between one literary generation and the next:

> ...Again with the obscurity of Mr. Eliot. I think that Mr. Eliot has written some of the loveliest single lines in modern poetry. But how intolerant he is of the old usages and politeness of society – respect for the weak, consideration for the dull! As I sun myself upon the intense and ravishing beauty of one of his lines, and reflect that I must make a dizzy and dangerous leap to the next, and so on from line to line, like an acrobat flying precariously from bar to bar, I cry out, I confess, for the old decorums...

Eliot has himself touched upon the question of difficulty in modern poetry. He said that difficulty is not something peculiar to certain writers, but a condition of writing in the contemporary world. In a context of 'great variety and complexity' the modern poet can only respond with 'various and complex results'. 'The poet must become more and more comprehensive, more allusive, more indirect, in order to force, to dislocate if necessary, language into his meaning.'* Eliot's proposition may sound stern and unsympathetic, likely to produce stern and unsympathetic poetry. But we know that the case is otherwise. Much of his poetry can be read with pleasure at first sight, although not always with immediate and full understanding. Eliot put the matter well. 'I know that some of the poetry to which I am most devoted is poetry which I did not understand at first reading.' He said that he was passionately fond of certain French verse long before he could be confident of translating it. Mallarmé he found 'very obscure' yet the poems 'worth while even when you don't understand them...' (Wyndham Lewis attacked this proposition in a searching essay, 'What is "Difficult" Poetry', *New Britain*, 7 March 1934.) Yet Eliot also insisted that when poetry calls for knowledge, the poetry-lover must be prepared to answer that demand. He found this with Dante's *Divina Commedia* and he advised other readers from his personal experience. 'If you get nothing out of it at first, you probably never will; but if from your first deciphering of it there comes now and then some direct shock of poetic intensity,

---

* This, anyway, was Eliot's theory in 'The Metaphysical Poets' (1921). Other people have argued differently, notably the poet and critic Yvor Winters, who describes Eliot's view as 'the fallacy of expressive, or imitative form'. Winters traces this fallacy back to the theory formulated by Henry Adams, 'that modern art must be chaotic in order to express chaos' (see Winters, *Primitivism and Decadence*, 1937, *The Anatomy of Nonsense*, 1943).

The shortest and most penetrating answer to Winters is to be found in the 1970 revision of *Poetries and Sciences* by I. A. Richards (first published in 1926), where he discusses the possibility of 'finding a new order through the contemplation and exhibition of disorder', a concept brought home to Richards by *The Waste Land*. Richards's footnote (to page 64) is worth looking at. He quotes a very telling extract from Joseph Conrad's *Lord Jim* on the idea that to survive in the destructiveness of the sea, we should immerse ourselves in it.

A more recent charge is that the literary modernism of Eliot, Joyce and Virginia Woolf was essentially a frightened reaction to the advent of mass culture at the beginning of this century, leading Eliot, amongst others, to cultivate irrationality and obscurity in his writing – 'the forces of deterioration are a large crawling mass, and the focus of development half a dozen men', wrote Eliot, a spokesman for those half a dozen, addressing the pre-*Waste Land* readers of *The Athenaeum*.

nothing but laziness can deaden the desire for fuller and fuller knowledge.'

This *Guide* is to meet precisely this latter instance. It is meant for the reader who has responded to Eliot's poetry and is seeking the means towards fuller knowledge. Essentially, it is designed to serve as a work of reference, to accompany the volume of *Selected Poems* (a selection made by Eliot himself for the Penguin edition published in July 1948, including the most important poems before the *Four Quartets*). It provides factual information about specific details in the poems – the source of literary quotations, the English meaning of foreign words and phrases, the presence of allusions, the identity of historical figures and events, and definitions for words adapted or invented by Eliot, and for rare or archaic terms usually included only in the largest dictionaries. I have also included helpful statements by Eliot himself. Although he was notoriously unhelpful, indeed, at times misleading, in the face of direct questions about this word or that line, Eliot was well aware of the importance, in the history of poetry, of his innovations and borrowings in language and form and tone.

Much of this information can be found elsewhere, for many of the critical and interpretative studies of Eliot necessarily deal with matters of fact. However, readers who want to arrive at their own understanding of the poetry may prefer to have the information provided systematically, poem by poem, free from critical comment, with no assumptions made about their knowledge of English literature, the Bible, and the other historical and cultural traditions upon which Eliot draws. In doing this, I have tried to observe what Eliot himself said about the proper relationship of critic and reader: 'the critic must not coerce, and he must not make judgements of worse and better. He must simply elucidate. The reader will form the correct judgement for himself.'

II

Many of the entries in this *Guide* cover precise and obvious points. Eliot sometimes signals his use of quotations by italics or quotation marks; many of the historical and factual references to people and events are equally straightforward and unmistakable. With allusions, however, there cannot be certainty. One reader may see an allusion that another reader denies. So I have used restraint and common sense, not straining to search for allusions, merely identifying those which seem relevant to the poem's meaning. We have to remember, however, that *allusiveness* was at the heart of Eliot's poetic method, something he brought home in 'The Three Provincialities' (1922): 'Whatever words a writer employs, he benefits by knowing as much as possible of the history of the words, of the *uses to which they have already been applied* . . . The essential of tradition is in this; in getting as much as possible of the whole weight of the history of the language behind his word.' He declared that the mark of the mature poet is that he 'retwines as many straying strands of tradition as possible'. Within these precepts, we have to be ready to meet both the familiar and the unexpected. Allusiveness is not inimical to originality and according to Eliot 'poetic originality is largely an original way of assembling the most disparate and unlikely material to make a new whole'. True to his word, such an assembly of 'the most disparate and unlikely material' is exactly what faces us in his poetry, some of this material very disparate and unlikely indeed, understandably so, remembering that Eliot regarded it as 'the business of the poet' 'to make poetry out of the unexplored resources of the unpoetical'.

Sources I have dealt with less exhaustively. By sources I mean the literary or other works by which Eliot's poetry is visibly influenced – in terms, say, of diction, imagery, verse form or subject-matter – to the extent of material obligation. Sometimes the borrowings are obvious and well-known, including the Greek and Roman classics, Dante, Shakespeare, Milton and modern classics, such as Dickens and Conrad; and Eliot would be expecting his reader to recognize these sources and follow his use of them. But sometimes the sources are little-known or obscure. In these cases we can assume that Eliot would not expect or require his reader to identify them; and sometimes, as the poet has admitted, the sources are 'unconscious', inasmuch as the borrowed material came to Eliot's mind without his having any sense of its external origin. As he pointed out in 1932, these 'unconscious' sources can be various and obscure: 'the mind of any poet would be magnetised in its own way, to select automatically, in his reading (from picture papers and cheap novels, indeed, as well as serious books . . .) the material – an image, a phrase, a word – which may be of use to him later. And this selection runs through the whole of his sensitive life.' To make an exhaustive inquiry into these areas would be an enormous and complex task, taking us into the remotest areas of literary history and the psychology of creation, well away from points of local and immediate meaning in the poetry.

This question arises, for example, with the impact of the French philosopher Henri Bergson (1859–1941), whose lectures Eliot attended for the first two months of 1911 at the Collège de France in Paris and recorded in extensive notes and two papers. He later recalled the packed lecture hall, the excitement which Bergson awakened, 'the epidemic of Bergsonism' and his own 'temporary conversion'. 'I was certainly very much under his influence during the years 1910–11, when I both attended his lectures and gave close study to the books he had then written.' One of these was *Matière et Mémoire* (*Matter and Memory*) (1896), which played a considerable part in forming Eliot's concept of 'memory' in 'Rhapsody on a Windy Night'; and Bergson's concepts of one's 'inner life' and time contribute to the other poems written in Paris. In 1945, Eliot confessed to being a Bergsonian when he composed 'Prufrock', a short-lived phase that lasted until 1913, when he escaped Bergson's 'meretricious captivation' for the 'melancholy grace' of the philosopher F. H. Bradley. To identify every trace of Bergson would call for a book in itself, an account which would tell us much about the intellectual climate of Paris at the time (over which 'swung the spider-like figure of Bergson', 'then the most noticed figure in Paris') and about the openness of *avant-garde* writers to new theories of the workings of the mind. It would, however, contribute little to an immediate understanding of local detail in Eliot's poetry.

The same issue arises with anthropology, a subject which Eliot studied at Harvard and continued to read as a student and reviewer into the 1920s. The importance of anthropology to *The Waste Land* is announced in Eliot's opening Notes, where the poem's title, plan and 'a good deal of the incidental symbolism' are attributed to Jessie Weston's recent study of the Grail legend, *From Ritual to Romance* (1920). Eliot also acknowledged his debt to *The Golden Bough* (1890–1915) by Sir James Frazer, which he read in 1913 and soon used in 'Sweeney Among the Nightingales' and other of the quatrain poems pre-1920, and there is a nod to Frazer in the title of his first collection of essays, *The Sacred Wood* (1920), in which Eliot carried out some ritual slaying of old reputations and rusty critical approaches. And elements of anthropology, particularly references to primitive ritual, are in Eliot's poetry well beyond *The Waste Land* – in 'The Hollow Men' and *Ash-Wednesday*; so much so that it calls for a work as compendious as *The Savage and the City in the Work of T. S. Eliot* (1987) by Robert Crawford to chart these elements in full.

Similarly, Eliot's knowledge of Indian thought deriving from his studies at Harvard, 1911–13, when he learned Sanskrit and Pali and read ancient religious and philosophical texts (see Jain, 1992). Eliot said that 'some of the early Buddhist scriptures affect me as parts of the Old Testament' and judged (as he tells us in the notes to *The Waste Land*, line 308) that the Buddha's Fire Sermon 'corresponds in importance to the Sermon on the Mount'. In his own poetry Eliot saw 'the influence of Indian thought and sensibility' – most obviously, of course, in Parts III and V of *The Waste Land*, where he maintains a direct counterpoint between the literary and religious traditions of the East and West, even to the poem's closing words. Eliot called the *Bhagavadgita* (one of the most important Upanishads in Vedic literature) 'the next greatest philosophical poem to the *Divine Comedy* within my experience' ('Dante', 1929). Rather than attempting to trace this Indian 'influence' throughout Eliot's poetry, I have provided detailed information at those places in *The Waste Land* where Buddhist and other Indian sources are drawn upon or alluded to (see notes to lines 308, 399–401 and

433); and Eliot wondered if he had not been unconsciously influenced by some aspect of Indian philosophy in the writing of *Ash-Wednesday*. Readers seeking fuller information can refer to Kearns, 1987.

The same question applies to Eliot's literary reading. The influence of such writers as Tennyson and Walt Whitman is so pervasive, with an abundance of verbal echoes and parallels, that readers wishing to pursue these paths will want to turn to such specialized studies as *T. S. Eliot and Walt Whitman* (1954) by S. Musgrove (covering Tennyson as well).

One Victorian poem of particular importance to Eliot was the translation from the Persian original by Edward Fitzgerald entitled *The Rubáiyát of Omar Khayyám* (1859), which he read in 1902 at the age of fourteen. Eliot later recalled 'the almost overwhelming introduction to a new world of feeling . . . It was like a sudden conversion; the world appeared anew, painted with bright, delicious and painful colours'. It is no surprise, then, to come across Rubaiyatian phrasing, cadences and details in 'Prufrock', 'Portrait of a Lady', the quatrain poems and 'Gerontion', described by D'Ambrosia as 'a monologue delivered under the mask of Fitzgerald', owing something too to the biography of Fitzgerald by A. C. Benson (see page 69, note to lines 1–2).

Similarly with Eliot's use of the French Symbolist poets, treated authoritatively by Edward J. H. Greene in *T. S. Eliot et la France* (1951), for which the author consulted Eliot himself. However, these poets are so important to the pre-*Waste Land* poetry that some brief introduction is called for here. Eliot recalled that at twenty 'the kind of poetry that I needed, to teach me the use of my own voice, did not exist in English at all; it was only to be found in French'. This discovery dated from December 1908 when, in a Harvard library, Eliot came across the revised edition of *The Symbolist Movement in Literature* (1899, 1908) by Arthur Symons. This book, he said, 'affected the course of my life'. It was remembered by him 'as an introduction to wholly new feelings, as a revelation'. For the first time he met the work of Laforgue, Rimbaud, Verlaine and Corbière. Symons's chapter on Laforgue drew a temperament very close to his own:

it was a case, he said, of 'a sort of possession by a stronger personality'. Although he found Symons's criticism 'execrable', the translations fascinated Eliot, especially of Laforgue; and, soon after, he ordered the three-volume *Œuvres Complètes de Jules Laforgue* (1901, 1902, 1903), which arrived the following spring. His discovery was *vers libre*, 'free verse in much the way that the later verse of Shakespeare, Webster, Tourneur, is free verse ... the form in which I began to write, in 1908 or 1909, was directly drawn from the study of Laforgue, together with the later Elizabethan drama' (whose blank verse 'accomplished a subtlety and consciousness, even an intellectual power, that no blank verse since has developed or even repeated'). A further debt, seen in 'Prufrock', was to the *dandysme* of Laforgue and Baudelaire (an aspect explored in Sigg, ch. 6). Eliot recalled (in 1950) that Laforgue was 'the first to teach me how to speak, to teach me the poetic possibilities of my own idiom of speech'; to teach Eliot a 'subtle conversational tone', as Ezra Pound shrewdly observed; to be to him, Eliot said, an elder brother; to whom, he recalled in 1961, he owed 'more than to any one poet in any language'. And through Laforgue and Baudelaire, Eliot came to glimpse the poetic possibilities of his seemingly prosaic existence:

> I learned that the sort of material that I had, the sort of experience that an adolescent had had, in an industrial city in America, could be the material for poetry; and that the source of new poetry might be found in what had been regarded hitherto as the impossible, the sterile, the intractably unpoetic. That, in fact, the business of the poet was to make poetry out of the unexpected resources of the unpoetical.
>
> ('What Dante Means to Me', 1950)

Under Pound's tutelage, other French poets played their part. Eliot recalled in 1958 that it was largely under Pound's influence that he studied Gautier and took 'a rest from *vers libre* in regular quatrains'. Gautier's 'L'Hippopotame' provided the point of departure for his own sardonic, anti-clerical Anglican 'Hippopotamus'. 'In Gautier', Eliot wrote in 1921, 'there is a large part' of the special kind of 'wit, a tough reasonableness beneath the slight lyric grace' he so admired in Marvell's 'Horatian Ode' and other Caroline poetry; and 'in the best of the light verse of Gautier' he found 'a satisfaction, a balance of inwards and form' ('Baudelaire', 1930). And from Laforgue and Corbière (who came to succeed Laforgue as a prime influence on his poetry) came the *fantaisiste* (whimsical) heritage, in which the poetry of feeling, of sensitivity is undercut by the detached amusement of the ironist, and (as John Middleton Murry put it) the irony 'verges on cynicism' coupled with 'an introspection that verges on egotism'.

The debt is undeniably extensive* – in diction and phrasing, in lines adapted or paraphrased from the French models, in subject-matter and in the attitude of romantic irony which Eliot holds towards the experience of life in cities – 'the more sordid aspects of the modern metropolis', whose 'poetical possibilities' he discovered through the poetry of Baudelaire. We have here a remarkable example of the way in which a powerful talent can ingest the materials of others, putting them, directly and indirectly, to an individual use. In practising this allusive method, Eliot saw himself employing the classical device of *imitation* in the particular definition he quoted from Ben Jonson – 'to be able to convert the substances, or riches of another poet, to his own use'. It is a process that should be studied by anyone who wants to determine the nature of Eliot's originality, to see what contributed to this new voice in English poetry, or who wants to trace the stages in his development. We need to catch the point of Pound's comment in 1920 to William Carlos Williams: 'Eliot is perfectly conscious of having imitated Laforgue, has worked to get away from it, and there is very little Laforgue in his Sweeney or his Bleistein Burbank, or his Gerontion.' Or of his guidance to the unsuspecting readers of *The Future* (an organ of the Esperanto movement) in June 1918, when Pound introduced them to the European aspect of Eliot's poetry. Quoting 'The Hippopotamus'

---

* Although this topic was treated extensively in Greene's book, there have been a number of later suggestions, the most recent being 'Gautier and Eliot's Openings' by Christopher Ricks, *Times Literary Supplement*, 11 June 1993.

complete, he added, 'This cold sardonic statement is definitely of the school of Théophile Gautier.' In April 1918, Eliot himself instructed readers of *The Egoist* to 'Try to put into a sequence of simple quatrains the continuous syntactic variety of Gautier or Blake.' But these insights and allusions can be grasped only through an extensive reading of the French poets. An accumulation of source references would merely be cumbersome, and positively obstructive to the reader whose prime use of this book is for the elucidation of specific points in the text.

Another source for one of the earliest poems was Dostoevsky. In the winter of 1910–11, when he was studying in Paris, Eliot read French translations of three of Dostoevsky's novels, *Crime and Punishment*, *The Idiot* and *The Brothers Karamazov*. When an American scholar, John C. Pope, suggested (many years later) that the figure of Prufrock and the poem as a whole bear the impress of Eliot's reading of *Crime and Punishment*, the poet agreed: 'These three novels made a very profound impression on me and I had read them all before *Prufrock* was completed.' Professor Pope also thought that the wording of 'Prufrock' had been influenced by Constance Garnett's translation of *Crime and Punishment*. However, as Eliot pointed out, he had never seen the Garnett translation.

When he came to Paris, Eliot was also struck by the novels of Charles-Louis Philippe (1874–1909) – *Bubu de Montparnasse* (1901) and *Marie Donadieu* (1904) in particular, both of which he drew upon for images and settings in 'Preludes' III and IV and 'Rhapsody on a Windy Night'. A translation of *Bubu* published in 1945 carried a Preface by Eliot in which he recalled that he first read the book 'at an impressionable age, and under impressive conditions'. It stood for him as 'a symbol of the Paris of that time', 'as some of Dickens's novels stand for London'. What appealed to Eliot was the novelist's 'grim humour', his integrity as 'a faithful recorder of things as they are, and events as they happened', the very qualities Eliot's contemporaries found in his poetry of that time. As with Dostoevsky, it would not be enough to catalogue the specific borrowings or allusions; Eliot's response was to the works entire.

Neither have I listed the multitude of possible sources for the passages of pastiche in 'Gerontion' and *The Waste Land*. Eliot's brilliant imitations of Elizabethan and Jacobean dramatic verse evoke for us, in a few lines, the way in which these writers – Marlowe, Webster, Tourneur, Middleton and Ford – experienced life and the style in which they communicated this experience. 'It was', Eliot wrote in 1961, 'from these minor dramatists that I, in my own poetic formation, had learned my lessons; it was by them, and not by Shakespeare, that my imagination had been stimulated, my sense of rhythm trained, and my emotions fed.' It was not a case of imitation. Pound put the matter fairly in commenting on Eliot's early poetry: 'His practice has been a distinctive cadence, a personal modus of arrangement, remote origins in Elizabethan English and in the modern French masters, neither origin being sufficiently apparent to affect the personal quality' (*Egoist*, June 1917).

I have dealt selectively with allusions intended for a closed circle of Eliot's family and friends and which appear to add little or nothing to the meaning of the poem. One source of such allusions is the Spanish satirical romance *Don Quixote* by Cervantes (1547–1616), known in the Eliot family, punningly, as 'The Donkey Book', this title also referring to the Don's steed. The Sherlock Holmes stories and historical romances of Sir Arthur Conan Doyle (1859–1930) were another family favourite, a source for this category of the private or semi-private allusion. Examples also come in Eliot's adult life. In May 1919 Eliot reviewed *The Education of Henry Adams* for *The Athenaeum*. In the review, he referred to the arrival in England of two Americans, Henry Adams himself in 1858, Henry James in 1870, both of whom, he wrote, 'land at Liverpool and descend at the same hotel'. No one can miss the similarity between these words and the opening lines of 'Burbank':

> Burbank crossed a little bridge
>   Descending at a small hotel;
> Princess Volupine arrived,
>   They were together, and he fell.

The poem was published (in the Summer 1919 issue of *Art and Letters*) a month or so after the review; and the phrasing of the review could not have been absent from Eliot's mind. But should we refer to the review as a significant source? Are we to suppose that Eliot would want us to catch some ironic parallel, or contrast, perhaps, between the arrival at Liverpool of those two highly civilized and cultivated American writers and the arrival at Venice of the *Baedeker*-carrying Burbank, a twentieth-century American tourist, and the promiscuous Princess with whom he is so unambiguously involved at their same 'small hotel'? The answer may be Yes; that Eliot would expect at least some of the readers of his poem to recall *The Athenaeum* for 23 May 1919, to catch and savour the comic parallel. Perhaps he advised his friends to look out for it. If there is any question of a deliberate allusion on Eliot's part, it can only be as a private joke; as may be his use of the adjective 'protrusive' for Bleistein's popping eyes: the word occurs in a passage of Henry James, *The Middle Years*, published as recently as 1917, quoted in that same review. Pound may also have contributed to the phrasing of this stanza. In his 'Henry James' essay published in the *Little Review* for August 1918 alongside 'On Henry James', an essay by Eliot, Pound referred to James's arrival at Liverpool and the possibility that he 'might have stayed at the same hotel on the same day as one's grandfather . . .'

Another allusive joke may have been going on with Pound, who had opened his piece on 'Henry James' declaring 'This essay on James is a dull grind of an affair, a Baedeker to a continent'; and within the essay itself, Pound mentions James's stay at Liverpool and a 'hotel' he may have visited. And Pound would have remembered Eliot himself as a *Baedeker*-carrying visitor to the National Gallery in London. Eliot and Pound were skilled at devising such patterns of cross-reference: a private joke for their own entertainment and to amuse their literary circle, it was an exchange of which readers outside the Eliot–Pound circle would have been totally unaware. In 1917, Pound saw the *Little Review* as serving this coterie, as an 'official organ' for himself, Wyndham Lewis, Joyce and Eliot, 'a place for our regular appearance and where our friends and readers (what few of 'em there are), can look with assurance of finding us'; and four of the quatrain poems duly appeared there, in all their allusive complexity. Such instances explain why Virginia Woolf described 'Mr Eliot' as 'an American of the highest culture, so that his writing is almost unintelligible'; and found 'kind of fun in unravelling the twists and obliquities of this remarkable man'. Although, then, these instances tell us about Eliot's associative mind, his sense of humour and the circles of his readership, they have little to do with the essential and permanent meaning of the poetry.

There are other 'Burbank'-*Athenaeum* parallels. For example, the issue for 25 April 1919 contains a translation of Cavafy's poem 'The God Abandons Antony'. On 2 May, there is a reference in a review by Eliot to Shakespeare's 'The Phoenix and the Turtle'. Echoes of the Cavafy title and Shakespeare's poem appear in the second stanza of 'Burbank'. Evidently, traces of Eliot's reading and literary journalism have found their way through to the poem. Similar instances of infiltration are to be found by anyone who searches the files of the periodicals which Eliot and Pound contributed to or edited. A comparison between this material and the poetry Eliot was currently writing can provide an insight upon the process of poetic creation. But it tells us little or nothing about the public meaning of these poems.

It is, however, worth noting that the jokiness of these semi-private allusions does not jeopardize the seriousness of the poetry. When 'Burbank' was published in *Poems* (1920), Eliot wrote to his brother: 'Some of the new poems, the Sweeney ones, especially "Among the Nightingales" and "Burbank", are intensely serious, and I think these two are among the best that I have ever done.' In the same spirit, exploring the meaning of 'wit', Eliot spoke of it in Laforgue as an 'alliance of levity and seriousness (by which the seriousness is intensified)' ('Andrew Marvell', 1921).

Another instance of what we might term an *irrelevant* source is 'Crapy Cornelia' by Henry James, a short story published in *Harper's Magazine* in 1909 and probably read then by Eliot, at the time 'Prufrock' was forming in his mind. The story opens to a distinctly Prufrockian note. The forty-eight-year-old bachelor

White-Mason is caught in a moment of hesitation, hesitating on a visit he has to make, a question he has to put, a point he has come to. The 'point', 'the important question', as we are to learn, is a proposal of marriage. The likeness to 'Prufrock' is also in the person of White-Mason as a self-conscious dandy, worried about his age; and the 'etherised' patient image may have been triggered by a reference to ether in the story. Perhaps, as with 'Burbank', Eliot's intimates would have spotted the joke. But 'Prufrock' has a life of its own. Its Jamesian elements – in matters of detail and in a light parody of the novelist's late style – exist only as points of departure, as ingredients, along with Dostoevsky and Charles-Louis Philippe, in a masterpiece which is Eliot's through and through, achieved by a marvellous assumption of the most varied materials. Thus to remark upon 'Crapy Cornelia' as a source is to make a historical and psychological observation rather than a point of meaning.

But the most striking and instructive example of an irrelevant source is found with *The Waste Land*. At some time between 1913 and 1920–1, Eliot met the Countess Marie von Wallersee-Larisch, an Austrian noblewoman, a niece and favourite of the Austrian Empress Elizabeth, and related to Ludwig II, the 'mad king' of Bavaria. Her reminiscences are set down in *My Past* (1913), a book now forgotten and at the time little known. The Countess was not a skilled writer (indeed the memoirs were worked up by that most accomplished of literary ghosts, Maude Ffoulkes); nor a very interesting woman; and the moments of her life were little more than the scandals of the court. Yet there is an undeniable fascination to this briskly told story of corruption, of sexual intrigue and domestic subterfuge in the royal circles of Europe.

For whatever reason, specific details from *My Past* stuck in Eliot's mind. They came to the surface again in the composition of *The Waste Land*. In the opening verse-paragraph we find unmistakable borrowings and adaptations: Marie's name (line 15) (unusual for central Europe; Maria would be the standard form); the Starnbergersee (line 8), the lake beside which stood one of her childhood homes; an arch-duke cousin (lines 13–14), of whom she had several; wintering in the south (line 18), corresponding to her own moves from Austria to Menton; the feeling of freedom in the mountains (line 17), to which Marie refers several times; an unexpected summer rain storm (lines 8–9), corresponding to the storm which overtook her and the Empress when they were out riding together. And there are extensive correspondences elsewhere – several passages about death by drowning, many references to Wagner and a striking section on fortune-telling (although the account of sledging, in lines 13–16, comes verbatim from Eliot's conversations with the Countess).

The discovery of this source was a matter of pure chance, the observation of an American scholar, Mr G. K. L. Morris, who happened to come across the book in a rented house in Provence in the early 1950s (as he recounted in *Partisan Review*, xxi, 1954). But for this fortuitous stroke we might never have known of this remote source; nor would it have mattered much; for Eliot's use of these details is quite independent of their forgotten origin. Their meaning arises wholly from the context of the poem in which they now stand. (I must record a different view argued by Herbert Knust in *Wagner, The King and 'The Waste Land'* (1967), where he proposes that *My Past* plays an important part in *The Waste Land* and that it points to a greater 'coherence of structure' and 'a more extensive range of symbolism' than have been revealed so far by the poem's critics and interpreters.)

On the other hand, my long note to lines 1 to 18 of *The Waste Land* (see pages 138–40) mentions Rupert Brooke's famous poem, 'The Old Vicarage, Grantchester'. This is not, in the strict sense, a source. But it is a work which I am sure Eliot wanted to call to the reader's mind. He evokes it through verbal, structural and thematic echoes. Eliot asserts the large and essential difference between the experience of life in *The Waste Land*, a subtle and complex experience, and Rupert Brooke's relatively simple, single view. To put the issue briefly: *My Past* is irrelevant to the meaning of *The Waste Land* for all that it supplies considerable detail; it is an *accidental* source. Whereas 'The Old

Vicarage, Grantchester' is a parallel we are required to keep in sight, not as a source, but as a term of reference, one aspect of Eliot's meaning.

Pound's importance to Eliot in transforming the 'sprawling, chaotic' manuscript of *The Waste Land* is described on pages 135–7. But something should also be said of his role in helping Eliot through stages in his earlier development and widening his literary experience. As Mario Praz (1937) puts it, 'through his book on *The Spirit of Romance* (1910), and still more through his table-talk', Pound made Eliot 'aware of the greatness of Dante' and brought the early Italian poets alive to him (this was Eliot's own testimony, communicated privately to Praz, whose 1937 essay remains the best account of the place of Dante in Eliot's poetry, and of Pound's active role). Wyndham Lewis was a contemporary observer, a friend to both men, who watched the process by which Eliot 'was lifted out of his lunar alleyways and *fin de siècle* nocturnes [of the Bergson/Laforgue period] into a massive region of verbal creation in contact with that astonishing didactic intelligence'. While Lewis acknowledged the connection between 'Prufrock' and 'Gerontion', he saw the latter as 'technically ... "school of Ezra"'. He might have described the quatrain poems likewise: 'Ezra performed the caesarean Operation,' said Pound, describing his part in their production (see his mock-Marvellian poem 'Sage Homme'). The evidence is in the typescripts held in the Berg Collection (in the New York Public Library); and, to take a single example, Pound's efforts to form a Gautier–Eliot are set out in the introductory note to 'Whispers' (see page 109). The endeavour throughout was to create what Pound called a 'counter-current' to the 'general floppiness' and 'dilutation' of *vers libre*.

There was the influence, too, of Pound's early verse, to be seen, for example, in 'La Fraisne' (The Ash Tree), first published in Pound's earliest volume *A Lume Spento* (With Tapers Quenched; 1908) and reprinted in later collections including *Personae* (1909), *Provença* (1910); and Eliot included the poem in *Ezra Pound: Selected Poems* (1928). The poem itself is an interior monologue. At one point, the speaker tells of a love hurt of long ago. In the hesitations and disconnections of the verse we can see the origins of the intimate psychological characterization that Eliot developed so finely in 'Prufrock', 'Portrait of a Lady' and 'Gerontion':

> Once when I was among the young men . . .
> And they said I was quite strong, among the young men.
> Once there was a woman . . .
> . . . but I forget . . . she was . . .
> . . . I hope she will not come again.
>
> . . . I do not remember . . .
>
> I think she hurt me once, but . . .
> that was very long ago.
>
> I do not like to remember things any more.

Eventually, Eliot came to feel under pressure from Pound's poetic proximity. When, in 1923, Pound wrote 'These fragments you have shelved (shored)', Eliot felt it was too close to his own 'These fragments I have shored against my ruin' in *The Waste Land* and complained, half-facetiously: 'I object strongly on tactical grounds to yr 1st line. People are inclined to think that we write our verses in collaboration as it is, or else that you write mine and I write yours.' In truth, the assistance was not just one way. Eliot helped Pound with his poetry. Regarding his early Cantos, Pound testified that Eliot was 'the only person who proferred criticism, instead of general objection'.

At the level of allusion, what immediately concerns us in the *Selected Poems* is that Pound and Eliot conducted an elaborate game in their poetry, exchanging private references and continuing personal jokes. Very little of this stratum of (largely) hidden meaning is recoverable, but I have indicated its presence, for example, at the end of 'Whispers of Immortality' and 'A Cooking Egg'. Doubtless such cross-references run throughout the poetry written between about 1915 and 1920. Such jokes were not just conducted with Pound. Eliot's Harvard friends were also privileged readers of the quatrain poems. A clue to their mysteries – the 'Sweeney' poems in particular – is to be found in the productions of the Cambridge (Massachusetts) Social Dramatic Club in which the poet and his friends took part. Further clues are to be found in his correspondence with these Harvard friends, in which he elaborated dramatic fantasies, fragments of which spill over, allusively, into poetry. Yet further clues are to be found in the literary quizzes he also conducted with his friends, notably those with questions on Boswell's *Life of Johnson* and the works of Conan Doyle and Wilkie Collins. This may help to explain the burden of elaborate and arcane allusions that sometimes sink the quatrain poems to the depths of obscurity. They are poems for the cognescenti – 'to be understood by a few intelligent people is all the influence a man requires', Eliot wrote in 1918. Addressed to the chosen few, their air of complacent superiority is caught perfectly in Pound's 'Causa': 'I join these words for four people,/Some others may overhear them,/O world, I am sorry for you,/You do not know these four people.' Eliot was surely one of those 'four'; and this little squib, seemingly so trivial, must have carried a special meaning for him, since he included it in his 1928 selection.

III

As a general rule interpretation is left to the reader. I have tried to respect Eliot's belief that in interpretation 'the chief task is the presentation of relevant historical facts which the reader is not assumed to know'. From his own experience of teaching literature, he went a step further, declaring that interpretation 'is only legitimate when it is not interpretation at all, but merely putting the reader in possession of facts which he would otherwise have missed'. So most of the notes simply carry the information relevant to single points in the text. On occasion, however, it has seemed sensible to depart from this rule. The last stanza of 'Whispers of Immortality' offers a knotty problem in philosophical vocabulary, complicated by a private joke with Pound. So I have proffered an explanation there; likewise at the end of

'Burbank', another private joke with Pound; and in one or two other minor instances. The two poems for which I have provided considerable interpretative background material are *The Waste Land* and 'The Hollow Men'. In the prefatory sections to 'The Hollow Men' is a brief note on Dante's *Divina Commedia*, possibly the most important single note in the entire *Guide*.

To read Eliot in ignorance of Dante is to neglect a dimension of meaning that the poet exploits throughout his major works – 'His was the true Dantescan voice,' wrote Pound after Eliot's death; and Eliot himself regarded Dante, as he said in 1950, 'as the most persistent and deepest influence upon my own verse'. The opening words of 'Prufrock' take their point from the Dante epigraph. Prufrock is conducting us through the realm of a twentieth-century Inferno and Purgatory; and in this and other poems, including the *Four Quartets*, Eliot relates the experience of modern man to the experience of mankind given to us in Dante's prodigious statement. In calling his third collection of poems *Ara Vus Prec* ('Now I pray for you'),* Eliot was trying to compel an informed response from his contemporary readers. How many of them could recognize the language as Provençal? The source as the *Purgatorio* XXVI, 145? If they were unable to catch the allusion ('unintelligible to most people', he told his publisher) Eliot was forcing them (at least, those with inquiring minds) to familiarize themselves with the *Divina Commedia*. According to his Harvard friend and fellow-poet Conrad Aiken, after 1910 Eliot was never without his pocket edition of Dante, carrying it with him throughout the time he was writing *The Waste Land*.

In providing notes to *The Waste Land* he was more positively helpful. Eliot brings the allusions to our notice. They cannot be ignored. The poet explained this quite clearly in a talk, 'What Dante Means to Me', given in 1950.

---

* There is a curious error within this. Eliot did not know any Provençal himself and relied upon an Italian edition of Dante which misspelt 'Vos' as 'Vus', an error Eliot unwittingly repeated, although according to one story it was Pound who suggested this faulty title.

Readers of my *Waste Land* will perhaps remember that the vision of my city clerks trooping over London Bridge from the railway station to their offices evoked the reflection 'I had not thought death had undone so many' [line 63]; and that in another place I deliberately modified a line of Dante by altering it – 'Sighs, short and infrequent, were exhaled' [line 64]. And I gave the references in my notes, in order to make the reader who recognized the allusion, know that I meant him to recognize it, and know that he would have missed the point if he did not recognize it.

In the same talk Eliot paid his tribute to Dante, first encountered at Harvard when he was twenty-one, as 'the most persistent and deepest influence' on his poetry. He has described his method: 'I have borrowed lines from him, in the attempt to reproduce, or rather to arouse in the reader's mind the memory, of some Dantesque scene, and thus establish a relationship between the medieval inferno and modern life.' He pointed to Dante's salutary influence on his earliest writing: 'In my youth I think that Dante's astonishing economy and directness of language . . . provided for me a wholesome corrective to the extravagance of the Elizabethan, Jacobean and Caroline authors in whom I also delighted.' It is an influence whose effect cannot be assessed by cataloguing references and allusions. Dante's thought, the simplicity and beauty of his language, the clarity and force of his images, the shape of his verse, all of these are felt anew in Eliot, and anyone coming fresh to the Italian poet can make no better start than by reading Eliot's 'Dante' essay of 1929, which tells us so warmly and lucidly of his response to Dante's art.

Alongside Dante, the dominant exemplars for Eliot were James Joyce and Joseph Conrad, their names linked, in Eliot's account of the 'language' which was then important to him: 'that which is struggling to digest and express new objects, new groups of objects, new feelings, new aspects, as, for instance, the prose of Mr James Joyce or the earlier Conrad' ('Swinburne as Poet', 1920). In 1923, Eliot hailed Joyce's *Ulysses* as 'the most important expression which the present age has found' (the very terms that many of Eliot's contemporary admirers would then have applied to *The Waste Land*); and he went on to point to *Ulysses* as 'a book to which we are all indebted, and from which none of us can escape', and to Joyce as 'one of the great writers, not of our time only, but of all European literature'. The nature of Eliot's own personal indebtedness is referred to in the prefatory notes to *The Waste Land*. It is also worth remarking that Eliot's use of allusion, as a device central to his poetic technique, becomes much more pronounced in the poetry of 1917–18 at the very time he was reading sections of *Ulysses* (see page 130). In September 1918, he commented on the difference between Joyce's use of allusion and Pound's in 'Three Cantos' (1917): Joyce 'uses allusions suddenly and with great speed, part of the effect being the extent of the vista opened to the imagination by the very lightest touch'. Eliot was quick to learn and three years later, in completing *The Waste Land*, he was to deploy allusion to the same effect, so densely, indeed, that in places it becomes the very language of the poem.

The pervasive influence of Conrad's story, 'Heart of Darkness', is described in the prefatory notes to 'The Hollow Men'. It is in Conrad, Eliot wrote in 1919, that we find 'a point of view, a "world", it can hardly be defined, but it pervades his work and is unmistakable.' The nightmare visions of Joyce and Conrad would have made sense to Dante; and one can feel the force of their presence in Eliot's imagination. In reading *Ulysses*, he confessed that he received 'all the surprise, delight, and terror that I can require'; he could have experienced these too in Dante and Conrad; and he found the Conrad of 'Heart of Darkness' comparable with James, Hawthorne and Dostoevsky in their 'essential moral preoccupation', their perception of 'Evil'.

That said, there remains a strictly *critical* issue regarding the weight of learning carried in Eliot's poetry. I. A. Richards tackled this question in *Principles of Literary Criticism* in 1926. He remarked that 'the charge most usually brought against Mr Eliot's poetry is that it is over-intellectualised. One reason for this is his use of allusion.' Richards drew attention to 'Burbank', with its wealth of reference:

> These things come in, not that the reader may be ingenious or admire the writer's erudition (this last accusation has tempted several critics to disgrace themselves), but for the sake of the emotional aura which they bring and the attitudes they incite. Allusion in Mr Eliot's hands is a technical device for compression. 'The Waste Land' is the equivalent in content to an epic. Without this device twelve books would have been needed. But these allusions and the notes in which some of them are elucidated have made many a petulant reader turn down his thumb at once. Such a reader has not begun to understand what it is all about.

This is an explanation that carries conviction. A Cambridge don, Richards was also himself a practitioner of learned and allusive poetry, highly individual, but in Eliot's vein. Impressed by *Ara Vos Prec*, he became an intimate friend of Eliot in 1920 and would have observed the composition of *The Waste Land* at close hand. So his advocacy is worth attending to. And Richards's concept of 'compression' is a valuable critical tool, leading to his account of *The Waste Land* as a compressed epic (cf. Ezra Pound's comment on the nineteen-page typescript of the poem: 'let us say the longest poem in the Englisch langwidge', and cf. Matthiessen's similar observation that Eliot's revisions were made 'in order that he might best create a dramatic structure that would possess at the same time a lyrical intensity'. Matthiessen also commented that the Notes 'are simply a consequence of his desire to strip the form of the poem to its barest essentials on order to secure his concentrated effect').

A further critical issue arises from a poetic method, such as Eliot's, which involves such extensive quotation, allusion and imitation. This was a matter which Eliot took up in 1920, in a review-essay, 'Philip Massinger':

> One of the surest of tests is the way in which a poet borrows. Immature poets imitate, mature poets steal, bad poets deface what they take, and good poets make it into something better, or at least something different. The good poet welds his theft

into a whole of feeling which is unique, utterly different from that from which it was torn; the bad poet throws it into something which has no cohesion.

Eliot is thinking as much about his own poetic method as Massinger's. What he does provide here is a scale for us to gauge the measure of his own success. Are his 'thefts' those of the 'good poet' welded 'into a whole of feeling which is unique, utterly different'?

IV

It is no surprise that an understanding of Eliot's poetry involves us in wide reading, a task indicated in Eliot's dictum that 'The serious writer of verse must be prepared to cross himself with the best verse of other languages and the best prose of all languages.' Likewise the serious reader. But seriousness should not lead us into solemnity. Kipling was a writer Eliot greatly admired, both his poetry and his stories. In addressing the Kipling Society, in 1959, on 'The Unfading Genius of Rudyard Kipling', he declared that 'Kipling has accompanied me ever since boyhood' and pointed to that writer's influence in the titles of 'Prufrock' and 'The Hollow Men'. The testimony was heartfelt. Yet Eliot's impishness broke through with a piece of gentle mockery: 'Traces of Kipling appear in my own mature verse where no diligent scholarly sleuth has yet observed them,' a taunt that has stood the test of time, since my note to line 378 of *The Waste Land* refers to the only trace of Kipling that the sleuths have so far found. Another face of the poet's wit is seen in that hilariously grotesque satire 'The Hippopotamus'; another in the charming fantasies in *Old Possum's Book of Practical Cats* (1939); and yet another in the thicket of quotations at the head of 'Burbank', an intellectual puzzle, challenging the reader to identify its parts and relate them to the poem they head, a standing example of Eliot's pronouncement that 'poetry develops a conscious virtuosity, requiring a virtuosity of appreciation on the part of the audience'. The body of the poem offers a similar challenge, and the detailed notes to 'Burbank' point to the complex interplay of sources – principally Gautier, Henry James and Ruskin – running through the poem, making it one of the most densely allusive of all Eliot's works, in part a configuration of allusive artistry, a performance of 'conscious virtuosity' in which, doubtless, he was egged on by Pound. Thirty years after its first appearance in 1919, only three of the six quotations had been identified. So a critic appealed to the author, who entered into the spirit of source-hunting, identifying the remaining three himself. Or there is 'Mr Eliot's Sunday Morning Service', a satire on pedantry, defiantly pedantic in its glancing references to the disputes of the early Christian Church and in its comically obscure diction, a parody of the language of scholasticism – a trick he may have taken from Laforgue's device of using learned or unexpected allusions in an ironic context, the side of Laforgue that Eliot quotes in 'The Metaphysical Poets'. Indeed, this poem can itself be seen as a 'metaphysical' pastiche with a sharp edge. Or 'Whispers of Immortality', with its spoof zoology and arcane dance amongst the 'Abstract Entities' and pneumatics of philosophy! Or 'A Cooking Egg', a mare's-nest of complexity and pedantic learning, which has generated yards of speculation, an exercise that Eliot himself thought futile. In all these cases, Eliot means us to admire and smile, to enjoy the lightness and skill with which he can turn his learning to a joke, to glimpse a poet-dandy, the virtuoso delighting with us in the bravura and impudence of his own performance. The 'alliance of levity and seriousness' he spotted in Laforgue was a tradition he would continue. As Harriet Monroe put it, 'his sense of humour ... stands at the gate of his mind, not to keep emotions out, but to whip them as they come in'.

Eliot's most elaborate joke concerns us directly in the use of this *Guide*, for it involves the notes he provided to *The Waste Land*. At a public lecture given at the University of Minnesota in 1956, Eliot explained that he had originally meant the notes only to be source references added 'with a view to spiking the guns of critics of my earlier poems who had accused me of plagiarism'. This intention was certainly in his mind by February 1922, when he mentioned them to Maurice Firuski, a possible publisher for the first book edition. According to Clive Bell, Roger Fry urged Eliot to elucidate the poem with explanatory notes. When Eliot wrote to his patron John Quinn in June 1922, he spoke of *The Waste Land* as 'a long poem ... which, with notes that I am adding, will make a book of 30 or 40 pages'. But when *The Waste Land* was first printed, four months later, it was without notes of any kind (it came out in two periodicals, in London and New York). The notes were only added to the first book edition, published in December, to oblige the publisher Liveright (of the New York firm of Boni and Liveright) who 'wanted a larger volume and the notes were the only available matter' (as Eliot explained elsewhere).*

Recounting this, Eliot remarked that over the years the notes 'have had almost greater popularity than the poem itself', a nice enough joke. But perhaps some members of that university audience, and scholars elsewhere, when they later read the printed version of the lecture in 1957, may have been rather less amused by his discomforting account of the notes as a 'remarkable exposition of bogus scholarship' which he had often thought of omitting. (An amusing and instructive essay by F. W. Bateson examines what he calls Eliot's 'Poetry of Pseudo-Learning' (*Journal of General Education*, 1968, vol. 20, no. i), questioning the actual range of knowledge that stands behind some of Eliot's allusions. A later version of this essay appears in *Eliot in Perspective* (1970), ed. Graham Martin, under the less pointed title 'The Poetry of Learning'.) Of course, the joke works both ways. Some of the notes are very far from being 'bogus scholarship', or at least they are good explication. The note to line 218 is our most important guide to the reading of the poem, to its fluid

* But this was not quite accurate. Valerie Eliot discussed the manuscript of the poem with Ezra Pound, who was anguished that he had ever suggested to Eliot that the poem should be cut: 'He should have ignored me. Why didn't he restore some of the cancelled passages when Liveright wanted more pages?' Such a restoration would have been conceivable since when Liveright wrote to Pound, on 11 January 1922, about the shortness of the poem, the text had yet to be finalized, as it was early in February.

categories; and Eliot's observation that the nineteen lines quoted from Ovid are 'of great anthropological interest' is not facetious (as some critics, as recently as 1988, have suggested) but reflects an abiding interest in anthropology dating from his time at Harvard. The first part of the note to line 279 is extremely helpful; and without the note to line 433 Eliot's use of the word 'Shantih' would be incomprehensible.

Nevertheless, many of the notes are bait for the unwary. In presenting them, Eliot shows little regard for accuracy, relevance or completeness, as if he is really indifferent to whether or not the reader uses them, as in the note to line 46, where he admits to not knowing 'the exact constitution of the Tarot pack of cards, from which I have obviously departed to suit my own convenience'. Familiar sources and allusions are ignored, such as the use of Stevenson in line 221 or the phrase from Donne in line 30. Indifference also explains why some of the references are so inexact. In the note to line 279, Eliot directs us to 'Froude, *Elizabeth*, Vol. 1'. In fact, the author is James Anthony Froude (1818–94) and the title of the work in question is *History of England from the Fall of Wolsey to the Defeat of the Spanish Armada* (1856–70) in twelve volumes, four of which are given to *The Reign of Elizabeth*. Again, the compiler of this *Guide* took the trouble to track down the work referred to so summarily in Eliot's note to line 264. P. S. King and Son Ltd turn out not to be the publishers, trade sponsors or authors but the agents of sale for a London County Council official report by the Council's Clerk and Architect. The reference to King is revealed to be a piece of mock-bibliographical detail which he picked up from his own 'London Letter' in *The Dial*, May 1921, when casting round for material to bulk out the notes. Some of the notes are personal asides, endearing, yet unhelpful, as to line 360, where Eliot confides to us that he has forgotten the precise account of the Antarctic expedition, 'but I think one of Shackleton's'. Or the amusing mock-pedantry of line 357, quoting from Chapman's *Handbook of Birds of Eastern North America* for the habitat of the hermit-thrush, the *Turdus aonalaschkae pallasii*. (Eliot relished the mild indelicacy of *Turdus* and found an occasion to invent another variety of *Turdus*, which he named in a 1953 address on 'American Literature and the American Language'). The reference to Chapman may also conceal a private family allusion, more an affectionate tribute than a joke, since his mother had presented him with a copy of the sixth edition on the occasion of his fourteenth birthday, so helping him to identify that bird in the neighbourhood of the family summer home on Cape Ann. Eliot treasured the memory of himself as 'the small boy who was a devoted birdwatcher' just as he treasured the book itself. Inscribed 'Thomas Stearns Eliot Sept. 26th 1902', it remained in his library for over sixty years, until his death. Also among his books was another title referred to in *The Waste Land* notes (to lines 366–76), *Blick ins Chaos* by Hermann Hesse, inscribed 'Berne Dec. 1921'. It seems that when Eliot had to put the notes together as an afterthought, he went no further than the books on his shelves!

Not surprisingly some early reviewers attacked *The Waste Land* both for its obscurities and its notes. In 1924, Pound retorted that the obscurities were no more than four Sanskrit words, three of which are 'so implied in the surrounding text that one can pass them by ... without losing the general tone or the main emotion of the passage. They are so obviously the words of some ritual or other'. The single word requiring explanation is 'Shantih': peace.

> For the rest, I saw the poem in typescript, and I did not see the notes till 6 or 8 months afterward; and they have not increased my enjoyment of the poem one atom. The poem seems to me an emotional unit ...
>
> I have not read Miss Weston's *Ritual to Romance*, and I do not at present intend to. As to the citations, I do not think it matters a damn which is from Day, which from Milton, Middleton, Webster or Augustine. I mean so far as the functioning of the poem is concerned.

Even if we choose to accept Pound's verdict, the mock-notes are not to be ignored. They are a useful reminder to us of the poet's presence, of a personality with individual quirks and a distinctive point of view.* Arnold Bennett wondered if the notes were 'a lark or serious?' and inquired 'Mr Eliot, did you mean it all seriously?' Eliot's reply was possum-like – enigmatic and deadpan. The notes were, he answered, 'not more of a skit than some things in the poem itself'. They remind us too that the author can properly regard his sources as playthings, to be followed verbatim, or imitated, or changed at will. In his 'Dante' essay, Eliot wrote that we do not need to know the precise meaning of the imagery 'but in our awareness of the images we must be aware that the meaning is there'. Mario Praz has suggested that this is the case in Eliot's use of certain images in Dante: 'It is as if Eliot had been reading Dante without giving much heed to the meaning, but letting himself be impressed by a few clear visual images: these he rearranges in his own mind, just as in a kaleidoscope the same coloured glasses can give a no less harmonious (though different) design than the previous one.' Eliot touches on this question in *The Use of Poetry and the Use of Criticism*, discussing an astrological image in 'Gerontion' which he originally found in a play by the Elizabethan dramatist George Chapman (see page 77, note to lines 67–9), who in turn probably took it from the Roman playwright Seneca. Eliot speculated, from his own experience, that 'this imagery had some personal saturation value, so to speak, for Seneca; another for Chapman, and another for myself...' He stressed that the feelings awakened by the imagery were possibly 'too obscure for the authors to know quite what they were'.

In discussing the astrological image in 'Gerontion', Eliot went on to point to another unfathomable mystery surrounding the source of imagery:

---

* Anyone interested in looking further at the issues which surround the authorial annotation of poetry, the function of the epigraph and Eliot's general allusiveness should look at W. K. Wimsatt's *The Verbal Icon* (1954), pages 14–18, and William Empson's 'Obscurity and Annotation', an essay c. 1930 and unpublished at the time. Empson had Eliot and *The Waste Land* in mind and he tackles the issues in provocative and pungent style (*Arguifying: Essays on Literature and Culture*, 1987, ed. John Haffenden).

Only a part of an author's imagery comes from his reading. It comes from the whole of his sensitive life since early childhood. Why, for all of us, out of all that we have heard, seen, felt, in a lifetime, do certain images recur, charged with emotion, rather than others? ... six ruffians seen through an open window playing cards at night at a small French railway junction where there was a water-mill: such memories may have a symbolic value, but of what we cannot tell, for they come to represent the depths of feeling into which we cannot peer.

In 'Journey of the Magi' we encounter these images again, now set in a time and place remote from twentieth-century France. These examples indicate the areas of knowledge which are beyond the scope of any handbook, and remind us that our surest guide in interpreting the use to which Eliot puts his sources is our own sense of his habits of mind, a context of meaning to be discovered in the poems themselves, not through notes.

In the passage I have just quoted, Eliot draws our attention to images, deriving from experiences in his own life, which carry a density of meaning that he is unable to explain. This accords with a central tenet in his theory of poetic creation:

> the more perfect the artist, the more completely separate in him will be the man who suffers and the mind which creates ... It is not in his personal emotions, the emotions provoked by particular events in his life, that the poet is in any way remarkable or interesting ... *significant* emotion, emotion which has its life in the poem and not in the history of the poet. The emotion of art is impersonal.
>
> ('Tradition and the Individual Talent', 1919)

V

The force of these remarks should restrain us from interpreting Eliot's poetry through the details of his life; and, in practice, such details are not needed for the understanding of his work. Nevertheless, there is some point in knowing that correspondences do exist, that places and people in real life were carried through, sometimes much modified or fragmented, to the poetry; that, for example, Eliot saw the name Prufrock-Littau, furniture-wholesalers, on advertisements in his home town of St Louis, Missouri (an appropriation into 'Prufrock' which he described as 'quite unconscious': 'I did not have at the time of writing the poem, and have not yet recovered, any recollection of having acquired the name in this way'); that Sweeney was a figure probably derived from Eliot's recollection of the Irish ex-pugilist with whom he took boxing lessons at Boston during his student days at Harvard; that the lines

> On Margate Sands.
> I can connect
> Nothing with nothing.

in *The Waste Land* were written when Eliot was actually at Margate for four weeks from 11 October to 12 November 1921, convalescing from a breakdown and finding it difficult to write; that snatches of speech and mannerisms in 'A Game of Chess' copied his wife and were applauded by her on the manuscript as 'wonderful', while Pound scribbled 'photo' as his comment, i.e. close to life (did he mean *too* close?).

Two years earlier, in 1919, Eliot had described the poet's task in 'Tradition and the Individual Talent': 'the struggle – which alone constitutes life for a poet – to transmute his personal and private agonies into something rich and strange, something universal and impersonal'. Eliot was writing of Shakespeare. But the vibrant tones embrace his own 'agonies' – and his own ambitions, too, towards a transcendent historical standpoint, expressed a few lines later in the pronouncement that 'The great poet, in writing himself, writes his time.'

Eliot's criticism is also to be consulted for what it tells us about the writing of his poetry. Their proximity is signposted in 'The Frontiers of Criticism' (1956), where Eliot speaks of his criticism as being 'a by-product of my private poetry workshop' and 'a prolongation of the thinking that went into my own verse'. (According to Pound, the sum of Eliot's 'poetic theory' was 'I have tried to write of a few things that really have moved me'.)

I have allowed myself some freedom in including historical and biographical notes which may seem remote from questions of meaning in the text but which touch on issues which I believe to be generally helpful in our understanding of the inspiration and nature of Eliot's poetry and the ways in which it was enmeshed with his life and the lives of those in his immediate circle. Such, for example, is the very first note in the book, treating the dedication to *Prufrock and Other Observations* and in particular the identity of the dedicatee, Jean Verdenal. Although we know virtually nothing about him, the dedication establishes clearly enough his importance to the poet, both as a friend and as one killed in the war, one of Eliot's own generation. There remained for Eliot, as he recalled in 1934, a precious memory of Verdenal 'coming across the Luxembourg Gardens in the late afternoon, waving a branch of lilac', a scene which belongs to the time when he knew him in Paris before the war. Can this image have been far from Eliot's mind when he wrote the opening lines of *The Waste Land*, and placed them beneath the title 'The Burial of the Dead'? This, of course, is pure speculation. But *The Waste Land*, for all its constructedness and intellectual design, reads as the creation of a poet who has suffered his own 'waste land'. It is a poem 'reticent, yet confessional' (Harriet Monroe's phrase for Eliot's poetry in general); carrying 'an objective and reticent autobiography' (as Eliot said of Pound's 'Three Cantos' in 1918); and before its publication he wrote to his mother that the poem contained much of his life. Its 'confessional' aspect is recorded for us in Virginia Woolf's diary:

> He sang it and chanted it and rhythmed it. It has great beauty and force of phrase; symmetry; and tensity. What connects it together, I'm not so sure. But he read till he had to rush — letters to write about the London Magazine — and discussion was thus curtailed. One was left, however, with some strong emotion. The Waste Land, it is called; and Mary Hutch, who has heard it more quietly, interprets it to be Tom's auto-biography — a melancholy one.

(Mary Hutchinson spoke from knowledge. Like Virginia Woolf, she first met Eliot in 1916. A Bloomsbury hostess, she came to know the Eliots well and became a close friend whose opinion Tom would seek on his new poems and in whom Vivien confided about the problems of her marriage.*) The error of biographicalism – the fallacy of interpreting a work of literature in terms of its author's life – is notorious as one of the prime critical fallacies. Eliot was plagued by such speculations; and had grown used, he confessed (in 1956), 'to having my personal biography reconstructed from passages which I got out of books, or which I invented out of nothing because they sounded well; and to having my biography invariably ignored in what I *did* write from personal experience'. But the issues are not simple; and there are occasions when a biographical approach can offer us literary insights. There is, for example, Conrad Aiken's comment, that the 'psychological realism' of 'Prufock' and 'Portrait of a Lady' – poems written when he was one of Eliot's closest friends at Harvard, exchanging poems and ideas with him – is 'autobiographic'. Again, biography arose in Edmund Wilson's immediate response to *The Waste Land*, which he read in a proof of the American edition in September 1922. Writing to his friend the poet John Peale Bishop, Wilson dismissed the poem's ambitious historical-cultural pretensions and fixed upon what he felt to be on the one hand its personal essence in Eliot's 'own agonized state of mind' and equally upon its pressing universal truth in the condition of modern man:

> ... it is certainly his masterpiece so far. He supplements it with a set of notes almost as long as the poem itself, explaining the literary, historic, anthropological, metaphysical, and religious significances to be found in it; but the poem, as it appears to me from two or three cursory readings, is nothing more or less than a most distressingly moving account of

* A cryptic entry in Virginia Woolf's diary for 16 May 1919 – reporting a conversation with Lady Ottoline Morrell, another Bloomsbury hostess: 'we talked personalities; investigated the case of Mary Hutch & Eliot' – suggests that the intimacy of their friendship gave rise to the suspicion of a liaison.

Eliot's own agonized state of mind during the years which preceded his nervous breakdown. Never have the sufferings of the sensitive man in the modern city chained to some work he hates and crucified on the vulgarity of his surroundings been so vividly set forth. It is certainly a cry *de profundis* if ever there was one – almost the cry of a man on the verge of insanity.

Two months later, in November 1922, Bishop was able to get a more intimate account of *The Waste Land* from Pound, who explained its autobiographical areas of reference (quoted here in the notes (to Section II, page 156; and to line 99, pages 158–9)), leaving Bishop with his own understanding of the poem, as he told Wilson: 'it's my present opinion that the poem is not so logically constructed as I had at first supposed and that it is a mistake to seek for more than ... personal emotion in a number of passages ... Thomas' sexual troubles are undoubtedly extreme' (quoted in Bush, 1991).

Mrs Eliot has located the poet's agony at this time in his relationship with Vivien, his first wife: 'it was the sheer hell of being with her that forced him to write it' – an insight shared by I. A. Richards in identifying Vivien as Eliot's Muse. This understanding of the poem is confirmed by a statement Eliot made in the 1960s: 'To her the marriage brought no happiness ... to me, it brought the state of mind out of which came *The Waste Land*' (*Letters I*); and the modern Cleopatra of Part II and 'The lady of situations' have both been identified with her (Bush, 1991). Her contribution to *The Waste Land* is discussed on page 132; and, according to Rebecca West, Eliot never stopped writing about Vivien until *The Confidential Clerk* (1953).

Although these facts and lines of interpretation should not set us off in pursuit of personal clues, none the less, the attachment of *The Waste Land* to Eliot's life is a dimension of its meaning, and this we should attend to however lightly and tactfully; and if I seem to take up the question rather heavy-handedly it is partly in response to Eliot's own insistence upon the impersonality of art and the semblance of impersonality that so much of his poetry strives to convey (a highly personal impersonality, it has to be said). Partly, too, it is in response to Eliot's throwaway remarks about the origin and reference of *The Waste Land*: 'Various critics have done me the honour to interpret the poem in terms of criticism of the contemporary world, have considered it, indeed, as an important bit of social criticism. To me it was only the relief of a personal and wholly insignificant grouse against life; it is just a piece of rhythmical grumbling.' On another occasion he said that the poem was written 'to relieve my emotions'. Eliot told Virginia Woolf that he wrote the final sections of the poem in a trance. And during an interview for the *Paris Review* in 1959, he averred that 'I wasn't even bothering whether I understood what I was saying.' But the poem itself tells a different story. Recent studies have uncovered biographical layers, hitherto unsuspected. In particular, in *Eliot's New Life* (1988) Lyndall Gordon identifies Emily Hale, the poet's first love, as the inspiration of his religious poetry, her presence seen in the Lady of *Ash-Wednesday* and in 'Marina', both poems calling up the New England coast with which she was associated in Eliot's evocative personal imagery of coast and sea.

In more general terms, we should not forget the importance to Eliot of his American origins. A man of European culture, at one period he felt himself to be more French than English or American – the language of 'Preludes' and 'Rhapsody' is sometimes closer to transliterated French than to colloquial English; and in 1916–17 he was writing poems in French. Yet he was still able to say of his poetry: 'in its sources, in its emotional springs, it comes from America'. Matthiesen has remarked 'how often a sudden release of the spirit is expressed through sea-imagery which, with its exact notation of gulls and granite rocks and the details of sailing, seems always to spring from his own boyhood experience off the New England coast'. That this information came from Eliot himself seems to be confirmed by a letter in which John Hayward writes that 'Some of the great passages in his poetry – the end of "Gerontion", the Phoenician Sailor, "Marina" etc are evocations of the coast of New England and of white sails flying'. These memories are drawn upon in Section VI of *Ash-Wednesday* in a passage of great power, touching with highly-charged imagery the 'lost' world of his childhood (see the notes to line 192 onwards). The shabby townscapes of 'Preludes' and 'Rhapsody on a Windy Night' found their origin in his St Louis childhood where, 'for nine months of the year my scenery was almost exclusively urban, and a good deal of it seedily, drably urban at that. My urban imagery was that of St Louis, upon which that of Paris and London have been super-imposed.'

St Louis was also a source of amusement. In the first six months of 1897, when Eliot was nine, the *St Louis Globe–Democrat* carried the advertisements of Dr F. L. Sweany, a specialist in 'Nervous Disability', who inquired of his readers 'Is your Body and Brain Fatigued? ARE YOU LACKING IN ENERGY, STRENGTH AND VIGOUR ... MEN WHO ARE WASTING AWAY! Do you want to be cured?' At the time, Eliot was sufficiently impressed to copy Dr Sweany's advertisement for *Fireside*, his childhood magazine. Later, Dr Sweany's message was to re-surface in Prufrock's anxieties and the doctor himself in his namesake, 'Apeneck Sweeney'.

VI

The truth which Eliot could never escape from, whether by poetic artifice or prose argument, is neatly put by Thoreau: 'Poetry is a piece of very private history, which unostentatiously lets us into the secret of a man's life.' It is a secret, of course, that we can never hope to share completely. The inscription in a copy of *Poems 1909–1925*, given to his first wife, on Christmas Day 1925, warns us of this: 'for my dearest Vivien, this book, which no one else will quite understand'. However, with the benefit of Eliot's letters, we can identify some of the most intense pressures on his poetry, as when he wrote to Conrad Aiken on 10 January 1916 that he had been so 'taken up with the worries of finance and Vivien's health' that he had 'written nothing lately. I *hope* to write when I have more detachment ... I have *lived* through material for a score of long poems in the last six months.' Eliot was thinking back to the death of Jean Verdenal in May of the previous year.

With these reservations and warnings in mind, I have not excluded biographical references from the notes, although they are not essential to the public meaning of the poetry. In an interview in 1962, Eliot said that Prufrock was made up of himself and a man about forty. It is a personal presence that we might have guessed without this confirmation – and does it matter? Does this information add anything that the poem does not already convey to us? In Eliot's choice of the name Prufrock, the origin is a purely accidental factor. What is significant is the range of verbal associations which the name awakens – prudence, primness, prissiness (and so on) – associations which seem to be answered by the character of the man who reveals himself in the poem. Eliot is playing off the slightly absurd ring of J. Alfred Prufrock against the romantic expectations aroused by the words *The Love Song of*; it is a joke against the convention that Love Songs are not the preserve of people with such laughably unromantic names. To catch this significance in the name and in the poem's title, the reader has to do his own thinking. It is not an instance where factual or historical notes will help. Another case is Pipit, the mysterious someone in 'A Cooking Egg'. Who is she? Our sense of her identity will affect our understanding of the poem. But one's own guess or reasoning is as good as anyone else's. The critics cannot agree. An old aunt? a former nurse or governess? a childhood playmate, now visited many years later? a mistress? These are some of the contradictory suggestions put forward.

In this trivial instance the reader must judge the evidence and come to his own conclusions, exactly as he must throughout his reading of Eliot. Freedom is our prerogative. Eliot pointed this out in commenting on a collection of essays entitled *Interpretations* (one of which provided an analysis of 'Prufrock'). He drew attention to the fallacy

> of assuming that there must be just one interpretation of the poem as a whole, that must be right ... as for the meaning of

the poem as a whole, it is not exhausted by any explanation, for the meaning is what the poem means to different sensitive readers.

At the other extreme, Eliot resisted the projections of his readers when they conflicted with his own sense of 'intention', as with *The Waste Land*: 'some of the more approving critics said that I had expressed the "disillusionment of a generation", which is nonsense. I may have expressed for them their own illusion of being disillusioned, but that did not form part of my intention.' Or we can remember his response to an inquiry about the meaning of a much-debated line in *Ash-Wednesday*, 'Lady, three white leopards sat under a juniper-tree.' Eliot answered, 'I mean ...' and simply read back the line to his questioner without any comment whatsoever. The same question was put to his hippopotamus: 'what in the name of sense *is* the hippopotamus?' asked one teacher of his students; and he reports that 'on a later occasion the poet himself, with his sly ironic smile, put me off by intimating the writer could not – he meant would not – expound my riddle'. Another professor, reporting to the poet that his students found difficulty with *The Waste Land*, was informed that they were looking for what was 'not there'. When the experts were squabbling over the identity of Pipit – whether, to quote Eliot, she was 'a little girl, an inamorata, a female relative, or an old nurse' – he remarked that they had reached 'the nadir of critical futility'. As Eliot himself said, we should be alert to the danger of 'mistaking explanation for understanding'; to the temptation of inventing 'the puzzle for the pleasure of discovering the solution'.

All else failing, we might turn to the poet himself as the final authority. Eliot was prepared to offer help, notably, for example, in his opening Note to *The Waste Land*, where he refers his readers to Jessie Weston's *From Ritual to Romance* as a book that 'will elucidate the difficulties of the poem much better than my notes can do'; and he also speaks there of the process of 'elucidation', which is the attempt made in this book. But ultimately Eliot declined to make any special claim to authority, deferring to the communion between reader and text.

> In one sense, but a very limited sense, he the poet knows better what his poems 'mean' than anyone else; he may know the history of their composition, the material which has gone in and come out in an unrecognizable form, and he knows what he was trying to do and what he was meaning to mean. But what a poem means is as much what it means to others as what it means to the author; and indeed, in the course of time a poet may become merely a reader in respect to his own works, forgetting his original meaning, or without forgetting, merely changing.
>
> (*The Use of Poetry and the Use of Criticism*, 1933)

Sometimes he even denied a conscious intention, or made light of it, as in quoting Byron to explain *Ash-Wednesday* (see page 219) or as in the *Paris Review* interview he gave in 1959: 'I wonder what an 'intention' means! One wants to get something off one's chest. One doesn't know quite what it is that one wants to get off the chest until one's got it off.'

The implication for this *Guide* is clear. Beyond the level of mere information, no external aid is of final use to us in our reading of T. S. Eliot or any other poet; and the sooner we are able to dispense with the aid that this book represents, the sooner we are able to read the poetry directly and fully, by way of a personal encounter. Our real understanding of the poetry, and of the poet, begins where these notes end.

Sources

In the Acknowledgements and Select Bibliography I have indicated the wide range of Eliot studies drawn upon in the preparation of the notes that follow. But six authors had the benefit of advice direct from Eliot himself. These are identified in the notes: Williamson, Matthiessen, Hayward, Stephenson, Greene and Howarth.

Hugh Ross Williamson's *The Poetry of T. S. Eliot*, published in 1932 (reprint 1971), was one of the earliest critical-interpretative studies. In a prefatory note, Williamson expresses gratitude to Eliot for 'supplying certain facts and ... for the stimulus of his conversation'.

F. O. Matthiessen found Williamson's book 'a useful manual of relevant explanation, to which I have been frequently indebted'. But we should consult it with a pinch of salt, in view of Eliot's remark to Cleanth Brooks (in 1937) that he considered Williamson 'went to rather fantastic lengths'.

Matthiessen was a Professor of English at Harvard when Eliot visited as Charles Eliot Norton Professor from October 1932 to April 1933. In *The Achievement of T. S. Eliot*, published in 1935, Matthiessen acknowledged 'the great benefit of conversation' with the poet during those seven months, sometimes quoting Eliot verbatim.

John Hayward, a notable English scholar and bibliographer, was a close friend of Eliot from 1930 until Eliot's second marriage in 1957. He gathered a collection of Eliot's letters and manuscripts, now in the library of King's College, Cambridge. In 1946–7, Hayward assisted Pierre Leyris in the preparation of *Poèmes 1910–1930* (Paris, 1947), a French-language selection, to which he contributed dates or places of composition, together with additional notes to *The Waste Land*, interspersed among Eliot's. As Eliot and Hayward were sharing a flat at this time, we can take it, at the very least, that these notes came with Eliot's approval. It is significant that the wording of some notes is very close to the wording of Matthiessen's comments on the same points. This may mean that Eliot advised both of them in very much the same terms. Or, if Hayward was following Matthiessen verbatim, this would have been with Eliot's endorsement.

Ethel M. Stephenson was the author of *T. S. Eliot and the Lay Reader*, first published in 1944, with a second, extended edition in 1946. The Acknowledgements open with thanks to Eliot, 'who has seen each manuscript and who has added so many interesting references which inspired his work'.

Edward J. H. Greene (latterly a Professor at the University of Alberta) consulted Eliot in person and corresponded with him on points of detail in the preparation of *T. S. Eliot et la France* (Paris, 1951), a work commenced in 1937, abandoned during the war, and taken up again after the Liberation of France in 1944.

Whereas Matthiessen is a standard work in the Eliot literature, the comments by Hayward and Ethel Stephenson seem to be unknown; at least, they have not been drawn upon by other commentators, and I have felt them worth quoting here.

In December 1961, Herbert Howarth sent Eliot a copy of the typescript of his *Notes on Some Figures Behind T. S. Eliot*, offering to omit anything Eliot might object to. In the event, Eliot objected to Howarth's central thesis: that his poetry could largely be explained in terms of his reaction (positive and negative) to his family. Howarth accepted this criticism and, to meet Eliot's objection, carried through an 'entire reconstruction'. Eliot was mollified and undertook to read and comment on the revised text and to assist him on factual points, which he did. But Howarth suspected that Eliot's 'I don't remember' answer to some of his questions was sometimes a means of concealment.

A further source (described by Jordan, 1990, and in a personal communication) is a copy of *Ara Vos Prec* which Eliot annotated, indicating sources and other information, a gift to Miss Lucy Thayer in 1927. In the notes I have identified these annotations as Thayer. Lucy Thayer was a cousin of Scofield Thayer, a friend of Eliot at school, Harvard and Oxford, and editor of *The Dial* 1919–25. She was also a close friend of Eliot's first wife and a witness to their marriage at Hampstead Registry Office. Unfortunately, many further notes were erased. But further scientific examination may recover them.

The play *Tom and Viv* (1984, revised 1992) by Michael Hastings is a reconstruction of Eliot's first marriage, important to this *Guide* since its historical content is based upon manuscript materials and interviews and it provides us with the best-informed account of Vivien Eliot that we have.

Note on Dating

For readers interested in tracing the course of Eliot's development in these poems, I have added the dates and places of composition, where these are known. I have also given details of their first publication. These indicate the circulation the poems enjoyed.

The details of composition I have checked with two works whose authors consulted Eliot: Greene and W. J. Pope, 'The Early Works of T. S. Eliot' (unpublished M.A. thesis, University of London, 1950). I also referred to *Poèmes 1910–1930* (Paris, 1947), and to its editor, Pierre Leyris, who was advised by Eliot and John Hayward. The full bibliographical details are to be found in Donald Gallup, *T. S. Eliot, A Bibliography* (1952, rev. edn. 1969). Further information is now available in Valerie Eliot's edition of *The Waste Land* manuscript, in *Eliot's Early Years* (1977) by Lyndall Gordon and in Valerie Eliot's first volume of the *Letters: 1898–1922* (1988).

PRUFROCK AND OTHER OBSERVATIONS

Published June 1917

Dedication: In 1910, Eliot first met Jean Verdenal, then a medical student a year younger than himself, at the *pension* in Paris where they were fellow lodgers and writers of poetry. They shared an enthusiasm for Laforgue, visited galleries together, discussed the latest books and corresponded after Eliot's return to America in the autumn of 1911. A verse notebook of this period is dedicated to Verdenal. In a letter to Conrad Aiken in January 1916, Eliot gave Verdenal's death as one of the circumstances that blocked his writing. He was killed on the Anglo-French expedition to the Dardanelles in May 1915.

Epigraph: The lines, from Dante (*Purgatorio* xxi, 133–6), are a testimony to the strength of their friendship; they are taken from what Eliot described as one of the most 'affecting' meetings in the poem. Dante is being conducted through the underworld by the spirit of the Roman poet Virgil, who is recognized by the spirit of another Roman poet, Statius, one of his followers. Statius stoops and tries to grasp Virgil's feet in homage. But Virgil stops him with the reminder that they are both insubstantial shadows. Eliot quotes Statius's answer: 'Now can you understand the quantity of love that warms me towards you, so that I forget our vanity, and treat the shadows like the solid thing.' (The translation of these lines, as in many of the Dante quotations in this *Guide*, is that used by Eliot in his 'Dante' essay (1929).)

Eliot referred again to his friendship with Verdenal, many years later, in *The Criterion* for April 1934, contrasting the richness of Paris with the cultural 'deserts' of England and

America: 'I am willing to admit that my own retrospect is touched by a sentimental sunset, the memory of a friend coming across the Luxembourg Gardens in the late afternoon, waving a branch of lilac, a friend who was later (so far as I could find out) to be mixed with the mud of Gallipoli.' According to Robert Sencourt (*T. S. Eliot: A Memoir* (1971), ed. Donald Adamson), letters in the Houghton Library, Harvard, provide a 'record of this affinity of hearts'. In *Letters I* all seven letters from Verdenal come from the Houghton Library. All are written from Paris and date between July 1911 and December 1912. There are no letters from Eliot to Verdenal.

George Watson has given a very interesting account of his search for details of Verdenal and his friendship with Eliot ('Quest for a Frenchman', *Sewanee Review*, Summer 1976). From this, we learn that Verdenal was born on 11 May 1890, that Eliot saw him last in Autumn 1911, that he served as a medical officer and was killed on 2 May 1915.

The dedication in the original 1917 edition of *Prufrock and Other Observations* read 'To Jean Verdenal, 1889–1915'. Then, for the next collection, *Ara Vos Prec* (1920), the dedication was dropped and the Dante epigraph appeared for the first time; while the American edition, *Poems* (1920), carried the dedication but not the epigraph. The words 'mort aux Dardanelles' were added and the 'To' changed to 'For' in *Poems 1909–1925* (1925). These additional words may have been suggested by Conrad Aiken's *in memoriam* sonnet 'Rupert Brooke': beneath the title came 'Died at the Dardanelles, April 1915'. (The Dardanelles was formerly called the Hellespont. Here the Greeks landed to attack Troy. Here too Ulysses (in Homer's *Odyssey*) set out for home. It has been suggested that Eliot so expanded the Dedication to effect these classical allusions.) The poem appeared in *The Atlantic Monthly*, July 1915. (For the possible connection between Rupert Brooke, Verdenal and *The Waste Land*, see page 139.)

The Dante quotation and the Dedication were brought together first in *Poems 1909–1925* (1925) at the head of the 'Prufrock and Other Observations' section, and the volume as a whole was dedicated to Eliot's father.

The Love Song of J. Alfred Prufrock

Written Paris, Munich February 1910 – July/August 1911;
Poetry *(Chicago) June 1915*

Composition: 'The poem of Prufrock was conceived some time in 1910. I think that when I went to Paris in the autumn of that year I had already written several fragments which were ultimately embodied in the poem, but I cannot at this distance remember which. I think that the passage beginning "I am not Prince Hamlet", a passage showing the influence of Laforgue, was one of these fragments which I took with me, but the poem was not completed until the summer of 1911' (Eliot to John C. Pope, 8 March 1946).

An early work that stands behind 'Prufrock' is 'Spleen', a 17-line poem originally published in *The Harvard Advocate* in January 1910. The final stanza draws a proto-Prufrock: 'And Life, a little bald and gray,/Languid, fastidious, and bland,/Waits, hat and gloves in hand,/Punctilious of tie and suit/(Somewhat impatient of delay)/On the doorstep of the Absolute.'

Matthiessen comments that ' "Prufrock", in the movement of its verse, its repetitions, and echoes, and even in its choice of theme, seems of all Eliot's poems to have been written most immediately under Laforgue's stimulus (though brought to a finished perfection of form which Laforgue's more impromptu verse scarcely attained).'

Further elucidation is provided in Eliot's remarks on the 'verse method' of Donne, Corbière and Laforgue: 'the pattern is given by what goes on within the mind, rather than by the exterior events which provoke the mental activity and play of thought and feeling'. The Epigraph and the opening lines establish both the importance of Dante and the structure of the poem and the parallels – ironic, pathetic and comic – which Eliot constructs between the poet of the *Divine Comedy* and Prufrock. This is touched upon in the notes here and explored fully in Manganiello.

The other major influence was Bergson (see Introduction, pages 6–7), in particular 'Introduction à la Métaphysique' (1903). This was a relatively obscure journal publication and Eliot probably met the essay in the authorized translation, *An Introduction to Metaphysics* (1913), by T. E. Hulme, which he put on the reading list for his lecture course on modern French Literature given in 1916.

Firstly, here is Bergson discussing 'the depth of my being, that which is most uniformly, most constantly and most enduringly myself' (exactly what Prufrock reveals about himself), where Bergson (like Prufrock) finds 'a continuous flux . . . a succession of states . . . all extend into each other'.

This second passage is a direct continuation of the first. Again, it appears that Eliot modelled Prufrock on Bergson's scheme, taking over some of Hulme's language:

> The inner life may be compared to the unravelling of a coil, for there is no living being who does not feel himself coming gradually to the end of his role; and to live is to grow old [cf. line 120]. But it may just as well be compared to a continual rolling up [cf. line 121], like that of a thread on a ball [cf. line 92], for our past follows us, it swells incessantly with the present that it picks up on its way; and consciousness means memory . . . let us, then, [cf. line 1] rather imagine an infinitely small elastic body, contracted, if it were possible, to a mathematical point.

In *Matter and Memory*, Bergson describes individual freedom as the state 'when our acts spring from our whole personality, when they express it', a concept which bears directly upon Prufrock's self-agonizings. The mechanism of Prufrock's fluid psychological processes, the 'visions and revisions' (line 39) and the recollections, associations and fantasies from line 50 onwards, accord with the scheme elaborated by Bergson in *Matter and Memory*.

For the influence of Charles-Louis Philippe, see Introduction page 11. Moreover, Howarth has a valuable section (pages 158–62) and suggests that 'Prufrock' 'displays the materials, colors, and mood of some striking sentences' in *Lettres de Jeunesse*, which was published serially during Eliot's stay in France.

For the influence of Dostoevsky, see Introduction, page 11.

For the origin and associations of 'Prufrock' see page 37.

Title: The name 'J. Alfred Prufrock' follows the early form of the poet's signature 'T. Stearns Eliot'. He also used this form in signing his letters (in 1915–16) to Harriet Monroe when writing to her about the poem, which appeared in *Poetry* (Chicago), the magazine she founded and edited.

'I am convinced that it would never have been called "Love Song" but for a title of Kipling's that stuck obstinately in my head: "The Love Song of Har Dyal".' The poem was originally entitled 'Prufrock Among the Women'. Later, Eliot commented: 'I'm afraid that J. Alfred Prufrock didn't have much of a love life.'

Epigraph: 'If I thought that my reply would be to someone who would ever return to earth, this flame would remain without further movement; but as no one has ever returned alive from this gulf, if what I hear is true, I can answer you with no fear of infamy.' These words are spoken by Count Guido da Monte-feltro (1223–98) in Dante's *Inferno* xxvii, 61–6. Dante recounts his visit to the underworld. In the Eighth Chasm of Hell he meets Guido, punished here, with other false and deceitful counsellors, in a single prison of flame for his treacherous advice on earth to Pope Boniface. When the damned speak from this flame the voice sounds from the tip, which trembles. Guido refers to this, and goes on to explain that he speaks freely only because he believes that Dante is like himself, one of the dead who will never return to earth to report what he says.

Barbara Everett (*Critical Quarterly*, xvi, 1974) proposed that a possible prose model was 'The Diary of a Superfluous Man' by the Russian novelist Ivan Turgenev (1818–83). The Scribner's translation (1904) by Isabel Hapgood shows verbal likenesses with the poem not so evident in other translations. Henry James thought highly of the story and it was generally thought one of Turgenev's best and most interesting. Later, Eliot wrote about the isolation of the Russian writer during his years of exile in Paris.

Some commentators see an element of self-portrayal. Conrad Aiken recalled Eliot's 'agonies of shyness' and his conviction of 'the necessity, if one was shy, of disciplining oneself, lest one miss certain varieties of experience which one did not naturally "take" to. The dances, and the parties, were part of this discipline...' In 1914 Eliot was taught by Bertrand Russell, then visiting Harvard. Russell reported to Lady Ottoline Morrell that his pupil was 'ultra-civilized ... altogether impeccable in his taste but has no vigour or life – or enthusiasm'. A year later, he found Eliot 'exquisite and listless'. In November 1918, Virginia Woolf observed in her diary: 'Mr Eliot is well expressed by his name – a polished, cultivated, elaborate young American, talking so slow, that each word seems to have special finish allotted to it.' But she also discerned 'beneath the surface' someone 'very intellectual, intolerant, with strong views of his own, & a poetic creed'. To this may have been added aspects of other people: Conrad Aiken thought that his uncle, Alfred Potter, was one such model, commemorated in the oddity of Prufrock's name.

l. 1: in the *Inferno*, Dante is conducted through the underworld by the Latin poet Virgil.

let us: see discussion of Bergson, page 46.

you: Eliot offered different identifications. At some time in the 1950s, he answered an enquirer that 'anything I say now must be somewhat conjectural, as it was written so long ago that my memory may deceive me; but I am prepared to assert that "you" in *The Love Song* is merely some friend or companion, presumably of the male sex, whom the speaker is at the moment addressing, and that it has no emotional content whatever'. On the other hand, in a 1962 interview, Eliot said that Prufrock was in part a man of about forty and in part himself, and that he was employing the notion of the split personality, a concept which was first studied and widespread a few years earlier. On yet another occasion, he referred to Prufrock as a 'young' man.

But the immediate source for 'you and I' is likely to have been Bergson's *Essai sur les données immédiates de la conscience* (1889), published in translation in 1910 as *Time and Free Will*, the work from which Eliot quoted most frequently when later he wrote about Bergson at Harvard. In the *Essai*, Bergson develops the idea of a double self: one aspect being the everyday self, experiencing common reality; the other, a deeper self, attuned to profound truths, and normally in subjugation to the superficial self.

l. 2 spread out: this metaphor occurs several times in Bergson's *Essai*.

ll. 2–3: the extended image evokes a style of formulaic phrasing used in classical epics, notably to introduce scenes and books in Homer's *Odyssey* (e.g. the opening to Book II: 'When primal Dawn spread on the eastern sky/her fingers of pink light').

l. 3: this unusual image may have been suggested to Eliot by 'Morte? Se peut-il pas qu'elle dorme/Grise de cosmiques chloroformes?' (Dead? Can it not be that she sleeps/Grey from cosmic chloroforms?) from 'Jeux' by Laforgue, whose method was described by Symons as using 'non-poetic' words. Another suggestion may have come from two poems in the *In Hospital* sequence (in *Book of Verses,* 1888) by William Ernest Henley (1849–1903). In nos. V and VI the patient is under an 'anaesthetic'. Some of the poems were regarded as too macabre and unpoetic for an English readership but were admired in America. Eliot's use of the image illustrates what he referred to in 1917 as the 'required' 'violent stimulus of novelty', 'the element of *surprise* so essential to poetry' ('John Dryden', 1921); 'surprise which Poe considered of the highest importance, and also the restraint, and quietness of tone which make the surprise possible' ('Andrew Marvell', 1922), a 'quality' which Eliot also found in Dante.

Harriet Monroe, the then editor of *Poetry*, recalled that when the typescript of 'Prufrock' arrived the first three lines 'nearly took our breath away. Here indeed was modern sophistication dealing with the tag ends of overworldly cosmopolitanism.'

l. 4: cf. 'In the deserted, moon-blanched street,/How lonely rings the echo of my feet', the opening lines of 'A Summer Night' (1852), a dramatic monologue by Matthew Arnold lamenting man's prison-like urban existence.

l. 10 overwhelming question: in *The Pioneers* (1823) by Fenimore Cooper occurs 'this overwhelming question' (ch. 23). This was a novel Eliot read and enjoyed in his boyhood, not least for its concern with his own passion for sailing and for its distinctive Americanness. (Also see page 248, note to line 28 of *Marina*.)

ll. 13–14: cf. Laforgue: 'Dans la piece les femmes vont et viennent/En parlant des maitres de Sienne' ('In the room the women come and go/Talking of the masters of the Sienese School'). In imitating Laforgue almost word for word, Eliot introduces an element of parody, re-rendering the French in a tripping rhyming couplet, set off as a chiming chorus (repeated at lines 35–6), following a section of *vers libre*, a device which Eliot also found in Laforgue.

l. 14 Michelangelo: (1475–1564), great Italian sculptor, painter and poet.

l. 15 fog: according to Eliot, this was the smoke that blew across the Mississippi from the factories of his home-town of St Louis, Missouri. This same 'fog' also features in the opening line of 'Portrait of a Lady'.

l. 23: cf. 'Had we but world enough and time', from the poem 'To His Coy Mistress' by Andrew Marvell (1621–78). The poet argues to his 'coy mistress' there would be time for delay only if their opportunities for love-making were endless.

ll. 23–48: in this section Eliot places considerable emphasis on the phrase 'there will be time' and variants upon it, echoing the words of the preacher in Ecclesiastes iii, 1–7: 'To every thing there is a season, and a time to every purpose under the heaven: A time to be born, and a time to die; a time to plant, and a time to pluck up that which is planted; A time to kill, and a time to heal; a time to break down, and a time to build up; A time to weep, and a time to laugh; a time to mourn, and a time to dance

... a time to keep silence, and a time to speak.' Prufrock's obsession with time is infused with the Bergsonian notions of 'le temps' (abstract clock-measured time), and 'la durée' (subjective time, as we experience its passing). His obsession is also a Laforguean trait, picked up by Symons, that he is 'terribly conscious of daily life, cannot omit, mentally, a single hour of the day'.

ll. 28, 38: may well allude to the indecisiveness of Hamlet in avenging his father's death. See also note to line 111.

l. 29 works and days: echoes the title 'Works and Days', a poem by the Greek writer Hesiod (eighth century BC). It contains an account of primitive conditions in the country, together with maxims and practical instructions adapted to the peasant's life.

ll. 42–3: according to Howarth, 'There was an element of Laforgue already in him: it was easy to progress to the pose from the urbane dandyism, the perfection of dress, manners, and accomplishments, which was the Harvard style of his time, and in which he excelled.' In London Eliot sustained his Harvard style. Clive Bell, who first met him in 1916, recalled his 'studied primness of manner and speech . . . deliciously comic'.

l. 42 morning coat: a tail-coat for formal occasions.

l. 44: the word order is French, not English.

ll. 45–6: a question to be found in a letter of Laforgue's, dated 1881.

ll. 49ff.: Eliot may have taken the 'know'/'have known' locution from *The Spirit of Romance* (1910) by Ezra Pound, who quoted from the French poet François Villon (1431–?): 'I know a horse from a mule,/And Beatrix from Billet,/I know the heresy of the Bohemians,/I know son, valet and man./I know all things save myself alone.'

l. 51: a gently sardonic measure of time's passing, mingling Bergson's concept of 'le temps' and 'la durée'. cf. Laforgue, 'Sirote chaque jour ta tasse de néant' ('Sip each day your cup of nothingness').

l. 52 a dying fall: cf. 'That strain again! It had a dying fall.' These are the words of Duke Orsino in Shakespeare's *Twelfth Night* I, i. He is love-sick; the music suits his mood and he orders an encore. Clearly, Eliot liked this touch and provided his own encore, repeating the allusion, with quotation marks, in the closing lines of 'Portrait of a Lady'.

ll. 56–7 formulated: the pejorative sense is caught in Carlyle: 'Man lives not except by formulas; with customs, ways of doing and living' (*French Revolution*, 1878).

l. 60 butt-ends: an image based on the butts or ends of smoked cigars or cigarettes.

ll. 63–4: cf. 'A bracelet of bright hair about the bone' in 'The Relique' by John Donne (1572–1631), a line whose 'powerful effect' Eliot remarks upon in 'The Metaphysical Poets' (1921).

ll. 73–4: cf. 'for you yourself, sir, should be old as I am, if like a crab you could go backwards'. The words of Hamlet in Shakespeare's *Hamlet* II, ii (a scene to which Laforgue refers several times in his poetry and prose). He is simulating madness and addresses the old courtier Polonius. There are further references to *Hamlet* in lines 111, 117–18, 119.

The concealed 'allusion', to which these lines present an unlovely antithesis, is the romantic escapist yearning expressed in the Victorian song, 'Oh for the wings of a dove!'

l. 81: this line has a Biblical ring (cf. 'they mourned, and wept and fasted', 2 Samuel i, 12; and 'I fasted and wept', xii, 22), perhaps in anticipation of the Biblical allusion of the following line.

ll. 82–3: John the Baptist was decapitated and his head brought into Herod's court by Salome. Herod presented it to her as a reward for her dancing before him. The story is told in Mark vi, 17–29; Matthew xiv, 3–11. Salome (like Hamlet, see note to lines 111–19) is one of three subjects of Laforgue's *Moralités légendaires* (1887).

l. 82: Eliot imitates one of Laforgue's devices, an apologetic diminution put in parenthesis.

l. 83: cf. the words of Amos, when addressed as a 'seer' and ordered by Amaziah not to prophesy at Bethel, the King's court: 'I was no prophet, neither was I a prophet's son; but I was an herdman, and a gatherer of sycomore fruit' (Amos vii, 14).

Prufrock's apologetic admission of weakness and inability,

continued in the following passages, and reasserted at line 111, echoes Dante's reply when Virgil invites him to take the arduous journey through the underworld, see *Inferno* i, 112ff.

l. 85 eternal Footman: a personification of death, possibly derived from the 'Heavenly Footman' in *The Pilgrim's Progress* (1678) by John Bunyan (1628–88).

l. 92: cf. 'Let us roll all our strength, and all/Our sweetness, up into one ball.' At the close of 'To His Coy Mistress' (see note to line 23) the poet urges his beloved to enjoy love with him urgently and intensely. Marvell provides the obvious allusion. But it may have been coupled, in Eliot's mind, with a sentence in *The Symbolist Movement in Literature*, where Symons writes: 'In Laforgue, sentiment is squeezed out of the world before one begins to play at ball with it' (p. 112). It was certainly one of Eliot's habits to provide such arcane references for the small circle of his intimates who might be expected to pick them up.

A further dimension of allusion may be to *An Introduction to Metaphysics* (1903), where Bergson describes life as a succession of psychological states, memories and roles, 'a continual rolling up, like that of a thread on a ball, for our past follows us, it swells incessantly with the present that it picks up on its way'.

ll. 94–5: two Lazaruses are mentioned in the Bible. One was the brother of Mary and Martha, the dead man whom Christ brought back to life, whose story is told in John xi, 1–44. This Lazarus said nothing of his experience. The other Lazarus is the beggar associated with the rich man Dives, in the parable told in Luke xvi, 19–31. When they died, the poor man went to heaven, the rich man to hell. Dives wanted to warn his five brothers what hell was like, so he asked Abraham if Lazarus could be sent back to tell them. But Abraham refused: 'if they hear not Moses and the prophets, neither will they be persuaded, though one rose from the dead.'

l. 95: 'to tell all' will be to do as Christ promised of the Holy Ghost: 'he shall teach you all things, and bring all things to your remembrance' (John xiv, 26). There is also a *Hamlet* echo: 'The players cannot keep counsel, they'll tell all' (III, ii, 140).

l. 101 sprinkled streets: a cart would water the streets in summer to lay the dust. 'sprinkled pavements' and a 'magic lantern' (line 105) occur in no. XXIII of Henley's *In Hospital* sequence.

l. 105: an image from Eliot's boyhood reading. His father took the *St Louis Globe–Democrat.* In January 1897 it printed an article 'Seeing the Brain'. The illustration showed a man seated in front of a powerful light which throws a patterned X-ray of his brain on to a screen.

nerves: cf. Symons: 'It is an art of the nerves, this art of Laforgue, and it is what all art would tend towards if we followed our nerves on all their journeys.'

l. 111 Prince Hamlet: the hero of *Hamlet,* the opening of whose best-known soliloquy, 'To be, or not to be' (III, i), is echoed at the end of this line. Hamlet was given to self-scrutiny and tormented by indecisiveness. Thus Prufrock's sudden exclamation is to cut short the Hamlet-like soliloquy he has just indulged in and to assert his own subordinate, unheroic role in life.

This line also combines a reference to the *Inferno* ii, 42: 'Io non Enea, io non Paolo sono' ('I am not Aeneas, and I am not Paul'). Dante's words are a retort to Virgil, who has just tried to reassure him about the safety of their path, with the fact that Aeneas and St Paul have already been that way.

In 1956, a Professor Seymour L. Gross suggested to Eliot that the line was taken from a letter of Laurence Sterne (where the wording is identical save for the opening of 'No!'). Eliot wrote back that he had never read Sterne's letter. Would he have given the same answer to another suggestion? – that he was alluding to a line in the essay by Walter Pater (1839–94) 'Shakspeare's English Kings' (1889) (*Appreciations,* 1889): 'No! Shakspeare's Kings are not, nor are meant to be, great men . . .'. The passage continues in terms which fit Prufrock very well: 'rather, little or quite ordinary humanity, thrust upon greatness, with those pathetic results, the natural self-pity of the weak heightened in them into irresistible appeal to others . . .' Such an allusion is possible since Eliot was familiar with *Appreciations,* which had been reprinted not less than ten times by 1910.

ll. 111–19: according to Eliot, this passage, 'showing the influence of Laforgue', was one of the early fragments, written at

Harvard (about February 1910), from which 'Prufrock' was eventually put together during his stay in Europe.

Ezra Pound tried to get Eliot to remove this Hamlet section. However, as he wrote to Harriet Monroe, January 1915, 'it is an early and cherished bit and T. E. won't give it up, and as it is the only portion of the poem that most readers will like at first reading, I don't see that it will do much harm.'

Again, Symons may have played a part in this, since Laforgue's prose meditation on *Hamlet* (*Moralités légendaires*) is quoted in *The Symbolist Movement in Literature* (p. 111). The verbal quality of these lines illustrates one of Symons's comments on Laforgue's language:

> The prose and verse of Laforgue, scrupulously correct ... making subtle use of colloquialism, slang, neologism, technical terms, for their allusive, their factitious, their reflected meanings, with which one can play, very seriously ... The verse is alert, troubled, swaying, deliberately uncertain, hating rhetoric so piously that it prefers, and finds its piquancy in the ridiculously obvious ... with a familiarity of manner, as of one talking languidly, in a low voice, the lips always tensed into a slightly bitter smile.

Alongside this we can place the comment of F. O. Matthiessen: ' "Prufrock", in the movement of its verse, its repetitions, and echoes and even in its choice of theme, seems of all Eliot's poems to have been written most immediately under Laforgue's stimulus (though brought to a finished perfection of form which Laforgue's more impromptu verse scarcely attained).'

l. 113 progress: in Elizabethan England, and often represented on stage, the ceremonial journey of the nobility or royalty in full pomp.

l. 116 Politic: in its archaic sense, diplomatic and with an eye to advantage.

cautious: cf. 'cautelous', crafty, cunning, as used by Shakespeare.

meticulous: in the obsolete sense of fearful, as would befit 'an attendant lord' in the service of his prince.

l. 117 Full of high sentence: cf. 'ful of hy sentence', meaning full of lofty sentiments and learned talk, a description of the conversation of the scholarly Clerk of Oxford in the General Prologue (line 306) of *The Canterbury Tales* by Geoffrey Chaucer (1343?– 1400).

ll. 117–19: a description that calls to mind the long-winded and moralizing Polonius (see note to lines 73–4).

l. 119 Fool: the Fool was a stock figure in Elizabethan drama. He was often a court entertainer whose patter, seeming nonsense, contained a paradoxical wisdom. The court jester in *Hamlet* was Yorick; Hamlet remembers him (now dead twenty-three years) from his boyhood with affection and pity (see v, i).

l. 120: Eliot said that this line reminded him of the words of Falstaff, 'There live not three good men unhanged in England, and one of them is fat, and grows old' (*Henry IV, Pt. 1* ii, iv). But its origin may lie closer to the time of the poem's composition, in the statement 'to live is to grow old' (Bergson's *Introduction to Metaphysics*, 1903).

l. 121: these would be trousers with turn-ups (in America, cuffs), then just coming into fashion. Also see Bergson, quoted on page 46.

l. 122 Shall I part my hair behind?: in his autobiographical essay, *Ushant* (1952), Eliot's Harvard contemporary Conrad Aiken tells us what a sensation was caused when one of their fellow students returned from Paris 'in exotic Left Bank clothing, and with his hair parted behind'. Clearly, at the time, such a hair-style was regarded as daringly bohemian.

ll. 123–31: in Dante, Ulysses sails to the end of the world in pursuit of knowledge, during which voyage he is held spellbound by the Sirens' song. The mock-epic strain of 'Prufrock' is emphasized in this final passage as Eliot elevates the poetic lyricism and intensity.

l. 123: an autobiographical touch, as Eliot himself did on occasion.

l. 124: cf. 'Teach me to heare Mermaides singing', from 'Song' by John Donne. This is one of a series of challenges, richly poetic, yet unattainable. As with line 92, an English poet provides the obvious allusion. But, once again, for Eliot and his friends it may have been coupled with a reference to *The Symbolist Movement in Literature*. At the close of the chapter on Gérard de Nerval (1808–55), a line is quoted from his poem 'El Desdichado' ('The Disinherited'): 'J'ai rêvé dans la grotte où nage la sirène' ('I have dreamed in the cave where the siren swims'). Eliot refers to this poem in his note to line 429 of *The Waste Land*.

ll. 124–5: a neat, ironic reversal: the Homeric sirens, equated by the Elizabethans with mermaids, traditionally tried to lure heroes from their great tasks (as in *The Faerie Queene*, II, xii and *Ulysses and the Siren* by Samuel Daniel, 1562–1619).

Before 'Prufrock' appeared in *Poetry* (Chicago), its editor, Harriet Monroe, voiced some criticisms, which Pound countered in a letter dated 31 January 1915 (doubtless advised by Eliot himself):

> 'Mr Prufrock' does not 'go off at the end'. It is a portrait of failure, or of a character which fails, and it would be false art to make it end on a note of triumph. I dislike the paragraph about Hamlet, but it is an early and cherished bit and T. E. won't give it up, and as it is the only portion of the poem that most readers will like at first reading, I don't see that it will do much harm.
>
> For the rest: a portrait satire on futility can't end by turning that quintessence of futility, Mr P., into a reformed character breathing out fire and ozone.

Note: When 'Prufrock' first appeared in 1915, it concluded with a line of dots. If this typography is faithful to the manuscript, it may be pointing to an 'incompleteness' to the poem, a supposition that seems to be supported in a letter Eliot wrote to the *Times Literary Supplement* in 1960 saying that in 1912 he made 'some additions to the poem' but had 'enough recollection of the suppressed verses to remain grateful to Mr Aiken for advising me to suppress them'. The American poet and novelist Conrad Aiken was Eliot's closest friend at Harvard.

Portrait of a Lady

Written I November 1910; II February 1910;
III November 1911
Others (*New York*) *September 1915*

Conrad Aiken identified the Lady of this poem as a Boston hostess, 'our dear deplorable friend, Miss X, the *précieuse ridicule* to end all preciosity, serving tea so exquisitely among her bric-à-brac'. (Miss X was Adelene Moffatt.) In his autobiographical essay, *Ushant* (1952), Aiken indicates that there are aspects of the poet himself in the poem: 'the oh so precious, the oh so exquisite, Madeleine, the Jamesian lady of ladies, the enchantress of the Beacon Hill drawing-room . . . was afterwards to be essentialized and ridiculed (and his own pose with it) in the Tsetse's *Portrait d'une Femme*'. When Eliot sent Pound the manuscript of this poem in February 1915, he wrote that he had received a Christmas card from the 'lady' in question.

The dramatic structure of the poem – a one-sided dialogue, in which the lady speaks and her visitor silently comments – is a form of 'conversation galante' which Eliot took from Laforgue's 'Autre Complainte de Lord Pierrot'. A closer imitation is Eliot's own 'Conversation Galante', written in November 1909.

Carol Christ has shown that Eliot places this poem in a nineteenth-century genre of female portraiture and gives the lady the conventional idiom of this mode ('Gender, Voice and Figuration in Eliot's Early Poetry', in Bush, 1991). Such Portraits, satires on Boston society, were a feature of Harvard undergraduate writing, now 'transformed' by Eliot and 'raised' 'to criticism and self-criticism (for who is most at fault, the lady or her admirer?)' (Howarth, p. 123).

Title: Echoes that of the novel *The Portrait of a Lady* (1881) by Henry James, and the poem itself is remarkably Jamesian in its tones and ironies, the subtlety of its observation, the style of the dialogue and its echoes and allusions.

Epigraph: A snatch of dialogue from *The Jew of Malta* (IV, i) by Christopher Marlowe (1564–93). The first line is spoken by a Friar. He is beginning to accuse Barabas (the villainous Jew of the title), who interrupts him and finishes off the sentence with his own words. It is a scene of double deception. The Friar is trying to blackmail Barabas, not simply charging him with sin. In turn, Barabas's self-accusation is callous and comically prompt. He wants to lead on the Friar by advertising himself as a sinner. In fact, his sins go far deeper. He comes fresh from a grotesque crime – the poisoning of a convent of nuns.

Greene finds the model for the poem's structure and versification in Laforgue's *Derniers Vers* (1886), in particular in 'Légende' and 'Solo de lune', interior monologues which convey the passing moments; it is, he says, 'the free verse of Laforgue adapted to English poetry'.

l. 6 Juliet's tomb: in Shakespeare's *Romeo and Juliet* the tomb is the vault in which Juliet's body is placed, her family supposing her to be dead. Actually, she is only in a coma, drugged, a ruse to escape an arranged marriage and save herself for Romeo. But the plan goes tragically wrong. Romeo kills himself and Juliet commits suicide over his body.

ll. 8–9: note the electrical pun in the transmitting Pole!

l. 9 Preludes: a group of piano pieces by the Polish composer Frédéric Chopin (1810–49).

l. 15 velleities: light inclinations.

l. 28 cauchemar: French for nightmare, a word used by Laforgue.

l. 30 ariettes: lively little song-like tunes.

l. 32 tom-tom: from Eliot's anthropological reading, associated with primitive peoples. Hence, as in line 35, a 'false note' in this polite social setting.

l. 40 bocks: bock is a strong, dark German beer.

l. 53 buried life: 'The Buried Life' (1852) by Matthew Arnold seems to be the source of this phrase. In Arnold, the 'buried life' is 'the mystery of this heart which beats /So wild, so deep in us' – the impulsive, passionate side of the human nature that we so often try to ignore or suppress. Throughout the 'Portrait' Eliot seems to suppose the reader's acquaintance with 'The Buried Life', on which he provides a kind of modern commentary, a rewriting of Arnold's serious dramatic monologue as a 'conversation galante', a complex statement, with shifting tones of irony, quite different from the relative simplicity of Arnold's singleness of tone and feeling.

The juxtaposition of the 'buried life' and 'Paris in the Spring' suggests that Eliot was also alluding to *The Ambassadors* (1903), a novel by Henry James, in which the hero Lambert Strether sees his own recovery of life as the emergence of seeds long dormant: 'Buried for long years in dark corners ... these few germs had sprouted again under forty-eight hours of Paris.' Much of this poem was written in Paris.

ll. 84–91: autobiographical detail may enter here: it was in October 1910 that Eliot left America for Paris 'to learn' (line 91) at the Sorbonne.

l. 93: another Jamesian echo. In *The Ambassadors*, Mme de Vionnet's parting words to Strether are 'we might, you and I, have been friends', words repeated by Maria Gostrey in the following chapter (34).

l. 97: a variant upon 'That is the true beginning of our end', *Midsummer Night's Dream* (5.i).

l. 114: Greene holds that a line in Laforgue's 'Autre Complainte de Lord Pierrot' is the principal literary source for the poem: 'Enfin, si, par un soir, elle meurt dans mes livres' ('At last, if, one evening, she dies in my books'). This may explain line 116, 'pen in hand'. Laforgue's line is quoted by Symons.

l. 122 'dying fall': see pages 51–2, note to 'Prufrock', line 52.

Preludes

Written I, II Harvard October 1910; III Paris July 1911;
IV Harvard c. November 1911
Published together in Blast *(London) July 1915*

In 1950, Eliot commented of the 'Preludes' that 'While they are probably not those of my early poems which showed the most promise, I think they are the most satisfactory to myself.'

In an early manuscript notebook these four belong to a group of fourteen 'city' poems written in 1909–11 from his experience of Boston, Paris and London, described in Mayer, pp. 69–96.

Title: The reference here is probably not to the piano pieces by Chopin referred to in 'Portrait of a Lady', line 9 but to Laforgue's 'Préludes Autobiographiques', published in *Les Complaintes*. This autobiographical reference would certainly accord with what Eliot had to say about the childhood source for his urban imagery (see below).

On the manuscript, 'Preludes' I, II and III were originally entitled 'Preludes in Roxbury'. Roxbury was a sleazy suburb of Boston, within visiting distance of Harvard. III was there subtitled 'Morgendämmerung' ('Dawn') and IV 'Abenddämmerung' ('Twilight').

For Eliot's use in these poems of the novels of Charles-Louis Philippe, see Introduction, page 11; more detailed references are to be found in Grover Smith (1974). Eliot confirmed that III draws upon *Bubu de Montparnasse* (1901) and he thought that in IV he might have taken details from *Marie Donadieu* (1904). At the time Eliot read the novel, in Paris, in 1910, it seemed to him that 'Bubu stood for Paris as some of Dickens's novels stand for London'.

In 1959, Eliot pointed to the autobiographical origin of his 'urban imagery' in an address entitled 'The influence of landscape upon the poet' (see Introduction, page 36). The American basis of this 'urban imagery' is also communicated by Americanisms in the diction and reference of these poems, as noted below.

But Eliot also acknowledged a literary, imaginative debt to Baudelaire: 'It is not merely in the use of imagery of common life, not merely in the use of imagery of the sordid life of a great metropolis, but in the elevation of such imagery to the *first intensity* – presenting it as it is, and yet making it represent much more than itself – that Baudelaire has created a mode of release and expression for other men' ('Baudelaire', 1930).

I l. 8 lots: ground for building (and IV line 16).
II l. 3 sawdust-trampled: many bars and shops sprinkled sawdust on their floors to take up the dirt and this sawdust was carried out on to the streets (see 'Prufrock', line 7).
l. 9 shades: blinds.
IV l. 5 pipes: the fingers are stuffing the pipes with tobacco.
ll. 12–13: according to Valerie Eliot, these lines were written with his brother in mind – Henry Ware Eliot (1879–1947), see footnote 2 to *Letters I*, page 54.

Rhapsody on a Windy Night

Written Paris March 1911; Blast *(London) July 1915*

Eliot appears to be exploring Bergson's method of approaching truth not by analysis but by entering a current of immediate perception flowing through time. He considered that the most important passage in Bergson was concerned with the difference between 'the heterogeneous qualities which succeed each other in our consciousness', discontinuous perceptions, and an underlying harmony to be discerned.

In particular, Eliot may have had in mind two early statements in Bergson's *L'Évolution créatrice* (1907) – authorized translation, *Creative Evolution* (1911) by the Harvard Professor Arthur Mitchell: that 'incidents' seem to be 'discontinuous' but they 'stand out against the continuity of a background on which they are designed . . . they are the beats of the drum [cf. line 9] which break forth here and there in the symphony' (p. 3); and 'Duration is the continuous progress of the past which gnaws into the future and which swells as it advances' (p. 5). In 1923, Eliot said that the seductive appeal of *L'Évolution créatrice* deeply influenced his intellectual development.

Gray (1982) discusses the significance of Bergson's *Matière et Mémoire*.

Details in this poem – including the sight of the street-lamps, the women in the doorway, the smells, the memories – are derived from the novel *Bubu de Montparnasse* (1901) and *Marie Donadieu* (1904) by Charles-Louis Philippe (see Introduction, page 11).

Further behind the poem may stand 'The City of Dreadful Night' (1874) by James Thomson (1834–82), in which the progress of the city-walker's route is marked by street-lamps and moonlight. Crawford (1987) has discussed the wider significance of this poem.

According to Eliot, the most powerful inspiration for his early urban poetry was the Scottish poet John Davidson (1857–1909), whose *Ballads and Songs* (1894), in particular 'Thirty Bob a Week', described by Eliot in 1936 as a 'great poem', enabled him to realize his own 'dingy images'. Eliot's concern with Davidson was long-lasting: in 1917, he reviewed a study of the poet; in 1957, he broadcast a tribute to him; and, in 1961, edited a selection of his poems. In the Preface he wrote warmly of Davidson's poetry: 'it prepared me for initiation into the work of some of the French symbolists, such as Laforgue, whom I came across shortly after'. Rather unexpectedly, considering the French idiom of 'Rhapsody', he wrote that he got 'the idea' from Davidson 'that one could write poetry in an English such as one would speak oneself. A colloquial idiom.'

l. 2 reaches: length, extent.
ll. 3, 4 lunar: Symons mentions this as a key word in the poetic diction of Laforgue (and see note to line 51).
l. 3 synthesis: a term employed by Bergson in *An Introduction to Metaphysics*.
ll. 5–7: a concept of Bergson in which images flow freely into the memory, where they combine.
l. 9: a note on the manuscript of the poem connects this line with the poet Henry Vaughan (1622–95).
ll. 9–12: cf. 'as a madman beats upon a drum', the words of Franford to describe the fearful feelings at his heart, in *A Woman Killed with Kindness* (IV, ii) by Thomas Heywood (*c.* 1570–1641). Eliot may also have had in mind two lines in *The Ballad of Reading Gaol* (1898) by Oscar Wilde (1854–1900): 'But each man's heart beat thick and quick/Like a madman on a drum'.
l. 12 geranium: one of Laforgue's flowers, as in 'O géraniums diaphanes' ('O diaphanous geraniums'), quoted by Eliot in 'The Metaphysical Poets' (1921).
l. 16 Regard: this construction mimics the French imperative

form, 'Regarde'; see also lines 35, 50 and 75.

ll. 23–5: cf. 'I notice memories which more or less adhere to these perceptions and which serve to interpret them' (Bergson, *An Introduction to Metaphysics*).

ll. 35–40: these lines seem to be based upon a prose-poem by Baudelaire, 'Le Joujou du pauvre' ('The Urchin's Plaything').

l. 38 automatic: cf. Symons on Laforgue: 'He thinks intensely about life, seeing what is automatic, pathetically ludicrous in it, almost as one might who has no part in the comedy.'

l. 40: cf. Laforgue, 'Pierrots', 'ces yeux! mais rien n'existe/ Derrière' ('Such eyes! but nothing behind them').

ll. 43–5: these lines may derive from Eliot's childhood. In *The Use of Poetry*, he cites such a moment:

> There might be the experience of a child of ten, a small boy peering through sea-water in a rock-pool, and finding a sea-anemone for the first time: the simple experience (not so simple, for an exceptional child, as it looks) might lie dormant in his mind for twenty years, and re-appear transformed in some verse-context charged with great imaginative pressure.

These last words certainly apply to this section of the poem, the only lines in which the poet is speaking emphatically in his own person. The only other use of 'I' is in line 8.

l. 51: 'The moon harbours no ill-feelings.' Eliot's line is a version of two lines from 'Complainte de cette bonne lune' ('The Lament of That Beautiful Moon') by Laforgue: 'Là, voyons mam'zell' la Lune,/Ne gardons pas ainsi rancune' ('Look, there we can see that fine young lady the moon, let's not harbour any ill-feelings').

ll. 65–6: cf. *Marie Donadieu*, 'des odeurs de filles publiques mêlées à des odeurs de nourriture' ('the odours of the prostitutes mingled with the smell of cooking').

l. 70: the first stage of Dante's journey in the *Divina Commedia* takes place between midnight and 4 a.m.

ll. 72–7: an aspect of memory, its practicality, according to Bergson.

l. 77: at a hotel, shoes were left outside the room at night to be cleaned.

POEMS 1920

'Any poet, if he is to survive as a writer beyond his twenty-fifth year, must alter; he must seek new literary influences; he will have different emotions to express.'

T. S. Eliot, 1917

'Some of the new poems, the Sweeney ones, especially *Among the Nightingales* and *Burbank* are intensely serious, and I think these two are among the best that I have ever done. But even here I am considered by the ordinary Newspaper critic as a Wit or satirist, and in America I suppose I shall be thought merely disgusting.'

Letter to his brother in America, 15 February 1920, a few days after the publication of his new collection of poems, the London edition entitled *Ara Vos Prec*, the American edition, *Poems* (1920).

Gerontion

Begun 1917, completed August 1919; London 1920

A version of the poem existed by July 1919; and Eliot produced the final version during August on a holiday in France with Pound.

Pound had known 'Gerontion' from its beginnings and advised Eliot in its writing. As Wyndham Lewis remarked the poem 'is a close relative of "Prufrock", certain matters filtered through an aged mask in both cases, but "Gerontion" technically is "school of Ezra" '.

Early in 1922 Eliot was undecided whether or not to print this poem as a prelude to *The Waste Land*. Ezra Pound advised against it and the two poems remained apart.

Northrop Frye regards 'Gerontion' as 'a parody of Newman's poem *The Dream of Gerontius*' (1866) (of which a new edition appeared in 1919), the dramatic reverie of an old man at the point of death. Unlike Eliot's 'old man', Gerontius is a Christian whose spiritual struggles are crowned with salvation. The poem was extremely popular; also the oratorio, with music by Elgar. In May 1916, it was performed daily for a week (a notable event, when there was so little large-scale musical activity in war-time London); and Newman featured in the syllabus of Eliot's University of London Extension Board tutorial classes in 1916. There seems to be a further allusion to Newman's writing in lines 57 and 59.

Ronald Bush (1976) points out that the soldier poets of the First World War – including Siegfried Sassoon, Isaac Rosenberg, F. S. Flint, Edmund Blunden, Herbert Read and Wilfred Owen – habitually took up the theme of youth dying at the front while the old men (Gerontion-like) remained securely behind the lines or at home.

In the writing of 'Gerontion', Eliot seems to have been influenced by 'Nestor', the second section of *Ulysses* (see Introduction, pages 21–2), which he would have read when it first appeared in the *Little Review*, April 1918, but which he got to know much more closely when he proof-read 'Nestor' for the January–February 1919 issue of *The Egoist*. Nestor is represented by Mr Deasy, 'a struggler now at the end of my days ... Old as I am', who has 'committed many errors and many sins'; and the theme is History: the scene opens with a lesson on Roman history and the nature of history is discussed. Several points of correspondence are given in the detailed notes that follow.

Title: The diminutive, disrespectful form of the Greek word 'gerōn', meaning an elder worthy of respect: could be translated as 'little old man'.

Epigraph: From Shakespeare's *Measure for Measure* III, i, 33–4. The Duke is addressing Claudio, a young man sentenced to death, telling him to value life lightly. Eliot has misquoted slightly. The correct reading is 'dinner's', 'Dreaming *on* both'.

ll. 1–2: when a critic suggested, in 1938, that the opening was an improvement upon some lines by Pound, Eliot replied that 'The line quoted from *Gerontion* was lifted bodily from a Life of Edward Fitzgerald.' In point of fact, these two lines derive from the biography *Edward Fitzgerald* (1905), by A. C. Benson, where the poet is described, in Benson's summary of a letter from Fitzgerald: 'Here he sits, in a dry month, old and blind, being read to by a country boy, longing for rain' (p. 142). Matthiessen quotes, with approval, a critic who suggested that Benson's 'whole book, with its picture of Fitzgerald in his pathetic, charming, and impotent old age, pondering on the pessimism of Omar, and beating out the futility of his final year, may have crystallized in Eliot's mind the situation ... of "Gerontion" '.

l. 3 hot gates: a literal translation of the Greek place-name
Thermopylae, a strategically important pass between Northern
and Central Greece, the scene of several battles, notably that
between the Greeks and Persians in 480 BC. Thayer: 'Thermo-
pylae cf. Ezra Pound's "The Wayfarer".' Since Pound wrote no
poem of this name, presumably Eliot is referring to 'The Seafarer',
first published in 1911 and included in Eliot's choice of Pound's
Selected Poems (1928). There is no specific allusion but a general
affinity, since Pound too writes of the endurance of a traveller.

l. 8 jew: likewise, Mr Deasy is concerned about Jewish
ownership.

l. 9 estaminet: a French word for café, brought into English by
soldiers returning from France and Belgium during the First
World War.

ll. 9–10 Antwerp, Brussels: these cities, in Belgium, may be
connected with London as trading and financial centres. Eliot
visited both in summer 1914.

ll. 10–11: Thayer: 'cf. Wyndham Lewis: "the Enemy of the
Stars".' This Vorticist, fantastic play was published in the first
issue of *Blast*, 20 June 1914, where Eliot would certainly have
read it. There is no direct allusion, but the squalid urban scene in
lines 7–16 may well stem from it.

l. 12 stonecrop: a moss-like plant.

   merds: excreta. The word is French but has been used in
literary English, including Ben Jonson's *The Alchemist* (1612)
and Robert Burton's *The Anatomy of Melancholy* (1621).

l. 14 peevish gutter: of Eliot's formulation, this must mean a
feeble spluttering fire, as if Eliot has adopted the German word
'gitter', which refers to all the ironwork (fender, grille, etc.)
attached to an open fire.

ll. 15–32: Matthiessen reports a conversation with Eliot in
which the poet said that 'the images here are "consciously con-
crete"; they correspond as closely as possible to something he
has actually seen and remembered'.

l. 17 'We ... sign!': the cry of the unbelieving Pharisees, calling
upon Christ to prove his divinity by performing a miracle:
'Master, we would see a sign from thee' (Matthew xii, 38).

Christ answered that 'an evil and adulterous generation seeketh after a sign' (39); 'signs' and 'wonders' are commonly found together in the Bible as evidences of God's power. But 'are taken' suggests gullibility: that the people are clamouring for a 'sign', ready to believe it a miraculous 'wonder', as in 2 Thessalonians ii, 9, where there are deceptive 'signs and lying wonders'.

ll. 18–19: Eliot's immediate source here and for the first part of line 17 is the Nativity Sermon preached before James I by Bishop Lancelot Andrewes (1555–1626) on Christmas Day 1618. His text for the sermon was Luke ii, 12–14: 'And this shall be a sign unto you; ye shall find the Babe wrapped in swaddling clothes, lying in a manger ... Signs are taken for wonders. "Master, we would fain see a sign," that is [,] a miracle. And in this sense it is a sign to wonder at. Indeed, every word here is a wonder. *Tò βρέφος*, an infant; *Verbum infans*, the Word without a word; the eternal Word not able to speak a word; 1. a wonder sure. 2. And the *σπαργανισμός*, swaddled; and that a wonder too. "He," that (as in the thirty-eighth [verse 9] of Job He saith) "taketh the vast body of the main sea, turns it to and fro, as a little child, and rolls it about with the swaddling bands of darkness;" – He to come thus into clouts, Himself!' ('clouts', the baby's swaddling clothes).

Line 18 is cited by Eliot in 'Lancelot Andrewes' (1926) as one of those 'flashing phrases' which 'never desert the memory'. But this particular 'flashing phrase' was Eliot's own construction. What Andrewes wrote was 'the Word *without* a word; the eternal Word not able to speak a word'. Eliot is quoting his own version of the line, given here in 'Gerontion'. However, Eliot did quote Andrewes correctly in *Ash-Wednesday*, line 153.

Andrewes and Eliot both use 'word' in its original Greek sense of *logos*, as in John i, 1: 'In the beginning was the Word, and the Word was with God, and the Word was God.'

l. 19 juvescence: Eliot's version of juvenescence, here meaning the spring. The rhythm calls for a trisyllabic word here and the usual Latin contraction would be 'junescence'.

l. 20 Christ the tiger: the contrary to the Biblical image of Christ the lamb. From Thayer, we know that this animal image was

derived from an image in Andrewes's Nativity Sermon, 1622:
whereas the Magi hurried to reach the child Jesus, there were
people who did not, who exclaimed 'Christ is no wild-cat ...
What needs such haste?' This is another of the 'flashing
phrases' Eliot quoted in the 'Lancelot Andrewes' essay
(although he misquoted in the Thayer copy – 'Christ is no
tiger'). In the poem 'The Tiger' by William Blake (1757–1827)
God's aspects of power and wrath, and of mercy and gentle-
ness, are signified in his creation of the tiger and the lamb.
ll. 21–8: details in this group of figures may be derived from
Pound's 'The Social Order', which includes a 'government offi-
cial' with 'a caressing air' and an old lady 'surrounded by six
candles and a crucifix'. Eliot would have met the poem in the
July 1915 issue of *Blast* which also contained his own 'Pre-
ludes' and 'Rhapsody of a Windy Night' (as it was then
entitled).
l. 21: this line is a concentrated allusion to a passage in *The
Education of Henry Adams* (1918) where Adams describes the
strange, pagan richness (as it seemed to him, brought up in
bleaker New England) of the Maryland spring:

> The Potomac and its tributaries squandered beauty ... Here
> and there a negro log cabin alone disturbed the dogwood and
> the judas-tree, the azalea and the laurel. The tulip and the
> chestnut gave no sign of struggle against a stingy nature. The
> brooding heat of the profligate vegetation; the cool charm of
> the running water; the terrific splendor of the June thunder-
> gust in the deep and solitary woods, were all sensual, animal,
> elemental. No European spring had shown him the same
> intermixture of delicate grace and passionate depravity that
> marked the Maryland May. He loved it too much, as though
> it were Greek and half human.   (p. 268)

Although Eliot identified this allusion to Thayer ('cf. Henry
Adam's autobiography'), he expressed amazement when years
later the scholar F. O. Matthiessen drew his attention to this
echo. Was this a joke? or mere forgetfulness? He knew the
book, having reviewed it in May 1919. Matthiessen suggests

that Eliot's 'theme is, of course, the loss of such ecstasy when cut off from the roots of faith'.

l. 22: refers to the presence of Christ in the sacrament of communion, the bread his body, the wine his blood, to be consumed in the mass by the priest and congregation.

ll. 23–9: there are hints of black magic here.

l. 24 Limoges: a French town famed for its china.

l. 26: the paintings of the Venetian artist Titian (d. 1576). This may not necessarily be an image of blind cultural obeisance, the uncomprehending East bowing before the prized art of the West, supposing Hakagawa to be a representative Japanese. In *The Wings of the Dove* (1902) by Henry James, there is a verbally similar occasion when Milly Theale 'among the Titians' in the National Gallery stands a chance of 'overtaking' 'great moments'.

ll. 27–8: suggestive of a seance. One of Eliot's students at his University of London Extension Board tutorial classes in 1917 was a spiritualist, another an astrologer who wanted to cast his horoscope, an invitation he declined.

l. 28 Kulp: cf. Latin 'culpa', guilt.

ll. 29–30: this may be an allusion to the lamentation of Job, whose days were passed in suffering and for whom life had lost its meaning: 'My days are swifter than a weaver's shuttle, and are spent without hope. O remember that my life is wind: mine eye shall no more see good' (vii, 6–7).

But there could have been a more immediate source for Eliot in Section I of *Ulysses*, where Stephen Dedalus reflects on the words of Mulligan, the parody priest: 'Idle mockery. The void awaits surely all them that weave the wind.' Also, in the following 'Nestor' section, Stephen reflects, 'For them too history was a tale like any other too often told . . . Weave, weaver of the wind.'

l. 32 knob: a rare dialect word for a rounded hill.

l. 33 knowledge: Eliot may have in mind 'that supreme moment of complete knowledge' in the quotation from Conrad's 'Heart of Darkness' which he originally intended to stand as the epigraph for *The Waste Land* (see page 134). Conrad's use of the word includes both the Biblical sense of knowledge of good and evil; also the specifically sexual, as in 'carnal knowledge'.

forgiveness: a word with strong biblical associations, as it is expressed in Daniel ix, 9: 'To the Lord our God belong mercies and forgivenesses.' The Apostles' Creed declares the Christian's belief in 'The Forgiveness of sins'.

Think: repeated in lines 36, 43, 48 and 50, together with the final line, indicating that the poem itself is a 'thought' of Gerontion; may derive from 'Nestor': 'Thought is the thought of thought'.

ll. 33–69: in this section Eliot is exploiting a wide range of Elizabethan and Jacobean dramatic verse. For reasons set out in the Introduction (see pages 11–12), the full extent of possible sources or models is not listed here, but Eliot's adaptive process can be illustrated through a single example, lines 55–8. Eliot follows the way in which the iambic pentameter of traditional dramatic blank verse had been loosened in the later work of Shakespeare, in Webster and Tourneur, where the 'poetry stretches, contracts and distorts the blank verse measure' into a form of free verse. One model Eliot seems to have had in mind is eight lines from *The Changeling* by Thomas Middleton (1580–1627):

> I that am of your blood was taken from you
> For your better health; look no more upon 't,
> But cast it to the ground regardlessly,
> Let the common sewer take it from distinction.
> Beneath the stars, upon yon meteor
> Ever hung my fate, 'mongst things corruptible;
> I ne'er could pluck it from him; my loathing
> Was prophet to the rest, but ne'er believed.

> (v, iii)

Eliot quoted these lines in his essay 'Thomas Middleton' (1927), prefacing them with this comment: 'He has no message; he is merely a great recorder. Incidentally, in flashes and when the dramatic need comes, he is a great poet, a great master of versification.'

Quoting lines 55–8 alongside these from Middleton, Matthiessen comments: 'The content of the two passages is not at all the same; but the contexts they rise from both express a horror of lust, and thus adumbrate the possible reason why Middleton's cadences stirred in Eliot's memory at the moment that he was shaping his lines.'

ll. 34–47: this account of 'History', and Gerontion's musings throughout the poem, may have been inspired by the remarks of Stephen Dedalus in *Ulysses*: 'history is to blame'; 'History . . . is a nightmare from which I am trying to awake.' This view of history also owes much to Eliot's reading of *The Education of Henry Adams*, particularly the sections where Adams discusses the increasing complexity of human knowledge, as in the area of evolution: at the beginning of the twentieth century the historian 'entered a far vaster universe, where all the old roads ran about in every direction, overrunning, dividing, stopping abruptly, vanishing slowly, with side-paths that led nowhere, and sequences that could not be proved' (p. 400).

l. 34 cunning: Eliot's choice of this word may have been guided by the passage from Chapman, an important one for him, used in the imagery of lines 67–9 (see note). In the earliest text of the play, 'burning axletree' was printed as 'curning axetree'; in the edition Eliot used (ed. W. L. Phelps, New York, 1895), 'curning' had been corrupted to 'cunning'.

contrived corridors: Eliot may have had a specific contemporary 'contrived corridor' in mind – the so-called Polish Corridor. This was a strip of land taken from Germany under the terms of the Treaty of Versailles (signed June 1919) and awarded to Poland. It was one of the most resented of the Treaty settlements.

l. 35 issues: the 'passages', 'corridors' metaphor is continued in the primary meaning, exits.

ll. 39–40: cf. 'Too soon, and with weak hands', 'Adonais: an elegy on the death of John Keats' by Shelley, line 257.

l. 45 fathered: carries strong Shakespearian echoes from its use in *Julius Caesar* (II, i, 297), *Macbeth* (IV, ii, 27) and *King Lear* (III, vi, 117).

l. 47 the wrath-bearing tree: probably an allusion to 'the tree of the knowledge of good and evil' in Genesis; 'wrath-bearing' in that Eve's disobedience in taking from it the forbidden fruit was one reason for the descent of God's wrath upon mankind.

In Blake's poem 'The Poison Tree', the tree is produced by wrath and watered by tears. Indic scholars suggest that it may derive from the imagery of the *Katha Upanishad* VI.1, and *Gita* 15, 1–3.

l. 48 tiger: possibly God in his fearful aspect, as in Blake's poem 'The Tiger'.

ll. 51–3: Thayer: 'v. Middleton: The Changeling'.

l. 51 show: a small play-within-a-play, to re-enact and reflect some aspect of the surrounding drama, a feature of the Elizabethan theatre.

l. 52 concitation: derived from the Latin *concitatio*, meaning moving, exciting. Obsolete since the seventeenth century.

l. 53 backward devils: the augurers and diviners in Dante's *Inferno* (xx), for having presumed to foretell the future, were condemned to walk backwards.

l. 55: cf. 'I that am of your blood was taken from you', Middleton, *The Changeling* (quoted p. 74).

ll. 57, 59: cf. Newman's (1801–90) sermon on 'Divine Calls' quoted in *Apologia Pro Vita Sua* (1864): 'Let us beg and pray Him day by day to reveal Himself to our souls more fully, to quicken our sense, to give us sight and hearing, taste and touch of the world to come.' For Eliot's knowledge of Newman, see page 68.

ll. 64–5: an arrangement of mirrors to enable a voluptuary to see himself enacting his pleasures from a variety of angles. From Thayer, we know that Eliot had in mind the words of Sir Epicure Mammon in Ben Jonson's play *The Alchemist* (1612):

> my glasses
> Cut in more subtle angles, to disperse
> And multiply the figures, as I walk
> Naked between my succubae.
>
> (II, ii)

Eliot quoted a passage containing three of these four lines in his essay 'Ben Jonson', published in 1919.

ll. 67–9: in *The Use of Poetry and the Use of Criticism* (1933), pages 146–7, Eliot explained that the imagery in these lines derives from a passage in the play *Bussy D'Ambois* by George Chapman (1559–1634). It is the dying speech of Bussy. He commands his 'fame' to warn the heavens of his coming:

> Fly where the evening from the Iberian vales
> Takes on her swarthy shoulders Hecate
> Crowned with a grove of oaks; fly where men feel
> The burning axletree, and those that suffer
> Beneath the chariot of the snowy Bear . . .
>
> (v, iv)

Chapman is drawing upon the classical tradition that sinners were punished by being sent into an eccentric, outward orbit which would carry them away into space. The bear (usually known as the Great Bear) is a constellation in the Northern Hemisphere.

Eliot quoted 'fly' onwards as illustrating the handing on of a 'tradition' – in this case from Seneca to Chapman and, by implication, onwards into his own poetry. ('Reflections on contemporary poetry', *The Egoist*, July 1919.) For Eliot's remarks on the personal value to him of this image, see Introduction, pages 29–30.

cf. *Ulysses*, 'Nestor': 'I hear the ruin of all space, shatter of glass and toppling masonry, and time one livid final flame. What's left us then?'

l. 67: these are random names, with cosmopolitan overtones. Fresca also appears in a cancelled pseudo-Popean section removed from 'The Fire Sermon' in *The Waste Land*.

l. 68 shuddering Bear: Chapman's bear is 'snowy'; Eliot's 'shuddering' may derive from a tradition that the bear's orgasm lasts nine days.

ll. 69–71: according to Hayward, this sea/sailing imagery is an evocation of Eliot's own experiences off the New England coast (see page 35).

l. 69 In fractured atoms: in 1920, a highly contemporary scientific concept of the ultimate in destruction. The previous June the physicist Ernest Rutherford published the evidence of his experiments involving the disintegration of the nitrogen atom – connected with Adams in Eliot's statement at this time that 'Wherever this man stepped, the ground did not simply give way, it flew into particles' (*Athenaeum*, 23 May 1919).

l. 70 Belle Isle: Thayer: 'Near Labrador (*not* Belle Isle *France*).'

   Horn: Cape Horn, the southern extremity of South America.

l. 71 Gulf: the Gulf Stream is a system of currents in the North Atlantic.

l. 72 Trades: the Trade winds.

ll. 72–3: again, Eliot seems to be using *The Education of Henry Adams*. In ch. 21, Adams describes how he came back from the South Seas with John La Farge: 'Adams would rather, as choice, have gone back to the east, if it were to sleep forever in the trade-winds, under the southern stars, wandering over the dark purple ocean, with its purple sense of solitude and void.'

Burbank with a Baedeker:
Bleistein with a Cigar

Probably written 1918–19;
Art and Letters (*London*) *Summer 1919*

Pound recalled the origins of the poetic form for 'Burbank': 'At a particular date in a particular room, two authors ... decided that the dilutation of *vers libre* ... had gone too far ... Remedy prescribed "Emaux et Camées" (or the Bay State Hymn Book). Rhyme and regular strophes.' (Properly, the *Bay Psalm Book*, a collection of metrical psalms used by the Massachusetts Bay Colony in the mid-seventeenth century.) Eliot later commented: 'We studied Gautier's poems [in *Émaux et Camées*] and then we thought, "Have I anything to say in this form which will be useful?" And we experimented. The form gave the impetus to the content.' In fact, as Eliot recalled in 1946, the initiative was Pound's: 'At a certain moment my debt to him was for his advice to read Gautier's *Émaux et Camées* to which I had not before paid any close attention'. Pound appreciated Gautier's gift for making 'perfectly plain statements' and Eliot alludes to this in 'Whispers of Immortality' (see page 110, note to lines 17–18). In 1918, Pound referred to Gautier as a sculptor cutting in 'hard substance', another quality which Eliot seems to strive for in the quatrain poems, echoing Pound's avowal: 'Gautier j'ai étudié et je le révère' (I have studied Gautier and revere him). The outcome was 'Burbank' and the earlier quatrain poems 1917–18. For Pound's specific contribution to the 'content' of 'Burbank', see below; and to 'Whispers', see the headnote to page 109.

Matthiessen defined Eliot's ambition: 'to write compact verse in which the mind of the poet should be actually felt to be moving';

and Eliot thought that 'freedom is only truly freedom when it appears against the background of an artificial limitation.'

Background: Through the quotations in the Epigraph and allusions within the body of the poem, Eliot attaches 'Burbank' to the literature of Venice, from Byron, Gautier and Ruskin to Henry James, all of whom spent considerable time in the city and gave it prominence in their writing. In Canto the Fourth of *Childe Harold's Pilgrimage* (1818), Byron gives an unforgettable and unsurpassed lyrical evocation of the city's mighty past, the sadness of its fallen state, and the magic of its lasting beauty and the spell it casts. Although Eliot makes only two allusions to *Childe Harold* (see notes to lines 29 and 31–2), Byron's romantic vision is clearly intended to stand as a backcloth to the quite unromantic and unrhapsodical character of 'Burbank'. Ruskin's loving, yet not uncritical, account of the city is set out in the three volumes of *The Stones of Venice* (1851–3), a work which came into the tutorial classes on Victorian literature Eliot was conducting in 1916–18 and which is discussed in the note to line 32.

James followed in the tradition of Byron and Ruskin, primarily in a series of Venetian essays, collected in *Italian Hours* (1909). The book opens with 'Venice' (1884) – a city so painted and rhapsodized, he apologizes, that 'There is notoriously nothing more to be said on the subject.' Eliot's riposte is this sharp and cryptic addition to the literature of Venice. A second essay, 'The Grand Canal' (1892), is alluded to later in the poem (see note to line 19). Ruskin-like, James celebrates the glories of Venice and laments its fallen state, its 'barbarian' visitors, with their 'money and little red books', their 'Baedekers' (as he names them). Eliot's device is to split these attributes: to Burbank with 'Baedeker' and Bleistein with the vulgar and ostentatious emblem of 'money', his 'cigar'.

Two sources are from James's fiction: the novella *The Aspern Papers* (1888) and *The Wings of the Dove* (1902), both with a Venetian setting, both with scheming 'scoundrels' (echoed in Bleistein). *The Aspern Papers* is quoted in the Epigraph and discussed under that heading. The connection with Byron is direct since the name 'Aspern' is a transparent substitution for Byron. This heavily Jamesian emphasis is related to the editorial work Eliot was engaged in from Autumn 1917 preparing the Henry James number of the *Egoist* (January 1918), to which he contributed 'In Memory of Henry James' and Pound 'The Middle Years'. Thereafter he was working with Pound on the Henry James issue of the *Little Review* (August 1918), to which Eliot contributed 'Henry James: The Hawthorne Aspect'. In April 1918, he recommended *The Aspern Papers* to a cousin as 'very good' and in May told his mother that he was writing the essay 'and trying to write verse again', 'verse' which may well have been 'Burbank'. Pound's contribution was a long, composite piece which included 'The Middle Years', and began with a newly-written section, 'In Explanation', whose opening sentence may have provided the trigger for 'Burbank': 'This essay on James is a dull grind of an affair, a Baedecker (*sic*) to a continent'.

In the course of this essay, Pound refers frequently to a collection of James's early literary criticism published in 1878 under the title *French Poets and Novelists*. Among the items included in this volume is 'Théophile Gautier', a review first published in the *North American Review*, April 1873. It was written just after Gautier's death and James paid tribute to the 'chiselled and polished verses' of *Émaux et Camées* and described the poet as 'of literary artists the most accomplished'. James also compared his account of Venice in 'Italia', one of his travel writings, with Ruskin's in *The Stones of Venice*. The body of Pound's essay stresses James's internationalism, his being 'On the side of civilization – civilization against barbarism . . . After a life time spent in trying to make two continents understand each other . . . In his books he showed race against race, immutable . . . Kultur is an abomination.' 'Burbank' provides a critique of these ideas. Commenting on Baudelaire, James once wrote: 'For a poet to be realist is of course nonsense.' Pound quotes this; and he also quoted, with approval, Ford Madox Hueffer's rejection of that view; and, in turn, 'Burbank' can be read as Eliot's poetic denial.

So 'Burbank' needs to be read within the context of these rich and immediate literary associations, a confluence in which Pound played a strong part, not only encouraging Eliot to attempt an imitation/adaptation of Gautier's poetic form and style, but also providing him with the inspiration for the Jamesian-Venetian setting and the idea of the American tourist. This allowed Eliot, in turn, to signal his personal tribute to Pound, for whom Venice had been an important staging-post in his poetic career. It was here that his first volume was published, an item of history that Eliot recorded in *Ezra Pound: His Metric and Poetry*, a pamphlet published anonymously in New York in January 1918. Section II opens: 'Pound's first book was published in Venice. Venice was a halting point after he had left America and before he had settled in England, and here, in 1908, *A Lume Spento* appeared.' Eliot continued by stressing Pound's Venetian connection. The essay was part of their mutual log-rolling and in February 1918 Pound wrote of the 'apparent boost' he was getting from Eliot's 'brochure'. In fact, he supplied the title himself and made changes to the typescript. Pound explained to a correspondent that it was issued anonymously because 'I want to boom Eliot and one can't have too obvious a ping-pong match at that sort of thing'. The text is reprinted in *To Criticize the Critic*, 1965.

'Burbank' is a joking yet heartfelt tribute to James, complementary to Eliot's *Little Review* essay. Yet it should also be read in the light of Pound–Eliot relations as a contribution to the 'ping-pong' match in their extended game of mutual advancement and mutual modernization. To *Poetry* for February 1918 Pound contributed 'The Hard and Soft in French Poetry', celebrating the Gautier of . . . *Émaux et Camées*: 'He exhorts us to cut in hard substance, the shell and the Parian' – an exhortation duly answered by Eliot in the following year with the publication of 'Burbank'.

Title: Burbank: Exactly the kind of name that James would choose for one of his East Coast heroes; and Eliot may be using, for deliberate effect, the name of Luther Burbank (1849–1926),

a famous American botanist, playing off the superior associa-
tions of this name with the evidently worldly and Jewish
Bleistein.

Baedeker: Baedeker's guide-books are famed and joked about
for their potted entries which enable the tourist to inform him-
self in the space of a few lines on matters cultural, historical,
geographical, etc., as some American tourists do, not always
sneered at, in the novels of James. Eliot himself owned a
Baedeker, London and its Environs (1908), purchased on his
visit in October 1910, following his Harvard Florentine Painting
course (see 'Mr Eliot's Sunday Morning Service', note to line
10). Eliot annotated heavily the National Gallery entries for
early Italian and Renaissance paintings.

His French poem 'Lune de Miel', written 1916–17, is in part a
satire on the *Baedeker* style of entry.

Bleistein: German-Jewish name, literally Leadstone. Eliot could
have seen the name over a furrier's shop (see line 24) in Upper
Thames Street in the City of London, not far from his place of
work in Cornhill.

Bleistein reappears, once again a rich Jew, in 'Dirge' (probably
written in 1921), one of the three poems accompanying the
original manuscript of *The Waste Land* and omitted at the
suggestion of Pound. 'Dirge' is printed in Valerie Eliot's edition
of *The Waste Land.*

Overall, the poem's title follows James's first and third princi-
ples 'for building a novel', as summarized by Pound at the end of
his 1918 essay: 'Choice of names for characters; names that will
"fit" their owners, and that will not "joggle" or be cacophonic
when in juxtaposition on the page'; 'One character at least is
hitched to his "characteristic".'

Epigraph: Tra . . . laire: this is a version of 'Tra la, tra la, la, la, la
laire', representing the call of the gondolier, the opening line of
the poem 'Sur les lagunes' ('On the Lagoons') from a group of
poems entitled *Variations sur le Carnaval de Venise (Variations
on the Carnival of Venice)* by Théophile Gautier (1811–72).
'The Carnival of Venice' is a popular traditional tune; it reminds

Gautier, at the close of his poem, of 'La ville de Canaletto!' (The city of Canaletto), a detail to which Eliot may be alluding in line 19.

nil ... fumus: 'only the divine endures; the rest is smoke'. This inscription (the first word is actually 'nihil') is in a painting of the martyrdom of St Sebastian by Mantegna (1431–1506) in the Ca' d'Oro, Venice. The words (source unknown) are on a scroll round a guttering candle, a detail to which Eliot may be alluding in line 20. Mantegna was Eliot's favourite artist and he saw this painting, on touring Italy in summer 1914, when it hung in the house of the Franchetti family on the Grand Canal in Venice.

Struck by Mantegna's depiction – the youthful saint is riddled with arrows – Eliot wrote 'The Love Song of St Sebastian', a strange and violent dramatic monologue, not yet published. An account of the poem is given by Harvey Gross, 'The Figure of St Sebastian' in Olney (1988).

the gondola ... pink: the words come from ch. 1 of *The Aspern Papers* (1888) by Henry James, narrated by an American visitor to Venice, the unnamed 'scoundrel' of the story whose 'companion' is Mrs Prest, an American woman resident in the city: 'The gondola stopped, the old palace was there; it was a house of the class which in Venice carried even in extreme dilapidation the dignified name. "How charming! It's grey and pink!" my companion exclaimed.'

Eliot's telescoped version of this passage is not taken directly from James but from a pastiche quotation put together by Ford Madox Hueffer in *Henry James, A Critical Study* (1913, new edition 1918), p. 141. Eliot's version introduces further variants upon Hueffer's.

The particular part of *The Aspern Papers* which connects with 'Burbank' is a sequence where the narrator recalls a time when he ate ices under the winged lion of Mark, sometimes chatting with 'a stray tourist, disencumbered of his Bädeker'. Eliot took over other details: the narrator's gondola trip with Mrs Prest, when they look out from the shade of the *felze* (the gondola's cabin) upon 'the golden glow of Venice', becomes the Princess in her 'shuttered barge' burning 'on the water' (lines 11–12) –

compare also James's 'roast all summer'; a 'dying fall' enters 'fell' next to 'Defunctive' in lines 4 and 5; the 'piles' of the story reappear in line 22; and Jeffrey Aspern, seen as a 'god', is matched by 'the god Hercules'.

With these examples, we can see the point of Eliot's comment made at this time, that 'the "influence" of James hardly matters: to be influenced by a writer is to have a chance inspiration from him; or take what one wants . . .' (*Egoist*, January 1918).

The Aspern Papers is also related, more generally, to the Venetian aspect of 'Burbank'. In 1933, Eliot said that James's success in giving the whole feeling of Venice, by the most economical strokes, and his method in the story – 'to make a place real not descriptively but by something happening there' – was the example which led him to compress so many moments of Venice's past into his own poem. (Of course, Eliot admired James deeply. But in suggesting a connection between the compressed and caustic ferocity of his little squib and the polite, urbane and leisured irony of *The Aspern Papers*, Eliot is cracking an equivocal joke.)

Pound may have played a part in this method of compression. He described his own poem *Hugh Selwyn Mauberley* (1920) as 'a study in form, an attempt to condense the James novel' (and in 1922 he wrote that 'The metre in *Mauberley* is Gautier.')

goats and monkeys: an explosive outburst by Othello in Shakespeare's *Othello* IV, i, a play largely set in Venice. Othello has been goaded by Iago into a jealous fury against his Venetian wife Desdemona and her supposed lover. The animals he swears by are those traditionally associated with rankness and lust. In *Henry James* (pp. 140, 143), Hueffer twice quotes the final words of James's story, 'The Madonna of the Future': 'Cats and monkeys, monkeys and cats – all human life is there!' Thus Eliot may be seeking to evoke James as well as *Othello*.

with such hair too!: a phrase from the final stanza of 'A Toccata of Galuppi's' by Robert Browning (1812–89). The poem is about the vitality and wonder of life and its destruction in age and decay. Browning invokes the memory of the Venetian composer Galuppi Baldessare (1706–85), associating him with

Venice as a city of youth and love, of great traditions and prosperity. Yet (says the speaker of this dramatic narrative) the toccata itself is 'cold', the composer a mathematical, scientific man. This train of association leads him on to thoughts of the decay and death of those who once enjoyed beauty and riches – 'Dear dead women with such hair, too.' Browning himself stayed in Venice for long periods and died there.

so . . . departed: these words are the stage directions which close the *Noble Lorde and Lady of Huntingdons Entertainement of their right Noble Mother Alice: Countesse Dowager of Darby the first night of her honors arrivall at the House of Ashby* by John Marston (1575?–1634). The masque is Marston's graceful and flattering tribute to the Countess, his patron. In classical myth, Niobe was the mother who boasted that her children were better than the offspring of Zeus, king of the gods; in the masque, she withdraws in favour of the Countess, whose 'arrivall', in all its ceremonious formality, contrasts with the stark and sordid modern 'arrival' in line 3.

Eliot identified these sources on the Thayer copy, and a further eight for the remainder of the poem. However, none of the Epigraph allusions elucidate any detail in the poem itself. In the extravagance of this Epigraph, Eliot may be imitating Corbière ('Epitaphe' carried a joke epigraph, half-a-page long, while 'Ça?' has a burlesque single-word epigraph, 'What', attributed to Shakespeare). Erik Svarny discusses 'Burbank's' epigraph in *The Men of 1914: T. S. Eliot and early Modernism* (1988), pages 149–53, advancing the idea that its 'aesthetic effect cannot be disassociated from its very impenetrability: that effect is to leave the reader disorientated, outside the poem . . .' Save the last, all these sources have a connection with Venice, the setting of the poem and in the latter part of the nineteenth century, a prime cultural trophy for Americans on their European tour.

ll. 1–4: the stanza is in the style of a stage direction, echoing the last allusion of the epigraph.

l. 1 little bridge: Venice has a multitude of side-canals crossed by such little bridges.

l. 2 Descending: in the French sense of 'descendre', staying at, see Introduction, pages 12–13.

a small hotel: this may allude to a novella by Wilkie Collins, *The Haunted Hotel* (in *The Belgravia Magazine*, June–November 1878), subtitled *A Mystery of Modern Venice* (see Ricks, 1988).

l. 3 Volupine: a constructed name, with suggestions of voluptuous and vulpine (foxy), half-echoing the title-character of Ben Jonson's *Volpone, the Fox.*

l. 4: cf. 'They were together, and she fell', a line from 'The Sisters', a poem by Alfred Tennyson (1809–93). Eliot's 'he' is an ironic variant; in 'The Sisters', the 'she' is a beautiful girl seduced by an Earl.

l. 5 Defunctive music: funeral music. Shakespeare uses this phrase in 'The Phoenix and the Turtle', a memorial poem for the passing of love and constancy symbolized by the death in a 'mutual flame' of the mythical phoenix and the turtle-dove. In *The Athenaeum*, 2 May 1919, Eliot called this 'a great poem'.

ll. 5–6: for its rhyme-words Eliot employs the key words in a memorable exchange between the scheming lovers Kate Cory and Merton Densher in *The Wings of the Dove* (see page 80):

> 'I'm a brute about illness. I hate it. It's well for you, my dear,' Kate continued, 'that you're as sound as a bell.'
> 'Thank you!' Densher laughed. 'It's rather good for yourself too that you're as strong as the sea.' (Bk. 6, ch. 4)

ll. 5–8: a reference to Shakespeare's *Antony and Cleopatra* IV, iii. It is just before the battle at Actium, where Caesar routs the Egyptian forces. A group of Cleopatra's soldiers hears mysterious music. ''Tis the God Hercules, whom Antony lov'd, Now leaves him,' says one, interpreting the sound as an omen of the defeat to come. Antony, once the man of action, justly loses the patronage of the god of strength, for he has abandoned war for the sake of life with Cleopatra.

l. 6 passing bell: sounded at someone's death; and, moreover, appearing in Ruskin's account of Venice itself, as the city is eroded by the sea: 'the fast-gaining waves, that beat like passing bells, against the STONES OF VENICE'.

l. 7 Hercules: Thayer: 'Hercules the God of sexual virility'.

ll. 9–11: these lines refer to the rising of the sun. From Venice it would be seen to rise over the peninsula of Istria, eastwards across the Adriatic Sea. In classical myth, the sun was figured as a chariot drawn across the sky by a team of horses. This imagery of dawn is usually associated with the awakening and parting of lovers. By contrast, Eliot's phrasing, 'Beat ... with even feet', echoes the words of Horace 'aequo pulsat pede' (*Odes* I, iv, 13) describing the movement of death among all mankind, kings and paupers alike. In Horace 'aequo' (literally 'equal' or 'even') takes on the meaning impartial, ruthless, unremitting.

Eliot's specific literary reference is to the Venetian tragedy *Antonio and Mellida* by John Marston (1575–1634):

> For see the dappled grey coursers of the morne
> Beat up the light with their bright silver hooves
> And chase it through the sky.
>
> (Pt. II, i, 1)

There is also a local Venetian reference, for the sun's chariot and team is represented on the sculptured bronze doors of the Cathedral of St Mark.

l. 9 axletree: literally, the crossbar bearing the wheels of a coach or chariot. But Eliot draws upon a figurative meaning, the sky (see the passage from *Bussy d'Ambois*, a favourite of Eliot's, quoted on page 77, the note to lines 67–9 of 'Gerontion').

ll. 11–12: cf. the description of Cleopatra's barge by Enobarbus: 'The barge she sat in, like a burnish'd throne, Burn'd on the water' (*Antony and Cleopatra* II, ii). In *The Athenaeum*, 25 July 1919, Eliot quotes this description to invoke 'The really fine rhetoric of Shakespeare'.

l. 13: cf. 'And this, or something like it, was his way', line 2 in 'How it strikes a contemporary' by Browning. The allusion effects an ironic contrast, since the hero of Browning's poem is a poet, particularly characterized for his close observation of people and places, and thus altogether unlike the Bleistein of lines 17–19.

l. 16: Chicago and Vienna are cities with large and distinctive Jewish populations; and in his 1918 'Henry James' essay Eliot associated Chicago with the spirit of American 'commercialism': Americans 'like to be told that they are a race of commercial buccaneers'; 'this show of commercialism which Americans like to present to the foreign eye'. 'Semite' is the technical classification for the descendants of Shem, son of Noah, mentioned in Genesis x. But as Eliot uses the word here, in the ordinary sense of Jew, it carries the tone of an anti-Semite sneer. Ricks (1988) considers the question of Eliot's anti-Semitism raised by this poem.

l. 17 protrusive: from Henry James (see Introduction, page 13).

l. 18 protozoic: associated with the simplest forms of living matter. Eliot's train of thought, here, about the primitive, animalistic Bleistein, and, in the next two lines, about the perspectives of culture and history, may be related to another passage in Hueffer's *Henry James*: 'That the forces of deterioration are a large crawling mass . . . It is essential that every generation should reappraise everything for itself' (an extract quoted by Eliot in *The Egoist*, May 1918).

l. 19 Canaletto: Antonio Canale (1697–1768), famous for the many paintings of his favourite subject – the canals of Venice. Such an artistic 'perspective' on a modern scene is found in James's 'The Grand Canal': 'the traveller emerging for the first time upon the terrace of the railway-station seems to have a Canaletto before him'.

l. 20: alludes to the smoking candle in the right foreground of Mantegna's painting referred to in the Epigraph.

l. 21 Rialto: the ancient building in Venice where the principal financial and mercantile business was transacted. 'On the Rialto' is a phrase used by Shylock the Jew in Shakespeare's *Merchant of Venice* I, iii, with variants of it elsewhere in the play, meaning 'in business quarters'. These associations with Shylock the money-lender are continued in lines 22–3.

ll. 23–4: here, Eliot satirizes a then commonplace prejudice against the Jews – that, unseen, power was in their hands, usually through money. He may have taken the idea immediately from the 'Nestor' episode in Joyce's *Ulysses* (which he proof-read for the January–February 1919 issue of *The Egoist*), where Mr Deasy remarks: 'England is in the hands of the jews. In all the highest places: her finance, her press. And they are the signs of a nation's decay. Wherever they gather they eat up the nation's vital strength.'

The idea is also reflected in Eliot's review of *The Education of Henry Adams* (see Introduction, pages 12–13), where he quoted Adams on the Palgrave family:

> Old Sir Francis, the father, had been much the greatest of all the historians of England, the only one who was un-English; and the reason of his superiority lay in his name, which was Cohen, and his mind, which was Cohen also, or at least not English. He had changed his name to Palgrave in order to please his wife.

l. 24 Money in furs: meaning both that there is a fortune to be made in the fur trade, which is a Jewish trade, and that the rich dress in furs. Venice was once a centre for the fur trade from the Black Sea. Eliot's home-town of St Louis prospered from the fur trade.

l. 26 meagre: (in the sense of the French 'maigre'; see 'Whispers of Immortality', note to lines 17–18), emaciated and 'blue-nailed' because it is a 'consumptive' hand, i.e. the Princess is suffering from tuberculosis, a wasting disease, physically and/or morally.

phthisic: consumptive, is a word of Eliot's invention, possibly suggested by the use of 'phtisie' by Laforgue ('L'Hiver qui vient'). Milly Theale, the 'immensely rich' heroine of *The Wings of the Dove*, spoken of as the 'princess', comes to Venice incurably ill, echoing the theme of sickness here and death in lines 5–8.

l. 27 waterstair: the steps from the canal to the formal entrance of a palace or hotel. The word, slightly archaic in tone, is not recorded in the OED and may be an invention. Henry James habitually referred to the 'water steps' of Venice, as in entering 'the old palace' of the Epigraph.

Lights, lights: cf. 'Light, I say! Light!' the cry of Brabantio in *Othello* I, i. He has just been aroused from sleep by the shouted news that his daughter Desdemona has stolen away to be married to Othello, 'the Moor of Venice', an action that is represented to him as being unnatural and treacherous, a view he accepts.

ll. 28–9 Sir Ferdinand Klein: an indicative name, suggesting a German Jew who has been successful in England, hence his title. Klein: in German, small.

l. 29 lion's wings: the winged lion, the emblem of St Mark, was the heraldic device of the Venetian Republic of which he was the patron saint. cf. 'Devouring Time, blunt thou the lion's paws', the opening line of Shakespeare's Sonnet XIX.

ll. 29–32: cf. 'have clipt his wings, pared his nails, filed his teeth', in *A Tale of a Tub* (1704) by Jonathan Swift (1667–1745); this is a passage where Swift is ironically praising the achievement of hack-writers in so triumphing over 'Time'. Also cf. 'St Mark yet sees his lion where he stood,/Stand, but in mockery of his wither'd power' (*Childe Harold's Pilgrimage* IV, xi).

The allusion may be many-layered. In Ariosto, *Orlando Furioso* (Bk XL, Stanza 3), Cardinal Hippolito d'Este (b. 1480) is credited with having 'par'd the Lyons teeth and pawes'. This is Sir John Harington's translation (1591). His footnote reads: 'The Lyons teeth and pawes meaning the Venecians, called Lyons of the sea.'

ll. 31–2 meditating on/Time's ruins: cf. 'To meditate amongst decay, and stand/A ruin amidst ruins', *Childe Harold's Pilgrimage* (IV, xxv). These lines occur in the stanza that concludes Byron's celebration of Venice, honouring its great past, deploring its present decay, which he sees to be moral, as well as political, financial and architectural, a decadence which he further portrayed in *Beppo: A Venetian Story*, 1818. Eliot is also referring to *The Ruins of Time* (1591), a poem of 'the World's Vanity', in which Spenser (before Byron) continued the classical tradition of the *encomium urbis*, verses in praise of the Roman City of Verulamium (modern St Albans), personified by a Princess and lamenting its decline and fall.

l. 32 the seven laws: Thayer: 'Ruskin'. Ruskin set out the seven
architectural laws relating to St Mark's Venice, in *The Stones of
Venice*. He associated the rise and fall of Venetian Gothic style
with the state of Venice's political, moral and cultural health,
writing of its 'corruption', 'dissipation', its fate as 'the dying
city': 'she rose a vestal from the sea' and 'became drunk with the
wine of her fornication'. This imagery of sexuality and ill-health
is echoed in Eliot's account of Princess Volupine; Burbank's fall
in what Ruskin formally termed 'the Fall of Venice'. The corrup-
tion of Venice was also that of money (just as Princess Volupine
prostitutes herself, turning from Burbank to Sir Ferdinand Klein
– his name suggestive of an armaments baron): 'her exertion
only aroused by the touch of a secret spring. That spring was her
commercial interest . . .' Ruskin's modern Venice is a 'ruinous'
city, a place of 'ruin and ruins'. His lament for this sad spectacle
lies heavy on the book and is offered for the reader to meditate
upon, just as Eliot quits Burbank. At the conclusion of volume
one of *The Stones of Venice*, Ruskin conducts the reader on a
return journey, from Padua to Venice, re-entering the modern,
fallen Venice of the mid-nineteenth century, past the 'railroad
bridge, conspicuous above all things', in sight 'a straggling line
of low and confused brick buildings', and over them, what 'first
catches the eye is a sullen cloud of black smoke brooding over
the northern half of it, and which issues from the belfry of a
church. It is Venice' – Ruskin's 'perspective' on the 'smoky
candle end of time' (line 20).

Sweeney Erect

Probably written 1917–19;
Art and Letters (*London*) *Summer 1919*

Title: The title neatly points the sexual aspect of the poem's situation; also the joke on Sweeney as a human animal, human by scientific definition as an 'erectus', a creature walking upright in contrast to the stooping stance of the anthropoid and higher orders of the ape family. Sweeney is also 'erect' in his sexual function, consonant with the setting of the poem, since the 'house' (line 40) is a house of ill-fame, i.e. a brothel. Eliot and Pound exchanged 'erection' jokes in their correspondence, a line of humour which here enters the poetry. Eliot wondered if it would shock his mother (*Letters I*, p. 363). The title also seems to refer to Ralph Waldo Emerson (1803–82), his essay 'Self-Reliance' (which also appears to be referred to in lines 25–6). In the essay's penultimate paragraph, Emerson discusses man's fulfilment: 'He who knows that power is inborn, that he is weak because he has looked for good out of him and elsewhere, and, so perceiving, throws himself unhesitatingly on his thought, instantly rights himself, stands in the erect position, commands his limbs, works miracles; just as a man who stands on his feet is stronger than a man who stands on his head.' This poem effects a grotesque and ironic comment on Emerson's view. Matthiessen quoted Eliot's words on Emerson: that he was not 'a real observer of the moral life' (*Athenaeum*, 25 April 1919); and went on to describe Eliot as being 'dissatisfied with the undefined spirituality of Emerson or Arnold: neither "Self-Reliance" nor "The Buried Life" was adequate'.

Eliot said that he thought of Sweeney (who appears in a

number of poems) 'as a man who in younger days was perhaps a
pugilist, mildly successful; who then grew older and retired to
keep a pub'. Conrad Aiken, recalling his Harvard days with
Eliot, has suggested that Sweeney is based upon the ex-pugilist,
with a name like Steve O'Donnell, with whom the poet took
boxing lessons at Boston. In her edition of *The Waste Land*
manuscript, Valerie Eliot notes that Eliot recalled in later life
that when an undergraduate at Harvard he would visit the
Opera Exchange in Boston, whose bartender was one of the
prototypes for Sweeney. For another, see Introduction, page 36.

The representation of the Irishman as an ape – 'one of the
monsters who shambled through the nightmares of literary
America during the second and third quarters of the nineteenth
century' – is discussed by Jonathan Morse, 'Sweeney, the Sties of
the Irish, and *The Waste Land*' (in Robey).

Epigraph: From *The Maid's Tragedy* II, ii, by Francis Beaumont
(1584–1616) and John Fletcher (1579–1625). The speaker is the
heroine, the broken-hearted Aspatia. Her attendants are at work
on a tapestry which tells the story of Ariadne, in Greek legend a
woman who lost her beloved, as Aspatia has. She criticizes their
work. The colours are 'not dull and pale enough', and she tells
them to take her as their model. The lines quoted in the Epigraph
are a continuation of these instructions.

ll. 1–8: these lines echo Aspatia's instructions, particularly her
words preceding the Epigraph:

> Suppose I stand upon the sea-beach now,
> Mine arms thus, and mine hair blown with the wind,
> Wild as that desert . . .

'This is a pastiche of Jacobean verse, too skillful to be taken
only as parody and too evidently artificial to be taken as wholly
straightforward' (Arthur Mizener, 'To Meet Mr Eliot', *Sewanee
Review*, 1957). The effect, of course, is tapestry-like, following
on from the Epigraph and imitating its Jacobean literary diction.
l. 2 Cyclades: a group of islands in the Aegean Sea, 'unstilled'

because in Greek legend they are floating islands.

l. 3 anfractuous: the dictionary meaning is 'winding, involved, circuitous'; whereas the context seems to require 'contorted, craggy', an instance of Eliot compelling a new meaning. Thayer: 'a favourite word of Dr Johnson's'; and Eliot would have found it in Johnson's *Dictionary* (1756), alongside 'anfractuose', 'anfractuousness' and 'anfracture'.

l. 4 snarled: an obsolete word meaning entangled, twisted.

yelping: Eliot is using the rare original meaning, the sound of the waves.

l. 5 Aeolus: Greek god of the winds.

l. 6 Reviewing: not looking over but in the obsolete sense of looking back.

insurgent: insurgency is rebelliousness, so these are rising gales, figuratively disobedient.

l. 7 Ariadne: according to Greek legend she was the daughter of Minos, King of Crete. She fell in love with Theseus, and helped him to find his way in and out of the labyrinth, where he killed the Minotaur. They fled from Crete together and were married. But Theseus abandoned her on the island of Naxos where she hanged herself in grief.

l. 8 perjured sails: Theseus had set out from Athens to destroy the Minotaur and so free his country from the annual tribute of young men and women who had to be sent as sacrifices. His success or failure was to be signalled by the colour of the sails of the returning ship. It had set out, with its doomed passengers, bearing black sails; and Theseus forgot to change these on his victorious return journey. His father, the King, saw these and threw himself to his death.

l. 10 Nausicaa: according to Greek legend she was the daughter of King Alcinous on the island of Scheria. She came across Odysseus on the morning after he had been shipwrecked and thrown up on the shore. He was naked, but covered himself with a leafy olive branch and so talked his way into her confidence that she had him brought to the palace under her personal protection. The story is told in Homer's *Odyssey*.

Polypheme: appears in another important 'morning' scene in the *Odyssey*. He was the leader of the Cyclopes, a race of one-eyed man-eating giants. He captured Odysseus and his crew and held them prisoner in his cave. They escaped by blinding him and then hiding in the thick wool on the underside of his flock of sheep, which he let out for their daily pasture.

l. 11 orang-outang: the 'orang-outang' is Sweeney, 'Apeneck Sweeney', as he is described at the opening of 'Sweeney Among the Nightingales'. It is an anthropoid ape, popularly supposed next to man on the evolutionary scale, hence the literal meaning of its name, 'man of the woods'. In *The Use of Poetry*, Eliot draws attention to a note by Shelley: 'the orang-outang perfectly resembles man both in the order and the number of his teeth' (*Queen Mab*, 1813).

Eliot is referring here to 'The Murders in the Rue Morgue', a story by Edgar Allan Poe (1809–49), in which the murders occur after an orang-outang takes its owner's razor, lathers its face in front of the mirror and tries to shave. Many years later Eliot referred slyly and obliquely to his use of Poe: 'And some of his tales have had an important influence upon authors, and in types of writing where such influence would hardly be expected' (*From Poe to Valéry*, 1948, in which he refers specifically to 'The Murders').

l. 13: Thayer: 'cf. Tristan Corbière. Rhapsode Foraine'. This is 'La Rapsode foraine et le Pardon de Sainte Anne'. As there is no obvious point of allusion, Eliot must have had the poem as a whole in mind (see page 118, note to *ll.* 17–20).

ll. 13–15: Details in the description of 'The epileptic on the bed' (line 31) seem to be drawn from the description of the French philosopher Rousseau in Shelley's 'The Triumph of Life':

> That what I thought was an old root which grew
> To strange distortion out of the hill side,
> Was indeed one of those deluded crew,
> And that the grass, which me thought hung so wide
> And white, was but his thin discoloured hair,
> And that the holes he vainly sought to hide,
> Were or had been eyes . . .

This passage was familiar to Eliot. He quoted these lines in *The Use of Poetry and the Use of Criticism* (1933), remarking that in this 'last' and 'greatest though unfinished poem', 'There is a precision of image and an economy here that is new to Shelley'. Such 'precision' and 'economy' are characteristic of 'Sweeney Erect' and the other quatrain poems. Eliot spoke of 'The Triumph of Life' again in 1950, where he named it as the 'greatest' of Shelley's 'great poems' and again quoted the passage in which these lines come, a passage 'which made an indelible impression upon me over forty-five years ago'.

ll. 25–6: Eliot seems to be referring to two statements that come in a single paragraph of Emerson's essay 'Self-Reliance': 'an institution is the lengthened shadow of one man' and 'all history resolves itself very easily into the biography of a few stout and earnest persons'.

ll. 33–8: the Emerson echoes continue: the great soul, he writes, must not bother about consistency: 'Ah, then, exclaim the aged ladies, you shall be sure to be misunderstood. Misunderstood! . . .Is it so bad then to be misunderstood? . . . To be great is to be misunderstood.'

l. 43 sal volatile: smelling salts.

A Cooking Egg

Written 1917; Coterie *(London) May 1919*

The poem was developed out of a discarded final stanza to 'Whispers of Immortality'.

Title: Cooking eggs are usually those which are too old to be eaten on their own, when their staleness might be detected.

Epigraph: 'In the thirtieth year of my life,/When I drank up all my shame.' These are the opening lines of *Le Grand Testament (The Great Testament)* by the French poet François Villon (1431–?). He reviews his sins, penitently, to prepare him to face the after-life; at the same time, he cannot deny his enjoyment of lust and greed.

Matthiessen comments: 'Thus the title relates to the epigraph from Villon, which also tells the age and condition of the hero of the poem.' Eliot's friends would catch the personal reference, since in 1917 he was on the verge of his own 'thirtieth year'.

Possibly the epigraph was added at the time of publication. In a book review that appeared in *The Athenaeum* in May 1919, Eliot quoted the two lines of Villon. This was the kind of cryptic cross-reference Eliot enjoyed dropping in the path of his readers. The review also made a reference to Sidney (see line 10).

l. 1 Pipit: perhaps a familiar, affectionate pet-name. According to Matthiessen, the name 'might suggest that she is a little girl, an impression that is reinforced by several other details in the poem'. But it may also carry a learned and obscure 'egg' joke. Pipi is the Greek misrendering of the Hebrew *Yahweh*, regarded by occultists as a word of power: written on a shelled hard-boiled egg, it is said to open the heart to wisdom.

There is long, well-documented debate on Pipit's identity, a topic on which Eliot refused to be drawn (see Introduction, page 38). Eliot's Cambridge friend I. A. Richards wrote in 1926 that she was the speaker's 'retired nurse' – but Eliot said he was wrong and that a clue was to be found in one of his French poems, 'Dans le Restaurant' (written in summer 1918), where a waiter confesses a sexual experience in early childhood. This suggests that the Pipit of stanzas 1–2 is a young girl and that the dots following the opening stanzas mark the passage of time and that the second division, after stanza 6, indicates a shift in the 'I', as the memories of childhood well up and swamp the brave stance of the central section. The debate can be followed in *Essays in Criticism:* F. W. Bateson, 'The Function of Criticism in the Present Time', January 1953; answered by Elizabeth Drew and other critics, July 1953.

Eliot's allusion to Ruskin's affection for Rose La Touche (see page 100) further supports the Pipit/little girl interpretation.

sate: an archaic form of sat, much used, to comic effect, in the nonsense poetry of Edward Lear (1812–88). It sounds like an allusion to the humorous language of childhood, lasting into adult life. Eliot sometimes wrote to his friends in a mock archaic English (see also line 15).

l. 3: presumably a volume of pictures showing the colleges of Oxford University, where Eliot was a graduate student, 1914–15.

l. 5 Daguerreotypes: photographs produced by one of the earliest processes, in use from about 1840–60; a word which Eliot now uses to challenge the reader, in the spirit of Edward Fitzgerald's comment to a correspondent in 1839: 'Perhaps you are not civilized enough to know what a Daguerreotype is.'

l. 8: probably a piece of sheet music with that title. There are several nineteenth-century songs and piano pieces of that name, the best-known of which is by Weber.

l. 9 want: in the slightly archaic/Biblical sense of 'be without', as in 'The Lord is my shepherd; I shall not want' (Psalms xxiii, 1).

ll. 9–13: the collocation of 'Honour', 'Sidney' and 'heroes of that kidney' looks very much like an elaboration of 'Bold Sidney, and his kidney', a line in 'A Lament for the Decline of Chivalry' by Thomas Hood (1799–1845).

ll. 9–24 in Heaven: the detailed account of these heavenly activities is in part a satire on a devotional love poem, 'The Blessed Damozel' by Dante Gabriel Rossetti (1828–82). Its central ten stanzas iterate what she and her beloved will do together when reunited 'in Heaven', with details precise and material to the point of absurdity, e.g.

> We two will lie i' the shadow of
> That living mystic tree
> Within whose secret growth the Dove
> Is sometimes felt to be,
> While every leaf that His plumes touch
> Saith His name audibly.
>
> (cf. Eliot's lines 15–16)

Matthiessen suggests that some of the material in this section of the poem may have come from a letter from Ruskin to Susan Bever about Rose la Touche, the little girl with whom he fell in love in his middle age: 'But, Susie, *you* expect to see your Margaret again, and you will be happy with her in heaven. I wanted my Rosie *here*. In heaven I mean to go and talk to Pythagoras and Socrates and Valerius Publicola. I shan't care a bit for Rosie there, she needn't think it.'

l. 10 Sir Philip Sidney: Sidney (1554–86) was the exemplary figure of 'Honour' in Elizabethan England. He was the complete gentleman-courtier, statesman, poet, patron of the arts, and soldier. His humanity is celebrated in the story of how, when wounded, he passed on his cup of water to another wounded man: 'Thy necessity is yet greater than mine.'

l. 11 Coriolanus: the hero of Shakespeare's *Coriolanus*, a Roman general whom Shakespeare presents as a leader driven by a destructive, selfish 'heroism'.

l. 12 kidney: character or temperament, from the idea that the kidneys played an important part in determining a person's constitution. Self-consciously literary (Shakespeare, Fielding,

Disraeli, etc.), the phrasing here seems to carry a mild sneer.

l. 14 Sir Alfred Mond: (1868–1930), the age's representative man of power and affairs: industrialist, capitalist (he founded Imperial Chemical Industries), politician (holding the government office of First Commissioner of Works in 1917) and member of numberless public bodies and committees.

l. 15 lapt: an archaic word for wrapped.

l. 16: financial bonds issued by the British Government, carrying an interest rate of 5 per cent.

l. 17 Society: not merely company, but good society.

l. 18 Lucretia Borgia: (1480–1519), Lucretia was one of the notorious Italian Borgias. Her brother, Cesare, was the poisoner. But Lucretia could undoubtedly provide good 'Society'. She was Duchess of Ferrara, daughter of Cardinal Rodrigo Borgia (afterwards Pope Alexander VI), engaged six times, four times married, and closely associated with the most noble and powerful Italian families. Eliot may have taken these details from a letter of Edward Fitzgerald's (quoted in A. C. Benson's biography: see note to lines 1–2, 'Gerontion', page 69), which he was reading at this time. Fitzgerald was irritated by his wife's aspirations towards 'Society' and so described her: 'My Contemporary looks in this chamber of horrors like Lucretia Borgia.' 'Bride' is fitting, since they were then only three weeks married.

l. 22 Madame Blavatsky: Helena Petrovna Blavatsky (1831–91), the famous Russian spiritualist and Theosophist, well known in England and America. Theosophy (literally, 'wisdom of god') claimed direct insight into the nature of god. Eliot had no interest in Theosophy as such; but Pound did, through his friendship with Yeats, who dabbled in spiritualism, Rosicrucian philosophy and other mystic and occult systems. These lines sound like a dig at Pound, although they may have been aimed at Dora Marsden, a leading Theosophist in the Pound–Eliot–Joyce circle, founder and sometime editor of *The Egoist*, of which Eliot was assistant editor 1917–19. Eliot did not get on with her. He told John Quinn in 1919 that she 'frothed at the mouth with antipathy' and objected to her using *The Egoist* as a vehicle for 'her philosophical articles' (*Letters*, i.315).

l. 23: the 'Seven Sacred Trances' belong to the secret doctrines of Theosophy, known only to the adepts; 'Seven' corresponding to the seven planes of Theosophical reality, for which full instruction is not possible on the earthly level of existence; hence it will be conducted in 'Heaven'.

l. 24 Piccarda de Donati: a nun, who was compelled to break her vows. She was consigned by Dante to the lowest level of Heaven, where remain the souls of those who were unable to keep their vows on earth. She addresses Dante (*Paradiso* iii, 25–30) as a child and explains to him the meaning of God's will (70–87).

l. 25 But where; l. 29 Where are: these line openings imitate a classical Latin device, *Ubi sunt* ('Where are'), commonly used in poetry to signal sections of regretful recollection, usually of worldly pleasures. This device is used by Villon in *Le Grand Testament* (see note to Epigraph) and Eliot would have encountered it in Pound's *Three Cantos* written in 1916–17, which he helped to revise.

penny world: this name has long been used in the confectionery and baking trades for various kinds of cakes and sweets. Perhaps Eliot is using the words specifically as well as in their wider, metaphorical sense.

l. 26: in some households (particularly in the nineteenth century) it was customary for the children to have some meals with the rest of the family, but at their own table and separated from the adults by a screen. Eliot may be referring to this custom, rather than to some kind of secretive eating.

l. 28: northern suburbs of London. Golders Green was a new suburb, preponderantly Jewish, which developed after the extension of the Northern Line of the Underground from Hampstead and the opening of the Golders Green station in June 1907. It became an in-joke for Eliot's closest friends and featured in 'King Bolo', a sequence of obscene limericks and limerick-like stanzas begun at Harvard, to which he added stanzas from time to time, e.g. in a letter to Conrad Aiken, 10 January 1916: 'King Bolo's big black bassturd kween/That airy fairy hairy un/She led the dance on Golder's Green/With Cardinal Bessarian' (*Letters I*, p. 125). He wrote in the same vein to James Joyce in May 1921:

'Bolo's big black bastard queen/Was *so* obscene/She shocked the folk of Golder's Green' (*Letters I*, p. 455).

Both Bolo and Bessarian (properly Bessarion) are historical figures. Bolo is King Shamba Bolongongo (known today as Shyaam aMbul aNgoong) (died *c.* 1628), ruler of the Kuba tribes, legendary for the number of widows and children he left. Eliot could have come across his name in *Notes ethnographiques* (1911) by the Hungarian ethnographer and explorer Emil Torday; and he could have seen a wooden figure of Bolongongo, hailed as one of the outstanding examples of Kuba art, which was presented to the British Museum by Torday and put on display in the Ethnography Galleries in Summer 1909.

Cardinal Joannes Bessarion (1395–1472) was Papal Legate to Venice, remembered as founder of the Library of St Mark's. Eliot would have met the name in his Italian Renaissance course at Harvard.

In June 1915, Eliot was married at Hampstead – only a mile from Golders Green and about two from Kentish Town – staying there on and off during the summer with his in-laws, the Haigh-Woods. While teaching at the Junior Department of Highgate School in 1916–17, Eliot was only a mile further from Golders Green. Hampstead is the setting of the opening section of 'The Death of the Duchess', a poem in *The Waste Land* manuscript.

ll. 29–30: the eagle was one of the emblems of Rome, displayed by the legions of the army; and while these lines suggest a reference to Roman forces defeated or lost while crossing the Alps in Northern Italy, the occasion is not specific but refers to the cycles of history, the idea that history repeats itself from age to age. This Roman imagery may have been suggested to Eliot by

> The Napoleonic épopée was really a resurrection of Julius Caesar; transferred from Rome to Paris and having Gauls to carry his triumphant eagles ... to the borders of Europe. The war of 1870 was the return of the barbarians. Will we see Caesar resuscitated or will the Latin eagles remain for ever vanquished by the other proud eagles?

This is Section 149 of Rémy de Gourmant's 'Poudre aux Moineaux' (Dust for Sparrows) in Pound's translation. Although this was published only in 1920, Eliot could have seen it during the writing of 'A Cooking Egg', since Pound received de Gourmant's unpublished manuscript in June 1915. Eliot paid tribute to de Gourmant's intellectual gifts, including his 'sense of history', in 'The Perfect Critic' (1920), a passage quoted by Matthiessen.

l. 32: on Thayer, Eliot wrote 'Blake' by this part of the poem and this is indeed the language of William Blake. Cf. 'I laid me down upon a bank/Where love lay sleeping/I heard among the rushes dank/Weeping, Weeping' (from the 1793 *Notebook*); and 'multitudes' are also a feature of his poetry. Here, as in the earlier references to Kentish Town and Golders Green and in the next line, Eliot may be seeking to evoke such a poem as 'London' in the *Songs of Experience*, from which he quoted in a review in February 1920, describing it as Blake's 'naked vision'. In *Jerusalem* (27:9), Blake refers to Kentish Town: 'Pancross & Kentish-town repose/Among her golden pillars'.

l. 33 A.B.C.'s: branches of the Aerated Bread Company's chain of tea-shops, inexpensive restaurants once found throughout London. They were a favourite resort of the group around Wyndham Lewis and Pound, which included Eliot. In the second issue of *Blast* (July 1915), Lewis (its editor) referred to 'All A.B.C. Tea-Shops (without exception)' in his poem 'Bless' (countering his poem 'Blast'). Eliot was also making a sly joke with Ezra Pound, whose poem 'The Tea Shop' (*Others*, November 1915) refers to the waitress who serves 'us our muffins' and whose 'glow of youth will be spread about us no longer./She also will turn middle-aged' – a cooking egg herself! Eliot was familiar with the poem since it was included in *Lustra*, Pound's 1916 collection published in London, which Eliot helped him to edit for an American edition, 1917.

A.B.C.s also featured in Wyndham Lewis's novel *Tarr*, serialized in the *Egoist* from April 1916 onwards: prominent, on the first page of chapter one, is Hobson, whose 'strong piercing laugh threw A.B.C. waitresses into confusion'; this carries an identifiable trait of Pound's. Eliot reviewed *Tarr* in the September 1918 issue of the *Egoist*.

A.B.C.s remained sufficiently alive as a shared joke for Pound to characterize Eliot – 'He writes of A.B.C.s' – in 'Sage Homme', a poem he sent to Eliot with his comments on *The Waste Land* (letter, 24 December 1921).

A further Eliot–Pound reference is in the first line of the Epigraph. Pound also used this line from Villon (altering 'mon' to 'son'), in the opening poem ('E. P. Ode') of *Hugh Selwyn Mauberley* (1920), which Eliot considered 'a great poem' and included in *Selected Poems* (1928). Pound's quatrain form in *Mauberley*, like Eliot's, owed much to Gautier.

The Hippopotamus

Written 1917; Little Review *(Chicago) July 1917*

A parody imitation of 'L'Hippopotame' by Gautier (see Introduction, page 9), copying the quatrain form and *abab* rhyme-scheme of the French original. Gautier's poem was recommended by Pound to readers of *The New Freewoman* on 15 September 1913 and Pound may have played some part in the writing of Eliot's version.

As Foreign Editor of the *Little Review* from May 1917 until spring 1919, Pound promoted Eliot's work: hence the appearance there of 'The Hippopotamus' together with three of his French poems in July 1917; and, in September 1918, of 'Whispers of Immortality', 'Mr Eliot's Sunday Morning Service', 'Sweeney Among the Nightingales' and a further French poem.

Eliot's circle would have seen an autobiographical joke in the title. In March 1917, the poet began work at Lloyds Bank, an event he signified here through an allusion to one of the Songs in *Sylvie and Bruno* (1889), the novel by Lewis Carroll: 'He thought he saw a Banker's Clerk/Descending from the bus:/He looked again, and found it was/A Hippopotamus:/"If this should stay to dine," he said,/"There won't be much for us!"'

Eliot's natural history, half-spoof, half-correct, is part of the joke. A four-ton beast, the hippopotamus is bulky and unwieldly, with short, stubby legs. So the 'feeble steps' of line 9 are feasible. Likewise lines 2, 21–2 and 26, since he enjoys the water, is a daytime sleeper and lives in savannah country. But the idea of his hunting (line 22) does not fit the grass-eating animal, nor is anything known to zoologists of his 'mating time' 'inflexions' (lines 18–19).

Epigraph: From St Paul's Epistle to the Colossians iv, 16. This was written from Rome in the first century AD for the benefit of the early Christians at Colossae and Laodicea. Both groups were wavering between Christianity and Judaism, lukewarm in their faith. The Epistle is to remind them of their Christian duties and beliefs.

ll. 7–8: the Roman Catholic Church claims direct descent from the ministry of St Peter to Rome, thus the 'True Church'; 'based upon a rock' recalls the words of Christ to Peter: 'thou art Peter, and upon this rock I will build my church' (Matthew xvi, 18).

ll. 19–20: The Song of Solomon is interpreted as representing the marriage of Christ to his Church.

l. 23: echoes 'God moves in a mysterious way,/His wonders to perform,' the opening lines of 'Light Shining out of Darkness' by William Cowper (1731–1800); and in general Cowper's poem seems to be a point of departure for Eliot's satire.

l. 27 quiring: an archaic form of 'choiring' preserved in the wording of the English Prayer Book. Eliot may also be taking in the meaning of 'quire'; in the heavenly hierarchy, the angels are divided into nine orders or quires.

l. 28 loud hosannas: cries of adoration (imitating the sound of the Hebrew word from which it is derived). A literary phrase, it is found in Milton, Pope, etc.

l. 29: Christ regarded as a sacrificial lamb, whose blood would cleanse man of sin, a metaphorical view of the death of Christ for the salvation of mankind, as in John i, 29: 'Behold the Lamb of God, which taketh away the sin of the world,' and Revelation vii, 14, where God's chosen people are described as made 'white in the blood of the lamb' (see line 33).

l. 33: cf. the prayer of the psalmist: 'wash me, and I shall be whiter than snow' (Psalms li, 7) and God's promise that man's 'scarlet' sins 'shall be as white as snow' (Isaiah i, 18).

l. 34 martyr'd virgins: pious unmarried women were particularly esteemed by the early Christian Church for their religious merits. Notable virgin martyrs included St Catherine (of the wheel) and St Ursula.

kist: an archaic, poetic form of kissed, as 'wrapt' (line 36) is of wrapped. These forms maintain the light tone of sardonic ridicule.

l. 36 *miasmal mist:* germ-laden gas from rotting matter.

Whispers of Immortality

Written 1917 to May–June 1918;
Little Review (*Chicago*) *September 1918*

Eliot's difficulty in writing this poem can be gauged by the fact
that there are no fewer than eight drafts in the Berg Collection
(New York Public Library). These reveal the influence of Pound
in directing Eliot to the style of Gautier (see head-note to 'Bur-
bank', page 79; and note below to lines 17–18). Pound sug-
gested the titles 'Night thoughts on immortality', 'Night
thoughts on Gautier'; and wrote on the back of one draft
'Webster Don[n]e Gautier'. So extensive are his corrections that
the poem is virtually collaborative. Pound saw these changes as
bringing 'us nearer the desired epithalamium of force, clearness
and beawtie', an ambition that explains why he pushed Eliot so
forcefully towards Gautier's vocabulary, phrasing and strict tet-
rameter quatrains (coupled with Laforguean satirical rhyming).

Pound's personal interest in this poem may have stemmed
from the fact that he had introduced Eliot to the original of
Grishkin (line 17), the subject of the second half of the poem.

'Whispers' took its 'impetus' (to use Eliot's term, quoted on
page 79) from the opening quatrain of 'Bûchers et tombeaux'
(Funeral pyres and tombs) in *Émaux et Camées* (the edition of
1858) by Gautier: 'Le squelette était invisible/Au temps heureux
de l'Art païen!;/L'homme, sous la forme sensible,/Content du
beau, ne cherchait rien', (The skeleton was invisible/In the joy-
ous days of pagan art!/Mankind, beneath the outward form,/
Satisfied with beauty/Sought for nothing). Lines 1–4 reverse this.
Eliot quoted the first two lines of 'Bûchers' in 'Andrew Marvell'
(1921), as an instance of the 'alliance of levity and seriousness

(by which the seriousness is intensified)', a quality he found also 'in the *dandysme* of Baudelaire and Laforgue'.

Title: A play upon 'Intimations of Immortality from Recollections of Early Childhood', an ode by William Wordsworth (1770–1850) concerned with the loss of innocence in experience.

l. 1 Webster: the dramatist John Webster (1580?–1625?) in whose works lust, violence and death are prominent in the plots and poetic imagery.

ll. 1–2: the skull, as a Death's-head, a *memento mori* ('remember death'), was a familiar image in Renaissance literature and art.

l. 5: cf. 'A dead man's skull beneath the roots of flowers!' the words of Flamineo in Webster's *The White Devil* v, iv, when Brachiano's ghost enters with a flower-pot of lilies and a skull beneath.

l. 9: the poet John Donne (1572–1631). Eliot's essay 'The Metaphysical Poets' (1921) provides a valuable comment on the entire stanza: 'Tennyson and Browning are poets, and they think, but they do not feel their thought as immediately as the odour of a rose. A thought to Donne was an experience; it modified his sensibility.'

l. 17 Grishkin: Serafima Astafieva (1876–1934), a Russian dancer with the Diaghilev company who opened her own ballet school in London. Pound introduced her to Eliot, 'with the firm intuito that a poem wd result & intention that it should'; and elsewhere Pound recollected that once 'I took Parson Elyot to see the Prima Ballerina and it evoked "Grushkin".' Eliot turned the joke against Pound at the end of the poem (see note to line 29).

nice: sexy (as well as agreeable), in the obsolete sense, used notably by Chaucer: wanton, lascivious.

ll. 17–18: these lines imitate the opening lines of Gautier's poem 'Carmen'(*Émaux et Camées*, the edition of 1863): 'Carmen est maigre, un trait de bistre/Cerne son œil de gitana' ('Carmen is thin, a touch of shadow/Outlines her gipsy eye').

Eliot would have come across them in Pound's 'To a Friend Writing on Cabaret Dancers' (*Lustra*, 1916), in which the dancers' jewels are spread out 'on the up-pushed bosom', echoed in Eliot's 'uncorseted' (lines 19–20). In *Ezra Pound: His Metric and Poetry* (1918), Eliot recommends his readers to 'turn at once to "To a Friend Writing on Cabaret Dancers"' to see Pound's mastery of tone. Pound regarded the lines from Gautier as touchstones of poetic technique: 'I think this sort of clear presentation is of the noblest traditions of our craft' (1913); 'Perfectly plain statements like his "Carmen est maigre" should teach one a number of things' (letter July 1916).

ll. 17–20: Eliot focuses upon Grishkin's animal magnetism, her sexual fascination; whereas in Astafieva herself Pound glimpsed a more subtle female quality. Thirty years later, he reflected critically on Eliot's portrait: 'Grishkin's photo refound years after/with the feeling that Mr Eliot may have/missed something, after all, in composing his vignette' (Canto 77).

l. 19 Uncorseted: the use of this remarkable word may have been suggested to Eliot by its appearance in the poem-sequence 'Paris' by Alan Seeger (1888–1917), where Mimi is described:

Uncorseted, her clinging dress with every step and turn betrays,
In pretty and provoking ways her adolescent loveliness.

Eliot reviewed the volume of *Poems,* in which 'Paris' appears, in *The Egoist* (December 1917). Both men were contemporaries and members of the same literary set at Harvard, and Americans-in-Paris, so that we may be detecting a private tribute on Eliot's part, rather than an insignificant plagiarism.

l. 20 pneumatic bliss: explained in a note by Pound, referring to 'Grishkin's Dunlop tyre boozum'. The 'bliss' could be spiritual (from the Greek *pneume*) as well as erotic joy. This also introduces a learned joke developed in the final stanza. The pneumatic philosophers regarded the spirit as no less a subject of study than the body; and this punning, between the attractions of the flesh and the spirit, is one of the levels of meaning in this second, Grishkin, part of the poem. In 1918, the phrase was remarkable, since while pneumatic tyres and pneumatic drills were familiar, the 'pneumatic bliss' of Grishkin's 'friendly bust' was Eliot's own innovation, copied by Ford Madox Ford in 1926 and Aldous Huxley in 1932.

Eliot may have first taken the idea from Pound's essay 'Cavalcanti' (published 1934 but written possibly as early as 1910). There, Pound writes on the ramifications of 'pneumatic philosophy', a term that Eliot uses himself in *After Strange Gods* (1934).

ll. 21–4: Gautier returns here: amongst the men captivated by Carmen, 'Et l'archevêque de Tolède/Chante la messe à ses genoux' (The Archbishop of Toledo/Says mass on his knees before her), a performance of lustful adoration that Eliot now parodies in the behaviour of his jungle animals.

ll. 21–2: the jaguar is the largest species of American cat and in South America spends much of its time in trees preying on monkeys. Hence Eliot employs the obsolete word 'couched', (not 'crouched'), meaning stretched out, as it may be, along a bough, in pursuit of the tree-dwelling marmoset, a small species of American monkey.

l. 22 Compels: in the rare and obsolete sense of.overpowers. In fact, this is a spoof. The quasi-scientific idea Eliot introduces here so convincingly (and in lines 25–7) – of the jaguar's 'effluence' (*l.* 23), its 'feline smell' serving to attract or overcome the marmoset – is wholly of his invention, since no such mechanism is known to zoologists to operate between these animals.

l. 24 maisonette: a flat or part of a house let separately, with its own entrance; here, signifying that Grishkin can entertain her men visitors in private. At this time, it was considered vulgar: see Huxley, *Antic Hay* (1923): '"It's a dreadful little maisonette," she explained.'

l. 25: cf. Revelation xx, 1: 'And I saw an angel coming down from heaven.'

l. 27 rank: to human nostrils, stinking offensively, as an animal on heat.

l. 29 Abstract Entities: following his study of philosophy at Harvard and Oxford, Eliot was well qualified to handle this kind of quasi-philosophical joke, indicating that Grishkin's powers of attraction can compel the attendance even of philosophical terminology. The explanation of these terms would require a philosophical discourse, but something of their meaning can be glimpsed in this quotation from George Berkeley, *Principles of Human Knowledge* (1710): 'The positive abstract idea of quiddity, entity or existence.'

Hence we have to visualize the Abstract Entities, captivated by Grishkin's 'charm', circling her in admiration. Whereas, the stanza continues, 'our lot' – i.e. poets such as Webster and Donne; you, Ezra, who introduced me to her; and myself – are left to find what comfort we can with fleshless bones. (Eliot explained that he is using 'lot' to mean 'kind' (as in mankind) not fate.) No Grishkin for us!

In 1917, within a book review, Eliot quoted a passage from *Principles of Logic* (1883) by F. H. Bradley, which provides a useful gloss on the 'metaphysics' of this last stanza: 'That the glory of this world is appearance leaves the world more glorious if we feel it is a show of some fuller splendour; but the sensuous curtain is a deception and a cheat – if it hides some colourless movement of atoms, some spectral woof of impalpable abstractions, or unearthly ballet of bloodless categories.' Eliot uses the poem to give his own answer.

It *is* a cheat!

Mr Eliot's Sunday Morning Service

Written 1917 to May–June 1918;
Little Review (Chicago) September 1918

Epigraph: From *The Jew of Malta* IV, by Christopher Marlowe (1564–93). These are the words of the servant Ithamore to the Jew, his master Barabas, as he catches sight of two friars. 'Caterpillars' because they exploit their religious office to make a rich living, profiting from their power over the laity. See also note on the Epigraph to 'Portrait of a Lady' (page 59).

l. 1: this curiosity is a word of Eliot's invention, meaning (adjectivally) that the 'sutlers' are highly productive of offspring. But this is not simply an amusing verbal extravagance. In *A New Life of Jesus* by Friedrich Strauss (the English translation 1865, ii, 41), the task of the Jews was 'to assimilate' Jesus 'to the philoprogenitive Gods of the heathen'. This occurs in a discussion of the 'myth' that Jesus was 'begotten' by the Holy Ghost, an area of speculation also closely related to the other controversies to which Eliot alludes in this poem.

Another form of the word, 'philoprogenitiveness', rapidly passed into circulation, appearing in 'The Student and His Vocation' (1868), an essay by Robert Buchanan criticizing the ideas of Matthew Arnold: 'If there is one quality which seems God's, and his exclusively, it seems that divine philoprogenitiveness, that passionate love and distribution and expansion into living forms.' In chapter 6 of *Culture and Anarchy* (1869), in the course of replying to Buchanan's attack, Arnold quoted the passage in which this sentence occurs, commenting 'It is a little unjust, perhaps, to attribute to the Divinity exclusively this philoprogenitiveness, which the British Philistine, and the poorer class of Irish, may certainly claim to share with him; yet how inspiriting is here the whole strain of thought! and these beautiful words, too, I carry about with me in the East of London ...' (i.e. the populous slum areas of the East End of London, in which Arnold went about his work as an Inspector of Schools and where the 'philoprogenitiveness' of the people was all too evident). Arnold's mocking riposte, which extends over several pages in a *tour de force* of scathing and sardonic humour, could well have been in Eliot's mind at this time since he was lecturing on Arnold in spring and autumn 1917.

An earlier and simpler form, 'philogenitiveness', comes in *Don Juan* (12, xxii) where Byron satirizes recent theories of 'procreation', in particular the controversial views on population control advocated by Thomas Robert Malthus (1766–1834). Byron uses the word twice in the same stanza and contrasts this Greek construction with the crude Anglo-Saxon word, unmentioned and unmentionable, a joke much to Eliot's taste.

> That's noble! That's romantic!
>   For my part,
> I think that "Philo-genitiveness" is –
> (Now here's a word quite after
>   my own heart,
> Though there's a shorter a good
>   deal than this,
> If that politeness set it not
>   apart;
> But I'm resolved to say nought
>   that's amiss) –
> I say, methinks that "Philo-genitiveness"
> Might meet from men a little
>   more forgiveness.

The use of a single eye-catching word to form a line is a device that Eliot would have seen in Laforgue; and it illustrates the value he placed upon '*surprise* so essential to poetry' (see note to line 3, page 49), a quality abundant in Laforgue and noted also by Pound, his comment applying equally to Laforgue the master and Eliot the apt pupil: Laforgue 'has dipped his wings in the dye of scientific terminology... "Un air d'hydrocéphale asperge". The tyro cannot play about with such things, the game is too dangerous. Verbalism demands a set form used with irreproachable skill. Satire needs, usually, the form of cutting rhymes to drive it home' ('Irony, Laforgue, and Some Satire', *Poetry*, November 1917).

l. 2 sutlers: provision merchants, usually to an army on the march. These are the bees (of line 25) seen as they pass the church window, their provisioning being the bearing of pollen from flower to flower, a fertilizing activity referred to in line 1. The other 'sapient sutlers' are the learned Christian scholars referred to in lines 31–2, controversialists whose arguments and commentaries on the Bible proliferate, in turn calling into existence further arguments and commentaries, a feature of Church history from the second to the sixth centuries.

l. 4: cf. 'In the beginning was the Word, and the Word was with God, and the Word was God' (John i, 1).

l. 6 Superfetation: a biological term meaning multiple impregnation of an ovary, resulting in twins or larger multiple births. In the doctrine of Origen (see note to line 8) this would refer to Christ: 'in relation to God this Logos or Son was a copy of the original and, as such, inferior'.

τὸ ἕν: Greek (to hen), the One.

l. 7 mensual: in a period of months. Is this Eliot's mistake for 'menstrual' (the form 'mensual' is not recorded in the *OED*)?

Ward (1973), looking forward to the next line: 'suggests an onset of barrenness ... analogous to the female change of life; the magnificent creativeness of God becomes represented by a Church and priests who choose sterility as a pledge of dedication'.

l. 8 Origen: (*c.* AD 185–254), the first and greatest of the early Christian theological scholars, famed for his output of a reputed 6,000 books and enormously long Biblical commentaries. His exegesis of John, ch. 1, was particularly elaborate. Hence one element of meaning in this stanza begins with Eliot's reference to

John i, and the offspring of the 'Word' in the many words of Origen and his fellow-commentators. Origen was 'enervate' physically, having castrated himself for the sake of his spiritual health, following Matthew xix, 12: 'there be eunuchs for the kingdom of heaven's sake'. Thus Eliot's reference in line 28 to the 'Blest office of the epicene', in which Origen would be numbered.

A second element of meaning in this stanza relates to particular points in the teachings of Origen: that God is an infinite being, endlessly creating; that Christ was the Word made flesh, the Logos that exists with God from eternity. These views furnished the matter for a number of early heresies, extensively declared and extensively refuted.

Origen was a 'sapient' (wise, learned) sutler in supplying the Christian doctrine of the Logos with ideas derived from the concepts of Greek philosophy.

ll. 9–13: Eliot is describing a real or imagined painting of the Baptism of Christ, a favourite subject in Western religious art. (The picture could well be Piero della Francesca's 'Baptism' which has been on view in London's National Gallery since 1861.) The usual treatment of this subject shows Christ standing in a stream or shallow pool, John the Baptist beside him, pouring water over his head from a small bowl. Above Christ's head, the Holy Ghost is often represented by a dove, and over the dove, God looks down from a gap in the clouds. According to the account of the Baptism in Matthew iii, just after the ceremony the Holy Spirit descended and God addressed his Son.

Eliot's own copy of the London *Baedeker* (see *Title* note to 'Burbank', page 83) carries heavy annotations made on visits to the National Gallery.

l. 9 Umbrian school: this was a school of painting, to which Piero della Francesca belonged, associated with the area of Umbria in fifteenth-century Italy.

l. 10 gesso: a prepared plaster surface for wall paintings. 'The *gesso* is much like ground chalk. Glue put on the panel first, then *gesso*' (in Eliot's notes for the course in Florentine Painting taken at Harvard, spring 1910).

l. 16 Paraclete: literally comforter or advocate, a title for the Holy Ghost, represented as a dove.

l. 17 presbyters: priests or elders of the early Church; Origen was an ordained presbyter; 'sable' because black-robed.

ll. 17–20: these lines may allude to Tristan Corbière's poem 'La Rapsode foraine et le Pardon de Sainte Anne' ('The Itinerant Rhapsodist and the Pardon of St Anne'), in particular to the section describing the sick who have come to the church seeking a cure: 'Qu'auréole un nimbe vermeil,/Ces propriétaires de plaies,/Rubis vivants sous le soleil' ('Haloed with a red nimbus, these owners of sores, living rubies in the sun').

Pound called this poem 'the proper introduction' to Corbière (*The New Age*, 2 October 1913). In this same article Pound asserted that 'the quintessence of style is precisely that it should be swift and mordant', terms which fit the quatrain poems perfectly.

In 1918, Pound described Corbière as 'the greatest poet of the period' and 'La Rapsode' as 'beyond all comment'.

ll. 18, 21: a formal procession and route for those repenting of their sins. There is a considerable body of Penitential Psalms, robes, confessions, exercises, manuals, etc. In his wide and arcane reading Eliot may have come across specific ceremonial penitential avenues and gates (the Eastern Church places four different orders of penitents in different parts of the church). Such obscure technicalities (as in line 20) belong to the entertaining, sometimes baffling, pedantry of this poem.

l. 20 piaculative pence: the collection money, with which the bepimpled young members of the congregation hope to gain remission for their sins: 'piaculative' is of Eliot's invention (the OED gives 'piacular' and 'piaculary') and he may have come across a French cognate in a recent anthropological work by Emile Durkheim (1858–1917), *Les Formes élémentaires de la vie religieuse* (1912), translated as *The Elementary Forms of Religious Life* (1915). The penultimate chapter, concerned with 'Rites piaculaires' ('Piacular Rites and the Ambiguity of the Notion of Sacredness'), opens with an explanation of the word's derivation from the Latin 'piaculum', its meaning and its associations of uneasiness and sadness. Eliot wrote about Durkheim in the *International Journal of Ethics* in 1916.

ll. 21–4: perhaps another painting, depicting the entrance to Purgatory, through which the souls must pass to be cleansed of sin before they may enter Heaven.

l. 22 Seraphim: a class of angel characterized by the fervour of love. The presumed derivation of the word from a Hebrew root meaning 'to burn' is reflected in line 24. In Isaiah vi, the prophet has a vision of God in which one of the seraphim lays a burning coal upon his lips, thus purging his sin.

l. 24: a note by Eliot on the manuscript shows that he had in mind the lines 'O for that night! Where I in him/Might live invisible and dim', from 'The Night' by Henry Vaughan (1622–95). Vaughan is a devout soul (line 23) *par excellence.*

ll. 25–8: these lines refer to the 'middleman' function of the bees, carrying on their 'hairy bellies' the pollen from the stamen (the 'male' organ) of one flower to the pistil (the 'female' seed-bearing part) of any other. In this work they can be said to be in contact with both sexes (thus 'epicene'), just as Origen could pass on the word of God to fertilize religious controversies and heresies, and, similarly, as he acted as a go-between, adapting Greek concepts of the Logos for use in Christian theology. That was on the spiritual plane. Physically, Origen was further 'epicene' as a eunuch: having the characteristics of neither sex, he was in a middle or common state between the sexes.

The abstruse word-play of line 27 seems to be borrowed from 'Ballade' by Laforgue: 'Une chair bêtement staminifère,/Un cœur illusoirement pistillé' ('A flesh grossly staminated,/A heart spectrally pistillated').

ll. 29–32: Sweeney's shifting in the bath parodies the logic-chopping of the schoolmen shifting from subtlety to subtlety in their dialectical exercises.

l. 29 shifts: a gloss on the word is provided by Eliot's comment on Donne's playing with theological terms: 'with a puzzled and humorous shifting of the pieces' (1933).

ham: back of the thighs and buttocks. But this is not a neutral anatomical term, since it was usually employed to describe the squatting posture of natives or animals.

ll. 31–2: Eliot's reference is to specialized and obsolete meanings.

l. 31 masters: men of learning, scholars of authority.

subtle: frequently used to describe disputants refined and discriminating in their use of dialectical controversy in the formal modes of logical disputation.

schools: gatherings of scholastic philosophers and theologians.

l. 32 controversial: as in the usage: 'controversial' theology or divinity.

polymath: learned in many fields of knowledge, as philosophers, ancient and medieval, were expected to be.

Sweeney Among the Nightingales

Written May–June 1918;
Little Review (*Chicago*) *September 1918*

Title: cf. 'Ode to a Nightingale' (1820) by John Keats, the most famous of all nightingale poems. A more specific allusion may be to 'Bianca Among the Nightingales', a poem by Elizabeth Barrett Browning (1806–61). At the end of each stanza there is a reference to singing nightingales, and the poem concludes with associations of hatred and death, echoing the death of Agamemnon (see *Epigraph*):

> They sing for spite,
> They sing for hate, they sing for doom,
> They'll sing through death who sing through night,
> They'll sing and stun me in the tomb –
> The nightingales, the nightingales!

Keats's poem and the death of Agamemnon in the play by Aeschylus, cited in the Epigraph and in the final lines, were connected by Eliot in 'Tradition and the Individual Talent' (1919), where he refers to these works as containing 'passages of the greatest poetry'.

The 'Nightingales' of the title are not only the birds of the final stanzas; the word is also a slang term for prostitutes; and Eliot once remarked to the critic Edmund Wilson that the action of the poem takes place in a dive.

Regarding the mood of the poem, Eliot said that 'All that I consciously set out to create . . . was "a sense of foreboding".'

Epigraph: 'Alas, I am struck deep with a mortal blow', the words of King Agamemnon as he is struck down by his wife Clytemnestra in the *Agamemnon* (line 1343) by the Athenian dramatist Aeschylus (525–456 BC).

l. 4 maculate: marked, literally, as the giraffe is spotted. But this rare word also carried overtones of 'foul' or 'polluted', see its antonym immaculate, meaning virgin, sexually innocent.

l. 5: meteorologically, the appearance of rings round the moon signifies the approach of stormy weather.

l. 6 River Plate: its estuary is on the coast of South America. From the hints in lines 5–6, it seems that these events take place in Montevideo, capital of Uruguay; not a casual location for Eliot since it was the birthplace of Laforgue.

l. 7 Raven: a constellation. Traditionally, the raven was a bird of death.

l. 8 hornèd gate: in classical myth, the gate of horn through which true dreams pass on their way from the underworld to the world of man (see *Aeneid* vi, 892ff., and *Odyssey* xix, 559ff.).

l. 9 Gloomy Orion: Thayer: 'Marlowe'. Eliot took the words from Marlowe's *Dido, Queen of Carthage* (1594), Act II. Orion (the hunter) is a constellation that includes the Dog Star (Sirius). It is one of the brightest in the sky. 'Gloomy', for clouded over, is a description Marlowe based on the *Aeneid* (i, 535), where Virgil refers to Orion as 'nimbosus' ('cloudy').

In the Egyptian calendar, the appearance of Orion forecast the coming of the harvest rain and the Dog Star the approach of the fertilizing Nile floods.

ll. 19–20: according to Frazer (see page 129), an Egyptian fertility ritual was to display images of Adonis and Aphrodite on couches and to place ripe fruits beside them.

l. 21 vertebrate: a term in zoology, referring to a division of the animal kingdom composed of those possessing backbones or spinal columns, including reptiles (as the next line suggests) as well as men.

l. 23: as Christopher Ricks (1988) has commented, 'it is more than odd to supply the sequence of the first name and the maiden name, linked by née, while withholding the married name' (see Ricks's fuller discussion of Eliot's strategy in 'this unsettling poem'). The names are distinctively Jewish.

l. 24 murderous paws: Thayer: 'Marlowe: Dido'. In *Dido*, Act II, Aeneas describes a 'band of Myrmidons,/With balls of wild-fire in their murdering paws,/Which made the funeral flame that burnt fair Troy'. The Myrmidons, a notably warlike race, supported Achilles in the siege of Troy. Eliot quoted the 'murdering paws' line in 'Some Notes on the Blank Verse of Christopher Marlowe' (*Arts & Letters*, Autumn 1919).

l. 36: a convent of nuns of the Roman Catholic congregation of the Sisters of the Sacred Heart of Jesus and Mary; there were branches of the congregation in South America. Here, Eliot introduces a neat Frazerian irony. The sacred heart, in the ancient world, was that of Dionysus, the god of fertility; in the modern world it is the emblem of nuns bound to celibacy.

ll. 37–40: Orestes was the son of King Agamemnon and Clytemnestra. His father was murdered in a bath-house in mid-January, neither the time nor the place for nightingales to be singing. When these anomalies were pointed out to him in 1958, Eliot claimed a wait of forty years 'for someone to question the presence of nightingales at the obsequies of Agamemnon'. He went on to explain that the wood he had in mind was the grove of the Furies at Colonus; he called it 'bloody' because of Agamemnon's murder (which was gruesomely bloody, as he was hacked to death). In *Oedipus at Colonus* by the Athenian dramatist Sophocles (495–406 BC) the grove of the Furies is described as filled with singing nightingales.

According to Frazer, one of the primitive rites to ensure the continuation of the cycle of the seasons was the ritual slaying of the old priest by his successor, an event which took place in the sacred wood, here perhaps echoed in the death of the king within 'the bloody wood'.

l. 38: Thayer: 'cf. Orestes', the *Orestes* by the Greek dramatist Euripides (480–406 BC).

l. 39 liquid siftings: as in 'liquid notes', Milton's Sonnet I, opening 'O Nightingale'; 'droppings' was the word Eliot originally used, until Pound made the striking change. Until we come to the next line, in the vocabulary of Romantic poetry, which Eliot is borrowing here, 'liquid siftings' would be ethereal bird-song, rather than a substance quite so comically banal. In 1958 Eliot explained:

> I suspect that they were suggested by the rain dripping on the coffin of Fanny Robin in *Far From the Madding Crowd*, the novel by Thomas Hardy. It was a simple matter to bring the dead Agamemnon into the open air, and to transfer the nightingales from one place to another. So they might as well continue to sing in January, though I confess to ignorance of the date of Agamemnon's death. But even had I known, it would have made no difference.

This off-hand explanation sounds suspiciously like one of Eliot's false trails laid to occupy earnest inquirers. But we know that Eliot did, in fact, associate Hardy with Greek tragedy. In the *Little Review* for August 1918, just after the poem was written, Eliot remarked that 'Hardy, with his eye on the Greek tragedians, has produced an epic tonality.'

The scene from *Far From the Madding Crowd* remained with Eliot and he referred to it again in *After Strange Gods* (1934).

l. 40: cf. 'dim,/Dishonoured brow', in 'Ichabod' (Hebrew, 'the glory that has fled') by J. F. Whittier (1801–92), a poem attacking the nineteenth-century American statesman Daniel Webster for compromising his stand against slavery in 1850. The theme of the poem is the loss of honour.

THE WASTE LAND

'It is for the elect or the remnant or the select few or the superior guys, or any word that you may choose, for the small numbers of readers that it is certain to have.'

John Quinn, on receiving the typescript, July 1922

'About enough, Eliot's poem, to make the rest of us shut up shop.'

Ezra Pound to John Quinn, February 1922

'Eliot's *Waste Land* is I think the justification of the "movement", of our modern experiment, since 1900.'

Ezra Pound to Felix E. Schelling, July 1922

The Waste Land

Some passages date from as far back as 1914.
Part One probably completed by October 1919.
The body of the poem was written and assembled
November 1921–January 1922. The Criterion (*London*)
October 1922, The Dial (*New York*) *November 1922*

Prefatory Note: The scale and organization of this poem, together with the unusual range of its reference, make it convenient to cover a number of general points in this Prefatory Note, so avoiding the need for lengthy and repetitious explanations in the detailed notes to the poem.

Eliot's immediate Waste Land is the world, as he saw it, after the First World War. The 'waste' is not, however, that of war's devastation and bloodshed, but the emotional and spiritual sterility of Western man, the 'waste' of our civilization. Eliot does not regard this as a single moment in history, particular to the West in the twentieth century, and the poem is organized to present an inclusive, comparative vision; a perspective of history in which (by succinct allusions and references) twentieth-century forms of belief and disbelief, of culture and of life, are kept in a continuous and critical relationship with those of the past.

The theme of the poem is the salvation of the Waste Land, not as a certainty but a possibility: of emotional, spiritual and intellectual vitality to be regained. Eliot develops this theme drawing upon related patterns in nature, myth and religion: the cycle of the seasons; the ancient fertility myths of Egypt, India and Greece, in which the god must die to be reborn, to bring fertility to the soil and potency to the people; a pattern known to us again in the life, death and resurrection of Christ. Eliot seems to have had this method in mind when he commented that 'The concentration resulting from a framework of mythology and theology and philosophy is one of the reasons why Dante is a classic, and Blake only a poet of genius' (lines added to a review in *The Athenaeum* (February 1920) when it was reprinted as 'William Blake' in *Selected Essays, 1930*).

In his notes to the poem, Eliot helpfully* refers us to *From Ritual to Romance* (1920) by Jessie Weston (a work based on literary rather than anthropological evidence, drawing heavily on *The Golden Bough*). The book appeared (as Matthiessen comments) 'at the very time when Eliot was seeking a coherent shape for the mass of intricate material that enters into his poem. For reading that book gave to his mind the very fillip which it needed in order to crystallize.' It is worth noting that Jessie Weston, a Theosophist, was concerned to trace the so-called 'secret doctrine' from its earliest beginnings in primitive religion and magic and the occult myths through which it was transmitted (see note to 'A Cooking Egg', line 23). One reviewer (F. L. Lucas, *New Statesman*, 3 November 1923), observed that 'Miss Weston is clearly a theosophist, and Mr Eliot's poem might be a theosophical tract.' Eliot made particular use of her account of the Fisher King, a figure which recurs in a number of fertility myths, and whose story is one of obvious relevance to this poem. His land is under a curse and laid waste. The Fisher King is impotent, by illness, maiming or old age; and his people are likewise infertile. The curse can only be lifted by the arrival of a stranger who must put or answer certain ritual questions.

Eliot follows Jessie Weston in relating this myth to the legend of the Grail. The Grail was the cup used by Christ at the Last Supper and in which Joseph of Arimathea is said to have caught the blood from the wound made in Christ's side at the Crucifixion, and brought it to Glastonbury in the West of England. The Grail was therefore regarded as a supremely holy Christian relic. It was lost, and the search for the Grail became a powerful narrative image for man's search for spiritual truth, an image used by many

*Although I say 'helpfully', Pound poo-pooed the idea: he had not read the book by 1924 and said then he had no intention of doing so (see page 28).

medieval writers. The searcher for the Grail is a Knight, whose quest takes him to the Chapel Perilous where he must (like the stranger in the Fisher King myth) put certain questions about the Grail and another holy relic, the Lance which pierced Christ's side. When this is done, the plight of the land and the people is eased.

Matthiessen notes that what in particular Eliot saw in *From Ritual to Romance* was

> the recurring pattern in various myths, the basic resemblance, for example, between the vegetation myths of the rebirth of the year, the fertility myths of the rebirth of the potency of man, the Christian story of the Resurrection, and the Grail legend of purification. The common source of all these myths lay in the fundamental rhythm of nature – that of the death and rebirth of the year; and their varying symbolism was an effort to explain the origin of life. Such knowledge, along with the researches of psychology, pointed to the close union in all these myths of the physical and spiritual, to the fact that their symbolism was basically sexual – in the Cup and Lance of the Grail legend as well as in the Orpheus cults; pointed, in brief, to the fundamental relation between the well-springs of sex and religion . . . Eliot found a scaffold for his poem, a background of reference that made possible something in the nature of a musical organization. He found the specific clue to the dramatic shaping of his material when he read in Miss Weston of the frequent representation of the mystery of death and rebirth by the story of a kingdom where, the forces of the ruler having been weakened or destroyed by sickness, old age, or the ravages of war, 'the land becomes Waste, and the task of the hero is that of restoration', not by pursuing advantages for himself, but by giving himself to the quest of seeking the health and salvation of the land.

Yet it is worth remembering that Eliot gave the poem its 'Waste Land' title only after it had passed through Pound's hands in the final process of reshaping and reduction. The uncut version was entitled 'He Do The Police in Different Voices', a sentence taken from ch. 16 of *Our Mutual Friend* (1864–5) by Charles Dickens, explaining why Sloppy is considered 'a beautiful reader of a newspaper', the court cases in particular. This relates to the highly dramatic nature of the original poem, calling upon a variety of voices and tones. The Grail legend, as a controlling myth, also seems to have been introduced at a late stage; and Eliot felt able to make a joke of it, expressing his regret at 'having sent so many inquirers off on a wild goose chase after Tarot cards and the Holy Grail'.

Eliot also refers to his other major source, *The Golden Bough* (12 volumes, 1890–1915) by Sir James Frazer. At Harvard, in 1913, Eliot studied the volumes so far published, discussing the work in a seminar paper. Altogether, it composed an encyclopaedic study of primitive myth and ritual, a possible line of continuity from these origins, through organized religion to modern scientific thought. Clearly, this hypothesis of continuity (as in *From Ritual to Romance*) is of importance to Eliot's interpenetration of past and present in *The Waste Land*. He drew particularly on Frazer's account of the vegetation ceremonies in Part IV, the two volumes treating the deities *Adonis, Attis, Osiris*: these ceremonies were rituals of sacrifice to conciliate the powers of nature and ensure the continuing cycle of the seasons, with the life of the new year to be born again out of the old. Eliot's use of Frazer is most fully documented in Vickery (1973).

In 1923, Eliot named Frazer, Bradley and Henry James as his 'masters' and a year later described *The Golden Bough* as a 'stupendous compendium of human superstition and folly'; and as being 'of no less importance for our time than the complementary work of Freud'. Frazer, he said, had 'extended the consciousness of the human mind into as dark a backward and abysm of time as has yet been explored'. Frazer was unable to return the compliment. When *The Waste Land* was read to him in his old age, both he and his reader 'soon gave up in bewilderment'.

In September 1921 Eliot discussed the ballet of Stravinsky's *Le Sacre du printemps* (*The Rite of Spring*), the sequences of which represent primitive vegetation rites. He felt that these ballet sequences were superficial and commented: 'In art there should be interpenetration and metamorphosis. Even *The Golden Bough* can be read in two ways: as a collection of entertaining myths, or as a revelation of that vanished mind of which our mind is a continuation.' These remarks clearly indicate how Eliot used Frazer in his poetry.

However, the manuscript of the original *Waste Land* shows us that much of the imagery from Frazer and Weston, together with the title itself, came into the poem at a very late stage and that Eliot's use of myth was, to quote his own words on Joyce, indeed 'simply a way of controlling, of ordering, of giving a shape' to disparate materials whose composition lay some time in the past, upon which the myth elements were superimposed to unify and provide a frame. Surrette (1993), however, asserts the importance of Jessie Weston and the theosophical elements.

Unreferred to in Eliot's notes is *Ulysses*, by James Joyce (1882–1941), an enormous and elaborate structure of myth, 'a book to which we are all indebted, and from which none of us can escape' (as he wrote in 1923). Joyce's novel was first published in Paris in 1922. But Eliot was familiar with much (perhaps all) of it before beginning work on *The Waste Land*. Five sections of *Ulysses* came out in *The Egoist* (January–December 1919) while he was assistant editor. Some of these had appeared earlier in the *Little Review*, where other sections also appeared over the period March 1918–December 1920. Pound first began to read the typescript in December 1917 and subsequently showed many sections to Eliot, who suggested improvements to Joyce.

Joyce also sent Eliot sections in manuscript. He found them 'superb', 'stupendous', 'truly magnificent'. Of 'Scylla and Charybdis' he wrote, 'I have lived on it ever since I read it' and of 'The Oxen of the Sun' and 'Circe' he wrote to Joyce, in May 1921, 'I have nothing but admiration; in fact, I wish, for my own sake, that I had not read it.' Perhaps he felt humbled by the magnitude of Joyce's creation; perhaps he also felt apprehensive of similarities* in their methods and their use of myth, similarities

---

*These similarities convinced Joyce that Eliot had stolen the substance and style of *The Waste Land* from *Ulysses*. He took his revenge in *Finnegans Wake* where Eliot's closing line is shorn of its reverential tone in Joyce's 'Shaunti! Shaunti! Shaunti!', a refrain he repeated no less than seven times. Many other such jokes are scattered through the novel, including a drunken version of line 76, 'my shemblable! My freer!' together with jibes at 'A Cooking Egg' and a 'wibfrufrocksfull of fun' directed at 'Prufrock'.

pointed to clearly in his note to line 218 which describes the mythical transfiguration of the merchant into the Phoenician Sailor, who is, in turn, 'not wholly distinct from Ferdinand Prince of Naples', of 'all the women' into 'one woman' and the meeting of the sexes in Tiresias: all these mergings of identity parallel Joyce's method of accommodating the years-long Homeric voyage of Ulysses round the Mediterranean to twenty-four hours in the life of Leopold Bloom in the city of Dublin. In the late 1950s, Eliot told an interviewer that the sight of the manuscript chapters of *Ulysses* arriving on his desk at the *Egoist* showed him that what 'he was tentatively attempting to do, with the usual false starts and despairs, had already been done, done superbly' in prose. Whatever admiration (and consternation) lay behind these comments, Eliot later paid a direct and generous tribute to Joyce's achievement in '*Ulysses*, Order and Myth' (*The Dial*, November 1923). One passage in that essay goes right to the heart of his own use of myth in *The Waste Land*: 'In using the myth, in manipulating a continuous parallel between contemporaneity and antiquity, Mr Joyce is pursuing a method which others must pursue after him. They will not be imitators, any more than the scientist who uses the discoveries of an Einstein in pursuing his own, independent, further investigations. It is simply a way of controlling, of ordering, of giving a shape and a significance to the immense panorama of futility and anarchy which is contemporary history.' (Significantly, in 1934, Eliot remarked that in *The Waste Land* he drew upon past and present as versions of 'futility'.)

Several of Pound's annotations on the manuscript of *The Waste Land* confirm the influence of Joyce: against line 64 he wrote 'JJ' and against line 125 'JJ' and 'Penelope' (referring to the final section of *Ulysses*). Many critics have commented on the extensive parallels between the two works. But as with other important influences on Eliot, the evidence is not to be reckoned up quantitatively in the number of direct allusions and borrowings. *Ulysses* is present in *The Waste Land* at a deeper creative level; and, to date, the fullest account of this is 'Joyce's Waste Land and Eliot's Unknown God' by R. A. Day in *Literary*

Monographs, vol. iv, ed. E. Rothstein (Madison, 1971).

Another important facet of the poem is its focus upon London: primarily upon the City of London, as a place of crowds and commerce; and also upon its character as a great river-city around and along the Thames. The manuscript suggests that early on Eliot envisaged a Drydenesque urban poem, his sordid London parodying the reborn Rome of Dryden's imperial city in *Annus Mirabilis* (1667). (Eliot was reading Dryden at this time, in February 1920 finding him 'a very great man', 'a great poet'; and he contributed a 'John Dryden' essay to the *Times Literary Supplement* in June 1921, collected in *Selected Essays*, 1932, where it is misdated 1922.) In developing this idea Hugh Kenner also sees *The Waste Land* as 'a kind of modern *Aeneid*' ('The Urban Apocalypse' in Litz, 1973; further explored by Gareth Reeves, *T. S. Eliot as a Virgilian Poet*, 1989).

In later life, Eliot remarked that when he wrote *The Waste Land* he 'seriously considered becoming a Buddhist'. It was a highly informed inclination, stemming from his extensive Indic Buddhist studies at Harvard (see note to lines 399–401), and emerges here in 'The Fire Sermon' and 'What the Thunder Said'. A full account is given in Kearns, 1987. Eliot's model for introducing Sanskrit and Pali into *The Waste Land* was Sir Edwin Arnold's *The Light of Asia* (1879), an epic poem based on the life of the Buddha, which Eliot read 'with gusto' in his boyhood and continued to admire as 'a good poem'.

The interpretation of 'the central impulse' of *The Waste Land* as 'personal tragedy' is discussed in the Introduction, pages 32–4. What remains of Vivien's contribution to the poem, following its revision, is difficult to say. Line 164 is in her hand and against line 172 she wrote 'Splendid last lines'. But according to Michael Hastings, 'her hand is all over the early drafts of *The Waste Land*, and to such an extent that it is impossible in some instances to separate her contributions from his'.

Readers seeking a plausible reconstruction of how *The Waste Land* was assembled, and the character of the earlier poems which went into its making, can consult chapter 5 of *Eliot's Early Years* by Lyndall Gordon. This supposes that the original version had a strong religious/visionary character, with the journey, in search of enlightenment, of a poet-pilgrim-saint-holyman-in-the-desert; and that Eliot drew upon the tradition of spiritual autobiography which flourished amongst the American Puritans of New England. Gordon suggests that for Eliot 'to experience the world as a waste land was a prerequisite to experiencing it in faith'. This aspect of the poem was largely to disappear in Pound's revision. Gordon again: 'Pound effectively blocked, at several points, Eliot's impulse to exhibit the whole truth – the strength as well as the sickness of a suffering soul . . . and he was forced to rewrite his saint's life in more explicit terms in "Ash Wednesday" and *Four Quartets*.'

But it has to be said that there is common agreement neither on the circumstances of the drafts nor on the character of the *Ur-Waste Land*. For example, examination of the manuscript leads Surrette (1993) to conclude that Pound's editing tended 'to remove the esoteric or mystical elements of the original draft'. Sultan (1987) provides an overview of the earlier debate.

Epigraph: 'Yes, and I myself with my own eyes even saw the Sybil hanging in a cage; and when the boys cried at her: "Sybil, Sybil, what do you want?" "I would that I were dead", she caused to answer.' (This is the translation in Eliot's own edition.) These words are spoken by Trimalchio in the *Satyricon*, a satire by the Roman writer Petronius (first century AD). Drunkenly boasting, he is trying to surpass his drunken companions in their tales of wonder.

In Greek mythology the Sibyls were women of prophetic powers, that of Cumae the most famous. She was granted long life by Apollo, at her own wish, as many years as she held grains of sand in her hand; but carelessly she forgot to ask for eternal youth. Hence she aged and her prophetic authority declined.

She was a source of cryptic knowledge and answered questions by throwing to the winds handfuls of leaves bearing letters.

Those that the inquirer caught, he had to arrange in the right order. Thus 'she divulged forbidden knowledge in riddles, fitfully'; and in these terms *The Waste Land* can be regarded as an organization of 'sibylline fragments' (see Hugh Kenner, 1959).

The Sibyl was also a gatekeeper to the underworld.

Grover Smith suggests that Eliot did not get the Petronius quotation directly from the *Satyricon* but took it, indirectly, from a verse version by D. G. Rossetti – 'Eliot frequently got quotations at second hand, thus displaying the practical economy of his learned resources.' This does less than justice to Eliot. In fact, he first read the *Satyricon* on a Roman novel course at Harvard in 1908–9; and it remained sufficiently in his mind for him to quote a passage in the original Latin at the opening of *The Sacred Wood*, a collection of his essays published in November 1920. Eliot's own copy of the Latin text, a German scholarly edition of 1904, is in the Library of King's College, Cambridge.

There may also be a private element in Eliot's choice, for under the pen-name Sibylla, Vivien contributed items to *The Criterion*.

Originally, Eliot had chosen for the epigraph a quotation from Conrad's 'Heart of Darkness' (1902) (see Prefatory Notes to 'The Hollow Men', pages 205–7): 'Did he live his life again, in every detail of desire, temptation, and surrender during that supreme moment of complete knowledge? He cried in a whisper at some image, at some vision, – he cried out twice, a cry that was no more than a breath – "The horror! The horror!"' However, Pound questioned this: 'I doubt if Conrad is weighty enough to stand the citation' (possibly unaware that lines 268–70 were derived from the opening page of Conrad's story). Eliot was puzzled by Pound's advice: 'Do you mean not use the Conrad quot. or simply not put Conrad's name to it? It is much the most appropriate I can find, and somewhat elucidative.' Pound replied that Eliot should do as he liked: 'who am I to grudge him his laurel crown?' These exchanges took place between December 1921 and January 1922. On 12 March,

Eliot advised Pound that he had 'substituted for the J. Conrad' the Petronius quotation he eventually used.

Title: Eliot's note explains that this was suggested by *From Ritual to Romance.* Most of its chapter 2 is devoted to an account of the 'Waste Land' (as it is styled). Jessie Weston's sources were literary rather than anthropological. So both she and Eliot may have encountered the words in *Morte d'Arthur* by Thomas Malory (*fl.* 1470), where the words have a significant context within the story of Galahad (Book 17, Ch. 3, in Caxton's text): 'And so bifelle grete pestylence & grete harme to both Realmes for sythen encrecyd neyther corne ne grasse nor wel nyghe no fruyte ne in the water was no fysshe werfor men callen hit the landes of the two marches the waste land for that dolorous stroke.'

A more immediate source is in the back-numbers of *Poetry* (Chicago), in which 'Prufrock' was first published in June 1915. Two years earlier, in the issue for January 1913, there had appeared a 'Waste Land' by Madison Cawein, a poem whose desolate landscape, like Eliot's, communicates a spiritual desolation, and whose imagery and themes are also similar.

A personal waste land closes Book II of the *Confessions* of St Augustine, to which Eliot refers in his notes to lines 307 and 309: 'I wandered, O my God, too much astray from Thee my stay, in these days of my youth, and I became to myself a waste land.'

Ezra Pound: (1885–1972), the American poet and critic, closely associated with Eliot's writing up to the 1920s, and tireless in working to gain recognition for him. Pound was instrumental in getting Eliot's early poems into print, arranged for the publication of his first collection, *Prufrock and Other Observations* (1917) and puffed it in reviews. More directly, Pound served as Eliot's closest mentor and critic, joining him in experiments, moulding his style to the point that at least one of the quatrain poems, 'Whispers of Immortality', is virtually a collaboration.

il miglior fabbro: 'the better craftsman' (*Purgatorio* xxvi, 117),
Dante's tribute to the twelfth-century troubadour poet Arnaut
Daniel, emphasizing his superiority over all his Provençal rivals,
words with a special attachment to Pound, since he used them for
the title of chapter 2 in *The Spirit of Romance* (1910), a chapter
devoted to Daniel as the great poet of the time; and Daniel was the
subject of twelve articles, published 1911–12, which Pound
intended to compose into a book. In fact, Pound's chapter-title
was adapted from Dante's tribute to Daniel ('fu miglior fabbro del
parlar materno') as a poet who 'was a better craftsman of the
mother-tongue', words placed in the mouth of Guido Guinicelli,
an admired love poet, in praise of Daniel as a yet more skilful
innovator 'in love poetry and tales of romance'. Pound referred to
Daniel as 'the best fashioner of songs in the Provençal', as 'il
miglior fabbro', at the opening of 'Arnaut Daniel' (1920).

In 1938 (answering a critic of Pound) Eliot expanded on this
tribute: 'the phrase, not only as used by Dante, but as quoted by
myself, had a precise meaning. I did not mean to imply that Pound
was only that: but I wished at that moment to honour the
technical mastery and critical ability manifest in his own work,
which had also done so much to turn *The Waste Land* from a
jumble of good and bad passages into a poem.' This happened
after Eliot left the original version with Pound in Paris in late
December 1921. There followed correspondence in which Pound
set out detailed advice and suggested extensive cuts. The
thoroughness of their joint revision is recorded in Eliot's remark
to a friend that the poem 'will have been three times through the
sieve by Pound as well as myself so should be in a final form' (letter
of 20 January 1922). Eliot recalled in 1946 that the 'sprawling,
chaotic poem' left Pound's hands 'reduced to about half its size',
virtually in the form in which it appeared in print.

In so reducing the original, Pound put into practice one of his
main tests for a writer (enunciated in 1915): 'his ability for . . .
concentration AND for his power to stay concentrated till he gets
to the end of his poem, whether it is two lines or two hundred'. He
was pleased with his work: 'let us say the longest poem in the
Englisch langwidge' was his benediction upon the nineteen-page

typescript (cf. I. A. Richards's account of the poem as a compressed epic, Introduction, page 23). In 1964, Eliot put this more graphically: 'the poem in the form in which it finally appeared owes more to Pound's surgery than anyone can realise'. In 'Sage Homme', a poem addressed to Eliot in December 1921, Pound characterized his part more graphically still: 'Ezra performed the caesarean Operation.' Eliot replied, 'Wish to use Caesarean operation in italics in front', to which Pound answered, 'Do as you like about my obstetric effort.' 'Sage Homme' never appeared. But Pound's cutting was largely responsible for the cinematic effects of the poem, in its sudden disjunctions and shifts of scene.

The Waste Land was first published without the dedication to Pound. Eliot added the words in January 1923 when he inscribed a presentation copy of the Boni & Liveright edition (the first in book form, published with the Notes in December 1922) for his fellow poet: 'for E.P./miglior fabbro/from T.S.E./Jan 1923'. This dedication was placed before the poem when The Waste Land was reprinted in Poems 1909–1925 (1925).

Fortunately, we have the material evidence of Pound's contribution in drafts of the poem. Their existence became public knowledge in October 1968, three years after Eliot's death. According to Mrs Eliot, the poet did not expect them to turn up, but wished them to be published if they did, as he wanted 'people to realize the extent of my debt to Ezra'.

There may also have been a direct indebtedness to Pound's recent poetry. For example, Eliot makes considerable use of Ovid's story of the rape of Philomela (line 99 etc.), a legend Pound had referred to in Canto IV, published in October 1919. Similarly, Eliot's note to line 221 mentions Sappho and it is this same poetic Fragment 149 that Pound alludes to in Canto V (published December 1921). And Tiresias (line 218) appears in Canto I (published September 1917).

Notes on The Waste Land: The Notes as a spoof are discussed in the Introduction (pages 26–9). Eliot's model for their mock-pedantry may have been similar bogus notes that Richard Harris

Barham supplied for his *Ingoldsby Legends*, a series of ghost stories and verse-tales (which came out in *Blackwood's Magazine* and *Bentley's Magazine*, beginning in 1826, and were first published as a collection in 1840 and much reprinted throughout the nineteenth century). Eliot was familiar with the *Legends* from his schooldays onwards and 'A Fable for Fakers', a narrative poem written at Smith Academy, is derived from Barham.

Another possible model is the elaborate and extensive body of notes which accompanied *The Dunciad* (1728, completed 1743), a mock-epic by Alexander Pope (1688–1744); and the notes are in part a smack at pedantry, one of Eliot's targets also.

I   THE BURIAL OF THE DEAD

Composition: In July 1919 Eliot told the publisher John Rodker that he had completed 'Gerontion' and thought he would 'have another about the same length by August'. This section of *The Waste Land* (76 lines, in its final version) is the same length as 'Gerontion' and is probably the poem in question, completed by October 1919.

Title: 'The Order for The Burial of the Dead' is the full title of the burial service in the Church of England. Stephenson alerts us to the cyclical process which Eliot elaborates in this section: 'Burial is sowing: resurrection is in the future crops.'

ll. 1–18: the character of Eliot's April as 'the cruellest month' is explained in *The Golden Bough*: 'from the middle of April till the middle of June the land of Egypt is but half alive, waiting for the new Nile'; 'it was essential that' primitive man 'should conceal the natural emotion under an air of profound dejection'; and festivals of mourning for Adonis often took place in the spring.

Critics usually contrast this account of April as 'the cruellest month' with the opening to the General Prologue to *The Canterbury Tales* by Chaucer (1343?–1400) which is conventionally energetic and cheerful in accordance with the traditional treatment of spring. But Eliot may also have had a contemporary

poem in mind, 'The Old Vicarage, Grantchester' (written and first
published 1912, then in *1914 & Other Poems*, 1915) by Rupert
Brooke (1887–1915). This opens with poignant flashes of mem-
ory of his childhood in the English countryside in springtime, so
different from the Berlin scene around him now:

> Just now the lilac is in bloom,
> All before my little room . . .
> Here am I, sweating, sick, and hot,
> And there the shadowed waters fresh
> Lean up to embrace the naked flesh.
> *Temperamentvoll* German Jews
> Drink beer around . . .

These lines were familiar to Eliot and he quoted the first two
approvingly in *The Egoist* for September 1917, commenting that
'"little" is used, not merely as a necessary piece of information,
but with a caress, a conscious delight'.

When the openings to *The Waste Land* and 'Grantchester' are
compared it can be seen that there are considerable likenesses in
detail and design; and it is likely that Eliot would be expecting the
reader to catch the essential dissimilarity between their two views
of life, as glimpsed through their accounts of spring memories and
awakenings.

More than this, Brooke himself was seen at the time as the
archetypal figure of the youth struck down in his prime, hand-
some and gifted, victim of the 'waste land' of war. In *1914 &
Other Poems*, published posthumously, the details of his life are
set out in seven lines, as if on a gravestone, concluding 'Died in the
Ægean, April 23, 1915' (cf. Eliot's memorial wording 'For Jean
Verdenal, 1889–1915/mort aux Dardanelles'; see page 44).

The heroic image of Brooke is drawn in the Preface that Henry
James contributed to Brooke's *Letters from America* (1916):
'young, happy, radiant, extraordinarily endowed and irresistibly
attaching . . . the interest and the charm that will henceforth abide
in his name and constitute, as we may say, his legend . . . his
blinding youth . . . '

The heroic image is also caught in a letter from D. H. Lawrence

to Lady Ottoline Morrell when the news of his death reached
England: 'fills me more and more with the sense of the futility of
it all. He was slain by bright Phoebus' shaft – it was in keeping
with his general sunniness – it was the real climax of his pose . . .
Bright Phoebus struck him down. It is all in the saga.'

Eliot himself discussed Brooke's poetry in 'Reflections on
Contemporary Poetry' (*The Egoist*, September 1917), quoting,
amongst passages from the poems, 'Just now the lilac is in
bloom/All before my little room'.

He also wrote about Brooke again, two months later, in *The
Egoist* for November 1917, in a mock-letter from one Helen B.
Trudlett.

(I should add that in answer to an inquiry Mr Conrad Aiken
told me that although it was possible, in his view, that this
section of the poem was written earlier than the rest, he could see
no evocation of Rupert Brooke's poetry in *The Waste Land*.)

Eliot's use of *My Past* (1913) by the Countess Marie Larisch,
from which come several details in these lines, is discussed in the
Introduction, see pages 15–16. Schwarz argues that Eliot drew
extensively on *My Past* in the writing of *The Waste Land*.

l. 1 April . . . cruellest: may have been suggested by 'Clair de
Lune Sentimental' by Gautier, in which occurs 'l'avril', 'si cruel'
(also 'mêle', 'mêlions' giving 'mixing' in the next line). Gautier's
poem comes in the sequence *Variations sur le Carnaval de Ven-
ise,* already drawn on in the Epigraph to 'Burbank' (see page 83).

l. 2 Lilacs: this may be an allusion to the elegiac poem 'When
Lilacs Last in the Dooryard Bloom'd' (1865) which Walt Whit-
man (1819–92) wrote at the death of Abraham Lincoln. There
seem to be further allusions in lines 356 and 360–65. The
opening lines attach the elegy to Spring (Lincoln was killed on
Good Friday, 14 April 1865): 'When lilacs last in the dooryard
bloom'd,/And the great star early droop'd in the western sky in
the night,/I mourn'd, and yet shall mourn with ever-returning
spring'. In his Introduction to *Selected Poems* of Ezra Pound
(1928), Eliot said that, following his Laforguean poetry of 1908
or 1909, 'I did not read Whitman until much later in life, and
had to conquer an aversion to his form, as well as to much of his

matter, in order to do so.' In the face of Whitman's imagery Eliot's objections dissolved. He found 'lilacs' among the most potent. Reviewing a Whitman biography in 1926, Eliot commented that whatever the inadequacy of his ideas, 'When Whitman speaks of the lilacs or of the mocking-bird, his theories and beliefs drop away like a needless pretext.' This 'aversion' may have been overcome in concert with Pound, who made 'A Truce' (*Lustra*, 1916) with Whitman: 'I have detested you long enough ... I am old enough now to make friends ... Let there be commerce between us.' Since Whitman used Lincoln's death as an occasion to mourn 'the debris and debris of all the slain soldiers' of the Civil War, there may well have been 'commerce' between 'When Lilacs Last' and *The Waste Land*, both of them post-war poems.

Eliot's memory of Verdenal, bearing 'a branch of lilac', and its connection with *The Waste Land*, is mentioned in the Introduction (p. 32).

ll. 2–3: in the mixing of 'memory' and 'desire' Eliot may have been recalling a passage in the opening chapter of *Bubu de Montparnasse* (see Introduction, page 11): 'A man walks carrying with him all the properties of his life, and they churn about in his head. Something he sees awakens them, something else excites them. For our flesh has retained all our memories, and we mingle them with our desires.'

ll. 6–7 feeding/A little life: cf. 'Our Mother feedeth thus our little life,/That we in turn may feed her with our death', from 'To Our Ladies of Death' by James Thomson (1834–82).

l. 8 Starnbergersee: a fashionable cosmopolitan lake-resort just south of Munich, visited by Eliot in August 1911.

ll. 8–22: in 1935, F. O. Matthiessen made the suggestion that the 'heap of broken images' (line 22) in these lines bears a similarity to the description by Rupert Brooke of the impact upon one of his friends on hearing the announcement 'We're at war with Germany':

> My friend ate and drank, and then climbed a hill of gorse, and sat alone, looking at the sea. His mind was full of confused

images, and the sense of strain. In answer to the word 'Germany', a train of vague thoughts dragged across his brain. The pompous middle-class vulgarity of the buildings of Berlin; the wide and restful beauty of Munich; the taste of beer; innumerable quiet, glittering cafés; the *Ring*; the swish of evening air in the face, as one skis down past the pines; a certain angle of the eyes in the face; long nights of drinking and singing and laughter ... certain friends; some tunes; the quiet length of evening over the Starnbergersee (pp. 92–3).

Cleanth Brooks followed Matthiessen's suggestion in his famous essay '*The Waste Land:* Critique of the Myth'. When he sent a typescript copy to Eliot in February 1937, Eliot replied that it was 'quite possible' that he had read Brooke's letter and that it might have been 'at the back of my mind, but actually this particular passage approximates more closely to a recollection of a personal experience of my own than anything else, and indeed is as nearly as possible a verbatim report'. Subsequently, Brooks withdrew this section in the published essay.

Whatever the origin of these lines, the rest of the verse-paragraph is cast in the form of a *poème conversation* in the style of the French poet Guillaume Apollinaire (1880–1918).

For the connection of this section with Marie Larisch, see Introduction, pages 15–16. According to Mrs Eliot, the description of the sledding (lines 14–16) 'was taken verbatim from a conversation with Marie Larisch'.

l. 10 Hofgarten: a public park in Munich, bordered by buildings with a colonnade (as in line 9).

l. 12: 'I am not Russian at all; I come from Lithuania; I am a real German.' Stephenson's translation renders this line in broken English: 'Am no Russian, come from Lithuania, genuine German.' This statement compresses the history of Lithuania's perilous nationhood. As a Baltic state, it had long been ruled by Russia. Its independence dated only from 1919 in the post-war partition. Most of its leaders were German.

It may be derived from a passage in *Tarr* (1918), a novel by Wyndham Lewis which Eliot reviewed in the *Egoist*: here a

Fraulein Vasek insists that she is 'a Russian. I'm thoroughly Russian' and explains the attraction to the Russians of German bourgeois life (p. 220).

In 1975, William Empson commented, 'She is the only person in the poem for whom the author expresses outright contempt, and surely we need to know what qualities he is despising.' Empson then quotes lines 19–20 and goes on to discuss Marie Larisch and the writing of *My Past*, suggesting that 'there remains a large field for enquiry' (*T. S. Eliot Review*, Fall 1975).

l. 17: in German, there is a romantic and somewhat clichéd expression with precisely this meaning. In Eliot's personal imagery, 'mountains' figure the heights of creative inspiration. See his letter to Dorothy Pound, 22 May 1921, when he was planning to visit the Pounds in Paris later in the year: 'I shall be ready for a little mountain air, after I have finished a little poem I am at present engaged upon. I see that the mountain air is about to produce *Ulysses* ... Tell Ezra that I am awaiting a testimonial to the ozone in the shape of some considerable opus from his Corona ...' His own 'little poem' was, of course, *The Waste Land*.

ll. 19–20: these are not direct Biblical allusions, but 'roots' and 'branches' are characteristic of its figurative language, as in 'if the root be holy, so are the branches' (Romans xi, 16). Likewise the 'stony places' (Matthew xiii, 5–6) where the 'seed' of faith springs up to be scorched in the sun and wither away. Possibly Eliot was drawing upon Job viii, 16–17: 'He is green before the sun, and his branch shooteth forth in his garden. His roots are wrapped about the heap, and seeth the place of stones.' In Job xviii, 16, the calamities of the wicked include 'His roots shall be dried up beneath, and above shall his branch be cut off.'

l. 20: Eliot's note refers us to Ezekiel ii, 1. God addresses his prophet, 'Son of man, stand upon thy feet, and I will speak unto thee.' Ezekiel is told of his mission, to preach the coming of the Messiah to a rebellious, unbelieving people.

l. 22 broken images: cf. Ezekiel vi, 4, 6, God's judgement upon the people of Israel for worshipping idols: 'and your images shall be broken.' Matthiessen: 'the lack of purpose and direction, the inability to believe really in anything and the resulting "heap of broken images" that formed the excruciating contents of the post-War state of mind'.

l. 23: Eliot's note refers us to Ecclesiastes xii, 5, where the preacher describes the desolation of old age: 'Also when they shall be afraid of that which is high, and fears shall be in the way, and the almond tree shall flourish, and the grasshopper shall be a burden, and desire shall fail: because man goeth to his long home, and the mourners go about the streets.'

l. 24: cf. the Lord's promise to Moses that when he shall 'smite the rock' with his rod 'there shall come water out of it' (Exodus xvii, 6).

l. 25: cf. Isaiah xxxii, 2, describing the blessings of Christ's kingdom: 'And a man shall be as an hiding place from the wind, and a covert from the tempest; as rivers of water in a dry place, as the shadow of a great rock in a weary land.'

Frazer also mentions rocks, one of them called Red Altar, figuring as rain-charms.

ll. 25–9: these lines are based upon the opening of one of Eliot's early poems, 'The Death of Saint Narcissus', probably written about 1912:

> Come under the shadow of this gray rock –
> Come in under the shadow of this gray rock,
> And I will show you something different from either
> Your shadow sprawling over the sand at daybreak, or
> Your shadow leaping behind the fire against the red rock . . .

'The Death of Saint Narcissus' was set up in type to be printed in *Poetry* (Chicago, 1915). A proof was printed, but then suppressed. The poem is now available in *T. S. Eliot, Poems written in early youth* (1967), ed. John Hayward.

l. 30 a handful of dust: this striking phrase is found in several sources: Meditation IV of *Devotions Upon Emergent Occasions* (1624) by John Donne: 'what's become of man's great extent and proportion, when himself shrinks himself, and consumes himself to a handful of dust . . .'; in Tennyson's *Maud*: 'Dead,

dead, long dead/And my heart is a handful of dust/And the wheels go over my head' (Part II, v.i); in Conrad's *Youth* (1902), where Marlow recalls finding 'the heat of life in a handful of dust'; and in a Conrad short story, 'The Return': 'He was afraid with that penetrating fear that seems in the very middle of a beat, to turn one's heart into a handful of dust'. Which one or more of these sources Eliot wants us to recall is an open question. However, the 'fearful' associations, raised in Eliot's line, are unquestionably Biblical. Dust is the symbolic reminder to man of his bodily mortality, his beginning and end in matter. Stephenson: Eliot 'is not speaking of the fear of death, but the fear of what the embryonic life, contained in a handful of dust, is likely to produce'.

Eliot may also be referring obliquely to the Sibyl's fateful request for as many years of life as there are grains of sand in her grasp (see note to the Epigraph, page 133).

ll. 31–4: Eliot's note refers us to the libretto of *Tristan und Isolde* (*Tristan and Isolde*), I, 5–8, the opera by Richard Wagner (1813–83). A sailor is singing about the sweetheart he has left behind him: 'The wind blows fresh to the homeland. My Irish girl, where are you lingering?'

The ship is Tristan's, carrying Isolde from Ireland to be the bride of King Marke of Cornwall, Tristan's uncle. A potion joins Tristan and Isolde in passionate love.

Allusions to Wagner run throughout the poem. In his sixties, Eliot discussed *Tristan* with Igor Stravinsky, who understood from him that it was 'one of the most passionate experiences of his life'. This may reflect something of Verdenal's enthusiasm for Wagner. He wrote to Eliot in July 1911, 'I went the other day to the Götterdämmerung, conducted by Nikisch; the end must be one of the highest points ever reached by man' (*Letters*, I.24–5). Writing to Eliot in 1912, Verdenal returned to this theme: '*Tristan and Isolde* is terribly moving at the first hearing, and leaves you prostrate with ecstasy and thirsting to get back to it again' (*Letters*, I.31). Thus a private tribute to Verdenal may be carried in Eliot's Wagner allusions.

l. 35 hyacinths: these flowers were a symbol for the resurrected god of the fertility rites. In Greek legend, they flowered where blood fell from the slain youth Hyacinthus. According to Frazer, the Greek festival of the Hyacinthia 'marked the passage from the youthful verdure of spring to the dry heat of summer'.

ll. 35–6: against these lines in the manuscript is written 'Marianne'. Asked to elucidate this, Ezra Pound thought that Eliot might have been referring to Tennyson's poem 'Mariana' – although there is no obvious connection.

ll. 37–41: Act I of *Tristan* ends with a scene of mystical love-recognition. Eliot seems to have merged this with a crucial step in the Grail legend, where the searcher meets the bearer of the Grail, fails to ask the right question and so misses his opportunity of success.

ll. 38–41: these lines seem to extend a notable poetic tradition rendering the experience of being overcome by beauty, to the point of losing one's senses. It originates in a lyric fragment by Sappho (to whom Eliot refers in his note to line 222), No. 2 in *Lyra Graeca* vol. i (1922), ed. J. M. Edmonds. The fragment was translated into Latin by Catullus and, in turn, into English by Byron under the title 'Translation from Catullus – Ad Lesbiam', which includes such lines and phrases as: '. . . my senses fly;/I needs must gaze, but, gazing die . . . My eyes refuse the cheering light . . . Such pangs my nature sinks beneath,/And feels a temporary death.'

l. 41 heart of light: is Eliot effecting a deliberate inversion of Conrad's 'Heart of Darkness' (see page 134)?

the silence: Eliot may have recalled these words, similarly separate and poised, in 'Days' by Joseph Campbell. The poem celebrates 'The days of my life', the first of which 'Is a black valley/Rising to blue goat-parks/On the crowns of distant hills./I hear the falling of water/And the whisper of ferns' tongues/And, still more, I hear/The silence.' Eliot reviewed Campbell's volume, *Earth of Cualann*, in the *Egoist*, December 1917.

l. 42: Eliot again refers us to *Tristan* III, 24. Tristan is mortally wounded, waiting for Isolde, who has the gift of healing, but the look-out reports that there is no sign of her ship: 'Desolate and empty the sea.'

Hayward: 'The absence of love in the Waste Land'.

l. 43 Madame Sosostris: in the novel *Crome Yellow* (1921) by Aldous Huxley there is a fake fortune-teller, a bank manager, Mr Scogan, who passes under the name of Madame Sesostris (ch. 27). Eliot said that he read the novel on its publication in November 1921 and that it is 'almost certain' that he borrowed the name from it, although he was 'unconscious of the borrowing'. But Eliot had forgotten quite how closely he had read the book, since his annotated copy survives. It appears that Eliot identified Mr Scogan as a portrait of the philosopher Bertrand Russell, by whom he was taught philosophy at Harvard in 1914 and whose acquaintance Eliot kept up when he came to England. Eliot and Huxley were both members of Lady Ottoline Morrell's set in Bloomsbury and at her country house, Garsington, near Oxford.

Madame Sosostris's 'bad cold' may carry an autobiographical detail in reverse. In 1917, Eliot reported that a spiritualist offered to give him 'mental treatment for a cold in the head' (see note to 'Gerontion', lines 27–8).

ll. 43–59: this section represents the ancient mysteries of the Tarot (see note to line 46) now reduced to the comic banality of fortune-telling. (Frazer: 'magic regularly dwindles into divination before it degenerates into a simple game'.) Eliot knew this first-hand since in 1921 he attended the lectures and seances of the fashionable 'mystic' of the day, P. D. Ouspensky. Jessie Weston comments, 'To-day the Tarot has fallen somewhat into disrepute, being principally used for purposes of divination.' cf. George Bernard Shaw's Preface to *Heartbreak House* (1919): 'It was superstitious, and addicted to table-rapping, materialization séances, clairvoyance, palmistry, crystal-gazing and the like to such an extent that it may be doubted whether ever before in the history of the world did soothsayers, astrologers, and unregistered therapeutic specialists of all sorts flourish as they did during this half century of the drift to the abyss'. Shaw is characterizing an aspect of life in England before the First World War.

In these lines, and elsewhere in the poem, Eliot makes use of

'Magic', an essay written by the Irish poet W. B. Yeats (1865–1939) in 1901 recounting a seance, during which he saw a 'vision' ('unfolded' by a 'seeress') denied to his companion, which 'he was forbidden to see' (cf. line 54), 'it being his own life'. There are other points of correspondence, verbal and in detail, between 'Magic' and *The Waste Land*, including a 'chapel' (line 387), an image which 'crawled' (line 381), 'gravestones' (line 387), arms 'without hands' (line 104). There is a section with the same horrific and phantasmagoric quality we find in lines 378–94; and another which carries the sense of danger and alarm in lines 401–9. In 1933, Eliot mocked Yeats's interest in magic and mysticism: 'He was very much fascinated by self-induced trance states, calculated symbolism, mediums, theosophy, crystal-gazing, folklore and hobgoblins...', a comment that accords with the satirical force of this 'Sosostris' passage. Yet Eliot seems to have been profoundly affected by other sections of 'Magic'. Yeats's portrait of Madame Blavatsky (*Dial*, August 1919) may also have inspired 'Madame Sosostris'. As Grover Smith comments, Yeats's account of his meeting 'preserves the posed image of that symbolic confrontation of Poet and Sibyl'.

l. 46 pack of cards: this is the Tarot pack, of 78 cards, sometimes increased to 100, first known to have been used in France and Italy in the fourteenth century, although many of the symbols and figures are of ancient origin, some of which are said to derive from Egyptian inscriptions, and all of which have been connected with fertility rites and folklore.

Eliot notes, jocularly, that he is not familiar with its exact details and that he has departed from them to suit his own convenience. In 1956, he said he was 'sorry to hear that *The Waste Land* has caused the rifling of Tarot Packs'. None the less, Jessie Weston does bring in the Tarot pack; so Eliot would have been familiar with her explanation of its significance. On this point, Matthiessen says:

> Miss Weston mentions that its four suits are Cup, Lance, Sword and Dish, which thus correspond to the sexual symbol-

ism of the Grail; and that the original use of these cards was 'not to foretell the Future in general, but to predict the rise and fall of the waters which brought fertility to the land' (p. 76). Through such knowledge the emotional relevance to the poem of this 'wicked pack' is obviously increased.

Critics offer a wide range of interpretations, some of them contradictory, for the six Tarot cards referred to in lines 47–55. (Eliot gives eight, but the drowned Phoenician Sailor and Bella-donna are not Tarot figures.) This diversity is not surprising since, although the designs are basically the same, in different packs the designs vary on points of detail. For example, the Hanged Man of line 55 need not be sinister, a corpse swinging from a gallows. In one set of cards, he is depicted as a young man, cheerfully smiling, suspended upside down by one ankle. Moreover, different Tarot masters explain the cards in different ways. So Eliot's note to line 46 – admitting to an unfamiliarity with the Tarot's 'exact constitution' and to changing it 'to suit my own convenience' – encourages us to elucidate the meaning of cards from the poem rather than spend time exploring the interpretations in the Tarot guides.

wicked: also in the American slang sense of effective, mar-vellous.

l. 47 your card: this is the first card to be turned, the Significator, which is chosen by the cartomancer to match the client's charac-ter or to direct the path of divination. The later cards are then turned at random, just as they come.

Phoenician Sailor: a type of the fertility god, whose image was thrown into the sea each year to symbolize the death of the summer (without which there could be no resurrection, the new year in the spring). Phoenicia itself was the part of the eastern Mediterranean coast now known as Lebanon and Syria. It was renowned for its sailors and traders. Here took place the annual ceremonies commemorating the death and resurrection of the god Thammuz.

Hayward: 'A kind of fertility god thrown into the sea each year to symbolize the death of summer. The Tarot pack is used to predict the rising of the waters.' This last detail comes directly from *From Ritual to Romance* (p. 76).

l. 48 a line from the Song of Ariel in Shakespeare's *The Tempest* I, ii. Ariel is singing to Ferdinand, telling him of the wonderful 'sea-change' that has taken place for his father, Alonso, King of Naples. In fact, Alonso has not been drowned; Ferdinand thinks he is; and Ariel sings a comforting song, leading him to Miranda, with whom he falls in love.

l. 49 Belladonna: literally, in Italian, beautiful lady; also the popular name for a flower from which is obtained a dangerous drug (*Atropa belladonna*), used by women to enlarge the pupil of the eye; also the name for one of the three Fates of classical legend (hence, perhaps, line 50).

Lady of the Rocks: the ominous, fateful overtones of the context suggest that Eliot had in mind a passage in *The Renaissance* (1873) where Walter Pater (1839–94) is discussing La Gioconda, more popularly known as the Mona Lisa, the portrait by Leonardo de Vinci of a woman on whose face there is the hint of a strange, haunting smile: 'She is older than the rocks among which she sits; like the vampire, she has been dead many times, and learned the secret of the grave; and has been a diver in deep seas, and keeps their fallen day about her; and trafficked for strange webs with Eastern merchants . . . .'

l. 51 man with three staves: a figure in the Tarot pack. Eliot notes that he associates him, quite arbitrarily, with the Fisher King.

Wheel: the wheel of fortune, figuring the reversals of fortune in life. Also, in many systems of ancient mythology, the wheel is the symbol of eternity, either of the divine or, as in Hinduism, the eternal human round of birth, death and re-birth.

ll. 52–4: according to Jessie Weston, the Syrian merchants transmitted the mysteries of the Attis cult and the Grail legend, although not necessarily comprehending their significance.

l. 52 one-eyed: Hayward explains that the merchant on the card is seen only in profile.

l. 55 The Hanged Man: see note to line 46. In Tarot lore the Hanged Man has attained a measure of perfection, short of complete freedom. However, in Eliot's Frazerian scheme he represents the god killed in order that his resurrection can renew the fertility of the land and its people. Eliot tells us that in his mind the Hanged Man is associated with the Hanged God (sacrificed to ensure fertility) of Frazer, and with the hooded figure mentioned in lines 360–66. Stephenson refers to the tradition that Judas, the betrayer of Jesus, hanged himself.

l. 57 Mrs Equitone: a synthetic constructed name.

ll. 60–76: in Matthiessen (pages 21–2), the function of the allusions in this section is analysed to the conclusion that they enable 'Eliot to condense into a single passage a concentrated expression of tragic horror'.

l. 60: Eliot refers us to 'Les Sept Vieillards' ('The Seven Old Men') by Charles Baudelaire (1821–67), quoting 'Fourmillante Cité, cité pleine de rêves,/Où le spectre en plein jour raccroche le passant' ('Crowded city, city full of dreams,/Where in broad daylight the spectre stops the passer-by'). In 1950 Eliot declared that these two lines summed up Baudelaire's 'significance' for him: 'I knew what *that* meant, because I had lived it before I knew that I wanted to turn it into verse on my own account.'

l. 62 London Bridge: a bridge across the Thames; the crowd is of workers on their way to the City district of London, the financial and business area.

l. 63: Eliot refers us to Dante, *Inferno* iii, 55–7, quoting 'si lunga tratta/di gente, ch'io non avrei mai creduto,/che morte tanta n'avesse disfatta' ('such a long stream of people, that I should never have believed that death had undone so many'). This is Dante's reaction to seeing the vast crowd of unhappy spirits – those who in life knew neither good nor evil, who never learned to care for anyone but themselves.

ll. 63–4: for the use of Dante in these lines, see Eliot's explanation, quoted in the Introduction, page 21.

ll. 63–8: Hayward: 'Those who have lived without praise or blame, without hope of death, the unhappy ones who have never really been alive. The crowd is the morning crowd with railway season tickets, spreading out into the City.' Hayward does not indicate that his first three lines are a translation of *Inferno* iii, 64.

l. 64: Eliot refers us to Dante, *Inferno* iv, 25–7, quoting 'Quivi, secondo che per ascoltare,/non avea pianto, ma' che di sospiri,/ che l'aura eterna facevan tremare' ('Here, there was to be heard no sound of lamentation, only sighs which disturbed the eternal air'). Dante is in Limbo. The sighs are those of the people who lived on earth virtuously but unbaptized, before the coming of Christ. Now they exist with the desire but without the hope of seeing God.

l. 65: see *Inferno* xxxiv, 15, the Traitors: 'altra, com'arco, il volto a' piedi inverte' (another, like a bow, bends face to feet).

l. 66 King William Street: leads directly on from London Bridge to the heart of the City of London, where at this time, Eliot was working at Lloyds Bank.

l. 67 Saint Mary Woolnoth: a notable City church, designed by Nicholas Hawksmoor (a pupil of Wren), built 1716–27. It stands on the corner of King William Street and Lombard Street, facing the offices of Lloyds Bank where Eliot worked from 1917 to 1925. Like the church of St Magnus-the-Martyr, this church was referred to in a report, 'Proposed Demolition of 19 City Churches' (1920), mentioned by Eliot in his note to line 264. The report, submitted to the London County Council by its Clerk and Architect, recommended the preservation of both these churches. In *The Dial* for June 1921 Eliot refers to the report and comments: 'To one who, like the present writer, passes his days in this City of London (quand'io sentii chiavar l'uscio di sotto) the loss of these towers, to meet the eye down a grimy lane, and of these empty naves, to receive the solitary visitor at noon from the dust and tumult of Lombard Street, will be irreparable and unforgotten.' The quotation is from Dante and Eliot provides the source (see note here to line 411), conveying the sense that 'his days' spent at the bank were prison-like. In his copy of the Baedeker guide to *London* (see *Baedeker* note, page 83), Eliot marked the entries for these two churches.

l. 68: Eliot provides a personal note to the effect that he has often noticed the 'dead' (flat) sound in the last stroke of the clock's nine o'clock chimes. But this rather trivial observation may be a derisive joke, a laconic distraction from the line's more serious possibilities of meaning. For the City worker in the 1920s 9 a.m. was the usual starting-time for the office day. Beyond this, attending to Eliot's use of the words 'dead' and 'final', some commentators have noted that the death of Christ took place at the ninth hour (this being not 9 a.m. but the ninth hour of daylight, i.e. about 3 p.m.). Eliot had already used the phrase 'dead sound' in a book review that appeared in *The Athenaeum* in May 1919, where he wrote of 'the "dead sound" of drums'. Frazer also records a fertility ceremony in which 'the effigy of Osiris in a coffin of mulberry wood was laid in the grave, and at the ninth hour of the night the effigy that had been made and deposited the year before was removed and placed upon the boughs of sycamore'.

l. 69 Stetson: it has been suggested that anyone then in Eliot's circle would have recognized this as referring to Ezra Pound, nicknamed 'Buffalo Bill' for his emphatic Americanism in London; his favourite hat was a sombrero-stetson; '*always* in appearance the Westerner in excelsis', 'A sort of Wild West turn', said the writer Wyndham Lewis who knew Pound from about 1911 onwards. Yet Eliot himself said that he was not referring to anyone in particular; that he just meant any superior bank clerk in bowler hat, black jacket and striped trousers; and to the suggestion that he had Pound in mind, he replied, 'My friend does not dress like that, and he would look rather out of place in King William Street!'

Hayward refers us to *Inferno* iii, 58–61: 'When I had made out some amongst them, I saw and recognized the ghost of one who, through cowardice, made the great denial.' (So Stetson is no better than anyone else in the crowd.) Hayward also notes that 'The name Stetson has no special significance: it is simply a typical businessman's name.' This is slightly disingenuous. As Hayward very well knew, Stetson is not a name met with in Britain.

Valerie Eliot reports that there was an American banker of this name, working in London and Copenhagen, and that Eliot may have met him through a mutual friend.

Donald J. Childs has devoted an article in *Essays in Criticism* (April 1988) to investigating the wider significance of 'Stetson' in the poem. He points out that felt slouch hats (a version of the stetson) were the characteristic and identifying head-gear of Australian and New Zealand soldiers in the First World War, and were a familiar sight in London. Childs connects this with the Australian reference that Eliot himself provides in the note to line 199; and further connects this to the sea battles over Mylae, which he takes as an oblique reference to the Dardanelles sea battle in which Jean Verdenal was killed (see page 43–4).

l. 70 Mylae: Hayward: 'The great naval victory of the Romans over the Carthaginians in the First Punic War. A trade war (cf. 1914–1918). All wars are one war.' Matthiessen, too, observes that this reference (assimilating the recent World War and Mylae) underlines 'the essential sameness of all wars'. The sea-battle took place in 260 BC.

ll. 71–3: cf. 'How are the dead raised up? and with what body do they come? Thou fool, that which thou sowest is not quickened, except it die. And that which thou sowest, thou sowest not that body that shall be, but bare grain, it may chance of what, or of some other grain', 1 Corinthians xv, 35–7; see the entire passage pursuing the analogy between the burying of the corpse and the planting of seed in The Order for the Burial of the Dead in *The Book of Common Prayer.*

l. 71: in ancient fertility rites images of the gods were buried in the fields.

This line has given rise to speculation. In 'The Frontiers of Criticism' (1956), Eliot reported that

> a gentleman from Indiana wrote to me a year or more ago, 'I wonder – it is possible that I am mad, of course' (this was his interjection, not mine; of course he was not in the least mad, merely slightly touched in one corner of his head from having read *The Road to Xanadu*) 'whether "the dead cats of civiliza-tion", "rotten hippo" and Mr Kurtz have some tenuous con-nection with "that corpse you planted last year in your

garden"?' This sounds like raving, unless you recognize the allusions: it is merely an earnest seeker trying to establish some connection between *The Waste Land* and Joseph Conrad's *Heart of Darkness*.

Eliot is evasive, for indeed there is some connection. Originally, he chose some lines from 'Heart of Darkness' to stand as the epigraph to *The Waste Land* (quoted on page 134). He also drew on the novel in lines 266–78. Parts of *The Waste Land* which were dropped in its final revision went towards 'The Hollow Men', which significantly carries an epigraph from 'Heart of Darkness': 'Mistah Kurtz – he dead'. So the 'gentleman from Indiana' was closer to the truth than Eliot allowed his audience to suspect. In 1933, he said that the Conrad of 'Heart of Darkness', together with Hawthorne, Dostoevsky and James, were the only novelists comparable in their 'essential moral preoccupation' with 'Evil'.

l. 72 sprout: Eliot wrote to Conrad Aiken, 'it's interesting to cut yourself to pieces once in a while, and wait to see if the fragments will sprout' (30 September 1914, *Letters*, I. 59).

l. 73: these questions seem to be answered in Whitman's 'This Compost':

> O how can it be that the ground itself does not sicken?
> How can you be alive you growths of spring?
> How can you furnish health you blood of herbs, roots,
>   orchards, grain?
> Are they not continually putting distemper'd corpses within
>   you?
> Is not every continent work'd over and over with sour dead?
> Where have you disposed of their carcasses?

l. 74: Eliot's note refers us to the dirge sung by Cornelia in *The White Devil* v, iv, by John Webster. She is singing for 'The friendless bodies of unburied men' – 'But keep the wolf far thence, that's foe to men,/For with his nails he'll dig them up again.' The change from 'wolf' to 'Dog' is easily made. In the Old Testament, the dog is no 'friend to man', but an unclean animal, living on human corpses. Sometimes the dog is figured as an agent of evil, as in Psalms xxii, 20: 'Deliver my soul from the sword, my darling from the power of the dog'; and Philippians iii, 2: 'Beware of dogs, beware of evil workers'. Frazer gives the dog and wolf as symbols of the Vegetation spirit.

Hayward: 'The suburban garden. The Englishman and his dog, his friendly "familiar demon". The substitution of the dog for the wolf, in this allusion, is a striking example of the use which Eliot makes of allusions in order to join the past and present. The idea also suggests that the dog, in digging up the corpse, is able to prevent its reincarnation.' Melchiori (1956) (pp. 74–80) discusses at length the significance of the 'Dog' in Eliot's work and suggests a source in *Ulysses*.

l. 76: Eliot refers us to *Les Fleurs du mal* (*The Flowers of Evil*), a volume of poems by Charles Baudelaire. Eliot's line (after 'You!') is the final line in Baudelaire's prefatory poem, 'Au Lecteur' ('To the Reader'): 'O hypocrite reader, my fellow man, my brother!' They share the sin of *ennui*, boredom heightened to a profound spiritual dissatisfaction, expressed in the modern term *anomie*.

II A GAME OF CHESS

Title: cf. the title of *A Game at Chesse*, a play by Thomas Middleton (1580–1627), who also wrote *Women beware Women* to which Eliot refers in his note to line 138 (correctly, 137), specifically to the chess game played there.

In some of the Grail romances, the hero comes to a chessboard castle, where he meets a water-maiden. In Elizabethan and Jacobean drama, to which Eliot refers within this section, chess is often used as a symbol for human life and government.

Originally, Eliot had entitled Part II 'In the Cage', a reference to the Cumaean Sibyl of the Epigraph.

Hayward: 'The contrast between the life of the great and that of the common people in a sterile and despoiled land. In Middleton's play [*Women beware Women*], the game of chess conceals seduction and rape. In the myth, the curse on the land follows the rape of the girls at the court of the Fisher King. Lust without love. Cf. also the "Thames Maidens".'

A key to the personal reference of this section is found in a letter (November 1922) from John Peale Bishop to Edmund Wilson following dinner with Pound, who confided in him about Eliot, Vivien and *The Waste Land*: 'Eliot's version of her is contained in "The Chair she sat in like a burnished throne" ', whereas the pub scene 'reflects the atmosphere immediately outside their first flat in London' (at Crawford Mansions, near Baker Street).

l. 77: Eliot refers us to *Antony and Cleopatra* 11, ii, the opening of Enobarbus's description of Cleopatra's ceremonial barge and her first meeting with Antony: 'The barge she sat in, like a burnish'd throne,/Burn'd on the water.' 'The great speech of Enobarbus in *Antony and Cleopatra* is highly decorated, but the decoration has a purpose beyond its own beauty' ('Rudyard Kipling', 1941).

ll. 77–96: details of the description suggest that Eliot also had in mind Exodus xxv–xxvii, where are set out the Lord's instructions to Moses for the furnishing of the Temple of Jerusalem: including a golden chair, flanked by golden cherubim and, set behind, a table with seven-bracketed candelabrum; and with elaborate directions for the right jewels, incenses, perfumes and unguents. Thus Eliot evokes the sacred and the profane.

A further source may have been Keats' *Lamia* ii, 173–98, the description of the banquet-room (discussed at length by Melchiori (1956), who also suggests the influence of *Ulysses*).

This passage is a pastiche of the style of 'wit and magniloquence' which Eliot describes in 'Andrew Marvell' (1921), 'magniloquence' which he found 'used and abused' by Milton and Baudelaire. Eliot seems to be conflating such models as the bedchamber in Pope's *Rape of the Lock* (1712, 1714) and Imogen's boudoir in *Cymbeline* (11, iv, 87–91), in which there is a reference to Philomel (11, ii, 44–6) as in line 99 below. Matthiessen comments: 'his intention is to keep up an impression of Renaissance splendour and luxuriance ... we are being given an entire sensation of magnificence'.

A further source for the language of this passage may be three stories by Edgar Allen Poe: 'The Murders in the Rue Morgue', 'The Assignation' and 'Shadow in a Parable' (the relevant extracts are given in Smith, 1983, pp. 123–4). These stories were in Eliot's mind at this time and he refers to them in 'Prose and Verse' (*Chapbook*, no. xxii, 1921).

l. 80 Cupidon: a cupid, the classical boy god of love, cast in gold.

l. 92 laquearia: a panelled ceiling. Eliot refers us to Virgil's *Aeneid* i, 726, quoting 'dependent lychni laquearibus aureis incensi, et noctem flammis funalia vincunt' ('flaming torches hang from the golden-panelled ceiling, and the night is pierced by the flaring lights'). The scene is the banquet given by Dido, Queen of Carthage, in honour of her beloved, Aeneas, who eventually deserts her.

l. 93 coffered: decorated with sunken panels.

l. 96 dolphin: in medieval art, the dolphin was associated with love.

l. 98 sylvan scene: Eliot refers us to Milton's *Paradise Lost* iv, 140. This is the wooded 'scene' before Satan when he first arrives at the borders of Eden.

l. 99: Eliot's note refers us to *Metamorphoses* vi by the Roman poet Ovid (43 BC–AD 18). Ovid's version of the Greek myth tells how Philomela was raped by King Tereus of Thrace (the husband of her sister Procne), how he cut out her tongue, and how she was eventually transformed into a nightingale and so escaped his murderous rage. Before her transformation, Philomela, now unable to speak, wove her story into a tapestry, which she got to her sister, who avenged the crime by killing her own son and serving his flesh as a dish to Tereus, his father. This tapestry-story is referred to as 'displayed' in line 97, as 'told' in line 105. In the poem, Eliot spells 'Philomel' without the 'a' which usually ends her name, the form he uses in the notes to lines 99 and 428. Apart from any metrical reason, this may be to connect her to Shakespeare's 'Philomel' in *Cymbeline* (see note to lines 77–96) or to Milton's nightingale, in *Il Penseroso*: 'Less Philomel will deign a Song/In her sweetest, saddest plight,/ Smoothing the rugged brow of night'.

John Peale Bishop sent his biographical interpretation to

Edmund Wilson (see page 157): 'The Nightingale passage is, I believe, important: Eliot being Tereus and Mrs E Philomela. That is to say, that through unbalanced passion, everybody is in a hell of a fix; Tereus being changed to a hoopoe [a hawk] and T.S.E. a bank clerk. Thomas' sexual troubles are undoubtedly extreme.' Wilson dismissed this as 'the wrong dope about the nightingale' and told Bishop that the bird was a reflection of the ' "sylvan scene" in *Paradise Lost*" ', and that Tereus was 'not Eliot, but the things which are crucifying Eliot'.

l. 100 forced: Jessie Weston quotes a Grail text in which a rape carried out by a King is described: 'One of the maidens he took by force . . .'

l. 101: in describing one of the centres of worship of the vegetation gods, an oasis in a desert land, Frazer notes that 'the place is a paradise of birds' where 'the thrush and the nightingale sing full-throated' (cf. Keats's 'Ode to a Nightingale': 'Thou . . . singest of summer in full-throated ease').

inviolable: secure and beyond violation.

l. 103 Jug Jug: in Elizabethan poetry this was a conventional way of representing bird-song, often in springtime (as 'Cuckoo, jug-jug, pu-we, to-witta-woo!', one of the tunes of 'Spring' in the poem by Thomas Nashe (1567–1601). The direct allusion is to Tricio's song in *Alexander and Campaspe*, a comedy by John Lyly (1554–1606): 'What bird so sings, yet so dos wayle?/Oh, 'tis the ravish'd nightingale. "Jug, jug, jug, jug, tereu", she cryes;/And still her woes at midnight rise.' (5.i.36–9). 'Tereu' is the Greek vocative form of Tereus.

Eliot repeats this reference in lines 203–6.

l. 104: cf. 'Conversation' by William Cowper, line 51: 'So wither'd stumps disgrace the sylvan scene'. The 'stumps' 'told upon the walls' could be those of Lavinia in *Titus Andronicus* and her tragic story (v, ii, 167ff.). There, she is compared to Philomela, for like her, Lavinia is raped and her tongue cut out, and her hands are cut off too, to prevent her, Philomela-like, from weaving a tell-tale tapestry. Lavinia is also associated with 'the tragic tale of Philomela' in iv, i, 51–8, and in ii, iv, 38.

ll. 108–10: Eliot took these lines, virtually unchanged, from 'The

Death of the Duchess', a highly autobiographical, unfinished poem that may have been written in the autumn of 1919 when he reviewed a production of *The Duchess of Malfi* (c. 1614) by John Webster. The 'Death' is printed with *The Waste Land* facsimile. It describes a couple trapped in their relationship, unable to communicate their needs, an experience explored here in lines 111 to 138.

Lines 108–10 allude to Act III, Scene 1 of Webster's play, where the Duchess is so absorbed in combing her hair that she fails to notice that her husband and maidservant have left the room and continues a bantering conversation she was having with them. This is overheard by her brother Ferdinand. As the Duchess is a widow, now secretly married, he accuses her of having a lover; and, eventually, she and her children are murdered on account of this, a course of events reflected in line 110.

In 1924, Eliot described Webster, in particular *The Duchess of Malfi*, as providing 'an interesting example of a very great literary and dramatic genius directed towards chaos'; and in 1941 he spoke of the 'breathless tension' of Act III, Scene 1, and of the poignancy of the words, 'Have you lost your tongue?' (perhaps taken up here in line 112) with which the Duchess betrays herself to Ferdinand.

l. 110 glowed into words: in Dante's *Inferno*, the damned souls can only speak through the tip of the flame that envelops them, an allusion that also relates to the fate of the Duchess, damned in the judgement of Ferdinand and her other brother.

ll. 111–14: against these lines, Pound wrote 'photography'. Could they render verbatim Vivien's complaints, the kind of experience which, to quote Eliot himself, 'brought the state of mind out of which came *The Waste Land*' (quoted, page 34). Similarly, against line 126, Pound wrote 'photo'. In 'Philip Massinger', written in 1920, Eliot employed the word 'photographic' to mean accurate and realistic: 'The comedy of Jonson is nearer to caricature; that of Middleton a more photographic delineation of low life' (*Selected Essays*, p. 216). It was a term he shared with Pound at this time, who in 1918 described a story by Henry James as 'a scandalous photograph from the life'.

ll. 111–23: there is a significant correspondence between these lines and a scene in 'The Fox', a short story by D. H. Lawrence (1885–1930), which first appeared in *The Dial* (May–August 1921). In the remarks of Jill Banford, Nellie Marsh and Henry, as they sit together in a room one evening, we encounter such words and phrases as 'My eyes are bad to-night ... My nerves are all gone for to-night ... I'm all nerves to-night ... Nothing! Nothing!' and the dialogue has an abruptness and a kind of aimlessness close to the pattern of Eliot's verse in these lines; moreover, Lawrence's dialogue turns on questions of what they are thinking about and the noise of the wind.

As a regular contributor, Eliot knew *The Dial* well and Lawrence's story appeared there while *The Waste Land* was in the course of being written; so the connection could be quite direct. On the other hand, in 1962 Eliot accepted the suggestion that in writing lines 117–26, Webster's *The White Devil* (v, vi, 223–7) 'was at the back of my mind':

> Nothing; of nothing: leave thy idle questions,
> I am ith way to study a long silence,
> To prate were idle, I remember nothing.
> Thers nothing of so infinit vexation
> As mans own thoughts.

l. 115 rats' alley: it has been suggested that this is soldiers' slang for the trenches on the Western Front in the First World War. Although no evidence of this specific usage has been found, it is plausible, since 'alley' was the slang term for the trenches, which were plagued with rats, ominous, familiar and detested. Writing to his mother in November 1915, Eliot reports the experience of Maurice Haigh-Wood (Vivien's brother) serving in the front-line: 'What he tells about rats and vermin is incredible – Northern France is swarming, and the rats are as big as cats.'

l. 116: in the First World War a source of particular grief for the bereaved was the loss of soldiers for whom there was no known grave.

l. 117: in *The Duchess of Malfi* IV, ii, Ferdinand sends madmen to torment his sister. As she hears them outside, she exclaims, 'How now! what noise is that?'

l. 118: Eliot refers us to, 'Is the wind in that door still?' from *The Devil's Law Case* III, ii by John Webster. The remark is made by one surgeon to another when he hears a groan from a man supposed to be dead. But in 1938 Eliot denied that this source was of any significance; his words, he said, were 'an adaptation of a phrase of Webster which Webster uses with quite a different meaning'. The modern equivalent of Webster's phrase is, 'Is that the way the land lies?' or, 'Is that the way the wind blows?'

ll. 120–26: cf. *The Duchess of Malfi* IV, ii: *Cariola:* 'What think you of, madam?' *Duchess:* 'Of nothing; When I muse thus, I sleep.' *Cariola:* 'Like a madman, with your eyes open?' Unwittingly, the two women are awaiting their executioner. This snatch of dialogue in part explains the 'nothings' of this passage; and the references to 'open' 'eyes' and a fateful visit seem to relate to line 138.

l. 125: see note to line 48. In his 'London Letter' dated July 1921 (*The Dial*, September) Eliot wrote: 'What is needed of art is a simplification of current life into something rich and strange.' The last five words are taken directly from Ariel's Song in *The Tempest*. The 'art' of *The Waste Land* at this point in the poem – in the fragmentation of the lines – represents visually and rhythmically such a 'simplification' and transformation into the poetically 'rich and strange'.

l. 126: Hayward: 'Cf. 'The Hollow Men': "Headpiece filled with straw"' (line 4). This note does nothing to help *The Waste Land* reader. But it may be a hint from Eliot of the connection between the two poems. Possibly this line was an insult actually thrown at Eliot by his wife in anger or exasperation and provided the trigger for Section I of 'The Hollow Men'. (See note on *Composition*, page 208.)

ll. 128–30: Eliot draws upon 'That Shakespearian Rag/Most intelligent, very elegant,/That old classical drag,/Has the proper stuff/The line "Lay on Macduff"'. This American ragtime hit from Ziegfeld's Follies of 1912 goes on to mention Desdemona (the tragic heroine of *Othello*), the fated lovers of *Romeo and Juliet* and Hamlet.

A style of jazz dance music, rag was very popular at the beginning of the First World War. The 'OOOO' and the extra syllable 'he', added by Eliot, catch the syncopated ragtime rhythm. Successive 'O's are a trade mark of a Shakespearian tragedy. Othello ends his last great speech with three; Hamlet's last utterance, in the Folio text, is four; Lady Macbeth, sleep-walking, utters three; and in moments of extremity Lear's speeches are interlarded with them.

But Hayward makes it clear that Eliot was thinking of 'The post-war ragtime world, the jazz world of 1920, restless, aimless, hectic, fearful, futile, neurotic.'

l. 135: Hayward: 'To get up late to shorten the boredom of an empty day. And, because of an afternoon downpour, an aimless car drive, to kill time.'

l. 136–8: lines taken from 'The Death of the Duchess', see note to lines 108–10.

l. 136 closed car: to distinguish it from cars with roofs but open sides. So a 'closed' car had the full enclosing body of a saloon car.

l. 137: Eliot's note refers us to the game of chess in Middleton's *Women beware Women* II, ii. In this scene the mother-in-law's attention is held by a game of chess with Livia, a procuress; every move corresponds to a step in the forceful seduction of Bianca, her daughter-in-law, which takes place in view of the audience in a gallery over the mother-in-law's head.

l. 138: see note to lines 120–26.

lidless: figuratively meaning 'watchful'.

Following this line, in the original typescript, came the line 'The ivory men make company between us'. According to Mrs Eliot, this line was omitted at Vivien Eliot's request (because it bore too heavily upon their personal situation?). But it was important to Eliot and when he wrote out a copy of the poem in 1960, he restored it from memory.

l. 139 demobbed: a slang abbreviation of demobilized, meaning released from military service, as conscripted troops were after the First World War. First recorded in 1919.

ll. 139ff.: Jessie Weston records that the ritual marriage should restore life to the waste land, provided that the test of love is passed.

l. 141: the call of the bartender at closing time in a British public house.

ll. 139–72: Eliot and Vivien used to mimic (what was then) working-class speech.

ll. 142–72: Eliot said that this passage was 'pure Ellen Kellond', the housemaid who told the story to the poet and his wife and whose cockney accent Eliot would mimic for the entertainment of his friends. Also see note to line 214, indicating the possibility that the cockney dialogue has connections with the music hall.

l. 143: Hayward: 'The bad teeth of the English working-class, especially amongst young men and women, is notorious. Moreover, false teeth, because they are very common and often badly fitting, are the subject of popular jokes.'

l. 148 four years: the period of the First World War, 1914–18.

l. 159: to induce an abortion, see lines 161–2.

l. 172: Eliot quotes *Hamlet* verbatim. Hayward: 'Cf. Hamlet IV, v. These are the pathetic farewell words of Ophelia, in her madness, to the ladies of the court of the King of Denmark. Hamlet has accused Ophelia of being a whore and telling her to retire to a "nunnery" – in Shakespeare's time, the slang word for a brothel.' Eliot later said that he also had in mind Laforgue's 'Hamlet', a poem in which these words are quoted as passing through the mind of Yorick.

III   THE FIRE SERMON

Composition: This part was probably begun in spring 1921. As distinct from the fragments of earlier writing that Eliot incorporated in constructing *The Waste Land*, this is considered to be the first part he wrote with a sense of the poem as a whole in mind. By 4 November 1921, he had completed what he described as a fifty-line 'rough draft', whilst convalescing at Cliftonville, Margate (see note to line 300).

The Fire Sermon was preached by the Buddha against the fires of lust, anger, envy and the other passions that consume men. It is one of the central texts of early Buddhism and was studied by Eliot at Harvard in 1912–13 (see his note to line 308), having begun his study of Indic Philology in 1911 and commenced learning Sanskrit and Pali. Stephenson explains that the Sermon was delivered by the Buddha to a congregation of priests or monks, expounding the canonical text of rules for their conduct in life.

l. 173 river's tent: the immediate, visual image is of the shelter provided in summer by the leafy boughs of the trees overhanging the river, a shelter now broken by the loss of the leaves at the close of the year. But the rhetorical ring of the first half-line suggests more solemn overtones of meaning; perhaps the loss is of some sacred or mystic quality. In the Old Testament 'tent' can mean tabernacle or holy place, arising from the use of a tent as a portable tabernacle by the wandering tribes of Israel in the wilderness. In Isaiah xxxiii, 20–21, the 'river' is linked with the 'tent' as an image of the power and security that God offers to his chosen people: 'Look upon Zion, the city of our solemnities: thine eyes shall see Jerusalem a quiet habitation, a tabernacle that shall not be taken down; not one of the stakes thereof shall ever be removed, neither shall any of the cords thereof be broken. But there the glorious Lord will be unto us a place of broad rivers and streams . . . '

ll. 175–9: for line 176, Eliot quotes his source, the refrain to 'Prothalamion' by Edmund Spenser (1552–99). The poem is a lyrical celebration of the ideals and joys of marriage written to precede the double marriage of the daughters of the Earl of Worcester in 1596. The setting is the Thames in a flawless pastoral vision, with the 'Nymphes . . . All lovely Daughters of the Flood' in attendance upon their river, which they strew with flowers to honour this 'Brydale day'.

l. 179 testimony: a formal, legal term for evidence, ironically formal in referring to the detritus and rubbish of the river. But 'testimony' is also related to the 'tent' as tabernacle (line 173), for in the tabernacle was carried the ark of the covenant, the chest containing the tablets of law, given by God to Moses, referred to in Exodus as 'two tablets of testimony, tables of stone, written with the finger of God' (xxxi, 18).

ll. 179–80: Hayward: 'The Thames, up-stream from London, from Richmond to Maidenhead and Henley, is the favourite rendez-vous of holiday-makers of the type described in lines 179–80: modern "nymphs", accompanied by their boy friends in cars, jolly fellows and their English marionettes . . . '

l. 180 loitering: here describing the idle sons of the rich. But, as with 'testimony', the word carries more formal and ironic associations, this time literary, through Keats's memorable use at the opening and close of 'La Belle Dame Sans Merci' (1819):

> 'O what can ail thee, Knight-at-arms,
> Alone and palely loitering?'

The Knight tells of his love-enslavement to the enchantress and his fate, to 'sojourn here,/Alone and palely loitering,/Though the sedge is wither'd from the lake,/And no birds sing' – an ending which accords with line 182.

l. 182: cf. the lamentation of the Israelites recalling their exile in Babylonia and yearning for their homeland, Psalms cxxxvii, 1: 'By the rivers of Babylon, there we sat down, yea, we wept, when we remembered Zion.' 'The waters of Leman' is a phrase associated with the fires of lust, from the meaning of leman as mistress or prostitute.

Lake Leman is the French name for the Lake of Geneva in Switzerland. At the suggestion of Ottoline Morrell and further encouraged by Julian Huxley, in mid-November 1921 Eliot travelled from Margate (see note to line 300) to the lakeside town of Lausanne for treatment by the well-known psychotherapist Dr Roger Vittoz, seeking a cure for what Eliot described as 'aboulie', a type of emotional frigidity. Here he continued work on *The Waste Land*, returning to England in late December. In February 1922, Ezra Pound reported, 'Eliot came back from his Lausanne specialist looking OK; and with a damn good poem (19 pages) in his suitcase . . . About enough,

Eliot's poem, to make the rest of us shut up shop.' In March, Pound wrote to William Carlos Williams: 'Eliot, in bank, makes £500. Too tired to write, broke down, during convalescence in Switzerland did *Waste Land*, a masterpiece.'

l. 184 loud or long: cf. a deflationary echo is 'I said it very loud and clear;/I went and shouted in his ear' (Lewis Carroll (1832–98), *Alice Through the Looking Glass*, 1871).

l. 185: cf. 'But at my back I always hear/Time's winged chariot hurrying near,' from 'To His Coy Mistress' by Andrew Marvell (see 'Prufrock', note to line 23). Biblical 'blasts' of punishment are frequent, see the word of the Lord as quoted by Isaiah: 'Behold, I will send a blast upon him' (xxxvii, 7).

ll. 186–90: details here seem to allude to the Hades episode in Joyce's *Ulysses*: on the way to Paddy Dignam's funeral, Mr Bloom recalls a jingle – 'Rattle his bones/Over the stones/Only a pauper/Nobody owns'; a rat crawls in the cemetery; and the funeral procession stops by Dublin gasworks near the canal.

l. 187 rat: see note to line 115.

l. 189: according to Jessie Weston, to find redemption, the Fisher King seeks the fish, synonymous with the Grail.

l. 190 gashouse: Eliot uses the American term, which does not exist in English. In *Ulysses*, Joyce uses the English word 'gasworks'.

l. 192: Eliot refers to *The Tempest* i, ii, where Ferdinand is thinking of his father (see note to line 48), reminded by Ariel's music: 'Sitting on a bank,/Weeping again the king my father's wrack.' Some critics suppose this to be a reference to the death of Eliot's father in January 1919, much pondered by Eliot, since it placed upon him, he felt, even more heavily, the onus of producing a book to prove that he had, after all, not 'made a mess of his life'.

l. 193: continuing the ritual referred to in the note to line 47, the image was taken out of the water to symbolize the god's resurrection.

l. 196: Eliot refers us to 'To His Coy Mistress', see note to line 185.

l. 197: Eliot refers us to *The Parliament of Bees*, a masque by John Day (1574–?1640), quoting:

> When of a sudden, listening, you shall hear,
> A noise of horns and hunting, which shall bring
>   Actaeon to Diana in the Spring,
>   Where all shall see her naked skin.

According to the Greek legend, the huntsman Actaeon surprised Diana (goddess of chastity) bathing with her nymphs. As a punishment he was turned into a stag and hunted to death.

ll. 197–8: in his 'London Letter' in *The Dial*, October 1921, Eliot described Stravinsky's music in *The Rite of Spring* as embodying, amongst 'other barbaric cries of modern life', 'the scream of the motor horn'.

l. 198 Sweeney: this is the hero of the 'Sweeney' poems, in his sexual character as 'Sweeney Erect'.

ll. 199–201: Eliot notes that these lines come from a ballad popular among Australian troops in the First World War; notably, it was sung as they landed in Gallipoli in 1915. It was reported to him from Sydney, Australia. Of the several versions, Eliot gives the polite wording, which obscures the point that Mrs Porter, a Cairo brothel-keeper, together with her daughter, was notorious among Australian troops for passing on venereal disease.

> O the moon shines bright on Mrs Porter
> And on the daughter of Mrs Porter.
> And they both wash their feet in soda water
> And so they oughter
> To keep them clean.

Years later, Eliot emphasized that the soda water is not the aerated drink but bicarbonate of soda solution. Concerning Mrs Porter and her daughter, Eliot told Clive Bell that 'These characters are known only from an Aryan camp-fire song of which one other line has been preserved: *And so they oughter.* Of such pieces, epic or didactic, most have been lost, wholly or in part, in the mists of antiquity . . . ' Eliot's friends were familiar with his style of parody-scholarship, a ponderous self-mocking of himself as Harvard doctoral candidate: e.g. see *Letters* I, p. 42, a letter to

Conrad Aiken 14 July 1914, in which Eliot provides learned annotation to a 'King Bolo' poem (for 'Bolo', see p. 102).

The soldier's ballad was derived from the chorus of a very popular ragtime and jazz song, 'Red Wing' (1907) by Thurland Chattaway: 'Now the moon shines to-night on pretty Red Wing, – the breeze is sighing, – the nightbird's crying.'

l. 202: Eliot refers us to his source, the final line to the sonnet 'Parsifal' by Paul Verlaine (1844–96): 'And, O those children's voices singing in the dome.' Having mastered the temptations of lust and cured the King, Verlaine's Knight adores the Grail and hears the voices. Verlaine is referring to Wagner's *Parsifal* and its music. In the Grail legend, the choir of children sings at the ceremony of the foot-washing which precedes the restoration of the wounded Anfortas (the Fisher King) by the Knight Parzival and the lifting of the curse from the waste land.

ll. 203–4: see note to line 103.

l. 205 forc'd: cf. line 100 'forced', whereas the spelling here is an archaic, literary form (e.g. 'with forc'd fingers rude' in Milton's 'Lycidas'), as if to underline a literary source (so far unidentified) allusively signalled in these skeletal lines. Possibly Eliot provided this pointer to steer the reader away from later Philomena poems, such as those by Matthew Arnold and Swinburne ('Itylus').

l. 206: Tereu (the Greek vocative form of Tereus) refers to King Tereus, who raped (line 205) Philomela (see note to line 99).

l. 207: Eliot is echoing Baudelaire's 'Fourmillante Cité', the city full of dreams, already mentioned in his note to line 60.

l. 209 Eugenides: literally well-born, of good family. Jessie Weston tells us that Syrian merchants played a part in spreading the cults of Attis and Mithra through the Roman Empire.

Smyrna: modern Izmir, in Western Turkey, formerly one of the great trading ports of Asia Minor. In 1919, it was taken from Turkey and handed over to Greece, a post-war settlement that brought a legacy of violence on account of the two countries' rival claims, events which kept Smyrna in the news from 1919 to 1923. By the treaty of Lausanne (July 1923), Turkey was given sovereignty. The Smyrna reference in the poem carries a particularly commercial emphasis, since the British case was that its loss by Turkey would damage British trade. Eliot was attentive to this dispute and so moved as to contribute to the public debate in a letter published in the *Daily Mail*, 8 January 1923.

ll. 209–14: the events described here actually happened. John Peale Bishop (see p. 34) reported: 'Mr Eugenides actually turned up at Lloyds with his pocket full of currants and asked Eliot to spend a weekend with him for no nice reasons. His place in the poem is, I believe, as a projection of Eliot, however. That is, all the men are in some way deprived of their life-giving, generative forces.' Years later Eliot told an inquirer that while working in the City he had in fact received such an invitation from an unshaven man from Smyrna with currants in his pockets. The homosexual implications that some interpreters have read into these lines did not, said Eliot, occur to him.

These lines parody the Grail legend, in which the Fisher King invites the quester to the Grail castle.

l. 211: curiously, since he handled such documents at the bank, Eliot's note explains 'C.i.f. London' incorrectly. The abbreviation does not mean 'carriage and insurance free' but 'cost, insurance and freight'. The second part of the line means that the documents of ownership and transport would be handed to the purchaser in exchange for a bank draft payable on sight. These were commercial matters with which Eliot was familiar. He recalled 'eight very satisfactory years', beginning March 1917, 'working in a bank, dealing with sight drafts, acceptances, bills of lading, and such mysteries', finding this 'a rest cure compared to teaching in a school'.

l. 212 demotic: common, colloquial (*OED* describes the word as 'somewhat rare').

l. 213 Cannon Street Hotel: a hotel attached to Cannon Street station in the City of London, which was then the main terminus for businessmen travelling to and from the Continent.

l. 214 Metropole: a fashionable luxury hotel at Brighton, on the south coast of England, sixty miles from London. A 'week-end at Brighton' is understood colloquially as an invitation carrying sexual implications.

Hayward's note in *Poèmes 1910–1930* quotes a verse (in French) of a song he attributes to the great music-hall entertainer George Robey (1869–1954) in which the 'Metropole' is mentioned. This does not throw any light upon line 214. But it does serve as a reminder of Eliot's attachment to the music hall, to which he was first introduced by Vivien when he settled in London in 1915 and thereafter began to build up his repertoire of music-hall songs. The original *Waste Land* opened with the monologue of a music-hall rake. This was dropped for the published version. But the cockney dialogue of the pub scene (lines 139–72), which was retained, may also come from the music-hall background. Eliot's *in memoriam* note on Marie Lloyd (December 1922; reprinted in *Selected Essays*) makes it clear that music halls not only gave him contact with the working classes, they also represented a special source of communal feeling and vitality and their disappearance was yet another aspect of the modern Waste Land. Eliot mentioned George Robey by name in contributions to *The Tyro* (Spring 1921), where music-hall artists are said to 'effect the Comic Purgation', and to *The Dial* (May 1921).

l. 215 violet: see Eliot's 1927 review of *Baudelaire* by Arthur Symons where he refers to the 'violet-coloured' London fogs of the 1890s (also line 220).

ll. 215–23: these lines seem to be modelled upon the evening scene at the opening to the *Purgatorio* viii: 'It was now the hour that turns back the desire of those who sail the seas and melts their heart, that day when they have said farewell to the dear friends, and that pierces the new pilgrim with love, if from far off he hears the chimes which seem to mourn for the dying day' (1–6).

ll. 215–56: Hayward: 'The sterile "love" of modern urban civilization'.

l. 216: in Eliot's case, the turning upwards was literal, since his office at Lloyds Bank was underground, its only natural light filtering through glass bricks set in the pavement outside the building.

ll. 216–17: Eliot remarked that 'perhaps the conditions of modern life (think how large a part is now played in our sensory life by the internal combustion engine!) have altered our perceptions of rhythms'.

ll. 218–20: many critics regard Eliot's note to line 218 as our most important aid in interpreting the poem. Some go so far as to identify Tiresias's vision with that of the poet himself. The note may have been triggered by the account of Tiresias given by Frazer in his edition of *The Library* by the Greek writer Apollodorus, published in autumn 1921. *The Library* is a summary of Greek myths and heroic legends, drawing upon literary records, written in either the first or second century AD. The story of Tiresias, considerably annotated by Frazer, is recounted in volume 1, pages 361–7.

In these lines Eliot refers to the prophetic powers and bisexuality of Tiresias, quoting the Latin text of Ovid's *Metamorphoses* which tells this legend: Tiresias came across two snakes copulating in a forest. He hit them with his staff and was turned into a woman. Seven years later he saw the same two snakes and hit them again. As he had hoped, he was turned back into a man. On account of Tiresias's male and female experience, Jove called him in as an expert witness to settle a quarrel with his wife Juno. Jove was arguing that in love the woman enjoys the greater pleasure; Juno argued that it was the other way round. Tiresias supported Jove. Out of spite Juno blinded him. To make up for this, Jove gave him the power of prophecy, and long life. Hence Eliot's reference to Tiresias's age, 'female breasts' and duality of experience in lines 218–19 and 228.

Eliot also draws our attention to the fluidity of the point of view in *The Waste Land*: 'Tiresias, although a mere spectator and not indeed a "character", is yet the most important personage in the poem, uniting all the rest. Just as the one-eyed merchant, seller of currants, melts into the Phoenician Sailor, and the latter is not wholly distinct from Ferdinand Prince of Naples, so all the women are one woman, and the two sexes meet in Tiresias. What Tiresias *sees*, in fact, is the substance of the poem.' (As Tiresias was blind, we have to understand this kind of seeing as his visionary or prophetic experience.) The word 'substance' in Eliot's note is used in the philosophical sense of the single essence which underlies the variousness of phenomena. Curiously, Eliot once signed himself 'Tiresias' in a letter to the Italian scholar Mario Praz.

Eliot may have originally taken the idea of Tiresias from Pound, who introduced this classical figure in Cantos I and III, published first in 'Three Cantos' (1917) and again in *The Dial* (1921).

l. 218 I Tiresias: this rhetorical opening may have been suggested by Swinburne's 'Tireas', which opens 'I, Tiresias the prophet, seeing in Thebes/Much evil'. It is also found in Revelation xxii, 8: 'And I John saw these things, and heard them.'

l. 221: Eliot refers us to Fragment 149 by the Greek poetess Sappho (seventh century BC), a prayer to the Evening Star: 'Evening Star, that brings back all that the shining Dawn has sent far and wide, you bring back the sheep, the goat, and the child back to the mother.' The Fragment may have been drawn to his attention by Pound, who referred to it in Canto V, on which he was working in 1919.

This is combined with an allusion to 'Requiem' by R. L. Stevenson (1850–94): 'Home is the sailor, home from sea.'

The 'dory' mentioned in Eliot's note is a two-manned flat-bottomed rowing-boat, much used by fishermen on the New England coast, where Eliot spent boyhood holidays. The 'longshore' fisherman works along the coast.

l. 224: cf. Keats's *Ode to a Nightingale*: 'Charmed magic casements, opening on the foam/Of perilous seas in faery lands forlorn'.

l. 228 dugs: breasts, but usually of animals. So, as spoken by Tiresias, it carries overtones of self-disgust.

ll. 231–48: Kenner (1971) points to a sonnet 'diffused' through these lines, recording a patently physical sexual encounter, contrasting with the delicately erotic sonnet, religious in imagery, to which Romeo and Juliet first exchange kisses (I.v.95–112).

l. 231: not just spotty but 'red like a carbuncle' too, according to Dr Johnson's *Dictionary* (1755). Odd as the word sounds, it carries a distinguished literary heritage; and Eliot told an

inquirer that he intended the phrasing of 'the young man carbun-
cular' to echo 'that old man eloquent' in Milton's sonnet 'To the
Lady Margaret Ley'. Eliot plays off this solemn rhetoric against
the comic image of the spotty youth. Wyndham Lewis recalled
that at what he described as 'the first reading' of *The Waste
Land* in 1922, a friend of Vivien Eliot, with spots on his face,
identified himself as the 'young man carbuncular'.

l. 243 Bradford: a manufacturing town in northern England,
reputed to have produced a crop of millionaires, men who made
their fortunes in supplying woollen goods during the First World
War. *Nouveaux riches*, they adopted the silk top-hat, the head-
gear that identified the traditional gentry.

An American scholar has argued strongly for the claims of
oil-rich Bradford, Pennsylvania. But Mrs Eliot confirms Brad-
ford, England: 'my husband told me that his millionaire came
from Bradford, Yorkshire, and did business with Lloyd's.'

ll. 243–5: Eliot is referring to bisexual Tiresias (see note to lines
218–20) and to the story of Tiresias in *Oedipus Tyrannus* (*King
Oedipus*) by Sophocles. Tiresias, the blind seer, recognizes that
the curse on Thebes has been called down by the unknowingly
incestuous marriage between Oedipus and his mother Jocasta
and Oedipus's killing (again, unknowingly) of his father. Thebes
has been turned into a waste land, the people and the land
infertile.

l. 245: cf. 'Under covert of a wall ... Of Thebes', in John
Dryden's play *Oedipus* (1679). These lines are quoted in *John
Dryden* (1921) by Mark van Doren, where it is pointed out that
of all the accounts of Tiresias, Dryden's is the only one to
mention a sheltering wall. Eliot reviewed the book in June 1921.
Grover Smith (1983) claims *John Dryden* as a significant source
(pp. 63–4, 99–101, 126–7).

l. 246: this probably refers to Homer's account of Tiresias in
Hades, where he is consulted by Odysseus (*Odyssey* xi).

l. 253: Eliot refers us to his source, the song of Olivia in ch. 24 of
The Vicar of Wakefield, the novel by Oliver Goldsmith (1730–
74). Returning to the spot where she was seduced, she sings this
song: 'When lovely woman stoops to folly/And finds too late

that men betray/What charm can soothe her melancholy,/What art can wash her guilt away?/The only art her guilt to cover,/To hide her shame from every eye,/To give repentance to her lover/ And wring his bosom – is to die.'

l. 257: Eliot refers us to *The Tempest* I, ii, the words of Ferdinand remembering the music that calmed both the storm at sea and his own storm of grief for his father's supposed death (see note to line 192).

l. 258 Strand: a London street, leading eastwards towards the City of London. Hayward notes that 'London, past and present, is evoked here' and that the Earl of Leicester lived at Durham House (in the Strand), where in 1566, Queen Elizabeth dined with him; and that he later lived in Essex House, also in the Strand.

Queen Victoria Street: in the City of London, leading into Cornhill, where Eliot was then working. This is at the heart of the City of London, taken up in the following line.

l. 259 O City city: this is not a precise Biblical allusion. But both Old and New Testaments carry many 'City' passages, such as the Book of Lamentations, in which Jeremiah bemoans the sinfulness, decay and sorrow that has befallen Jerusalem, see i, 7: 'Jerusalem remembered in the days of her affliction and of her miseries all her pleasant things that she had in the days of old' – the very note of regret that Eliot sounds in the lines that follow here.

l. 260 Lower Thames Street: near the river at London Bridge.

l. 261: Hayward: 'The sound of the mandoline doubtless was one of the "buskers" or walking musicians who played inside and outside London bars.' Also a private joke: when he was working on this part of the poem, in November 1921, Eliot diverted himself by practising scales on the mandoline.

l. 263 fishmen: as on the original manuscript, not 'fishermen', as in some editions, since there would have been few fish, if any, at this point of the Thames, sweating as it does with 'Oil and tar' (lines 266–7). These 'fishmen' are workers from Billingsgate fish market, just along the road from the pub; lounging 'at noon' because they start early and now their day's work is done. As 'fishmen' (or fishman) is not normally found in English, it is understandable that an officious editor or printer should have made the 'fishermen' mis-correction.

ll. 263–5: the City church of St Magnus-the-Martyr (1671–6), on Lower Thames Street, next to London Bridge and designed by Sir Christopher Wren, is one of those mentioned in the report cited in Eliot's note and referred to in the Introduction, page 27.

Hayward: 'its interior is remarkable for the beauty of the slender ionic columns separating the nave from the aisles'.

l. 265: some commentators gloss 'Inexplicable' as unexplainable, beyond explanation; others, as inexpressible, unutterable. But Eliot may also be playing on a more specialized sense, to describe the interior design and decoration of the church as being highly intricate. Ionic is one of the three orders of classical architectural style. Eliot originally wrote 'Corinthian', later changing the word to the unusual form 'Ionian', a revision in the direction of historical accuracy (since the columns which dominate the church interior are in a composite Roman order, more richly decorated than strict Ionic and approaching Corinthian) and subtlety of phrasing. There are also some Corinthian columns. But these are in wood carving and much smaller. 'Gold' because this is used to pick out lines and designs on the stonework. This was how the recently redecorated church looked to Eliot. Prior to 1921, it was a gloomy interior, described by John Betjeman as 'dead and dusty'. An architectural account of the church is to be found in *The Buildings of England: London Volume One*, rev. ed. 1973, Nikolaus Pevsner and Bridget Cherry.

The full significance of the City churches for Eliot is brought out in his 'London Letter', *The Dial*, May 1921. Few visitors, he surmised, bother to visit these empty sanctuaries, 'but they give to the business quarter of London a beauty which its hideous banks and commercial houses have not quite defaced ... the least precious redeems some vulgar street'.

l. 266: Eliot notes that the Song to the Three Thames-daughters begins here and that in lines 292–306 they speak in turn, and he refers us to Wagner's opera *Die Götterdämmerung* (*The*

Twilight of the Gods) III, i. The beauty of the Rhine has been lost with the theft of the river's gold, but the Rhine-maidens are anticipating its immediate return. As in the Grail legend, the violation has brought down a curse. The Nymphes in Spenser's 'Prothalamion' are called 'Daughters of the Flood' (see note to lines 175–9).

ll. 266–78: the river is the River Thames at London. Some details of this scene are taken from the description of the river at the opening to Conrad's 'Heart of Darkness': 'the tanned sails of the barges drifting up with the tide seemed to stand still in red clusters of canvas'.

Also in 'Heart of Darkness': 'nothing is easier ... than to evoke the great spirit of the past upon the lower reaches of the Thames' – as in lines 279–91 treating Elizabeth and Leicester. Elizabeth, by name, and Leicester, as 'that great Lord', are referred to in stanzas 8 and 9 of Spenser's 'Prothalamion' (see note to lines 175–9).

l. 275 Greenwich reach: Hayward: 'The Thames at Greenwich, down-stream from London, curves sharply to flow round the Isle of Dogs (Parish of Poplar, a poor dockland district) to the North, and to the South passes the magnificent group of buildings known as Greenwich Hospital, one of Sir Christopher Wren's most remarkable masterpieces. The marked contrast in the poem between the two banks is certainly intentional.'

l. 277–8: the lament of the Rhine-maidens (see note to lines 292–303), much abbreviated, as though Eliot was recollecting the libretto rather than the score (bars 97–102 and continuing) which gives them a long and lingering wail.

l. 279: an accurate citation is provided in the Introduction, page 27. Eliot refers us (loosely) to the *History of England* vii, 349, by J. A. Froude, which quotes a letter, dated 30 June 1561, from Alvarez de Quadra (Bishop of Aquila) to King Philip of Spain, whose Ambassador he was to the English court. De Quadra is reporting his observation of Queen Elizabeth and Lord Robert Dudley, the Earl of Leicester, whom he reported to be Elizabeth's lover: 'In the afternoon we were in a barge, watching the games on the river. She was alone with the Lord Robert and

myself on the poop, when they began to talk nonsense, and went
so far that Lord Robert at last said, as I was on the spot there was
no reason why they should not be married if the Queen pleased.'
The river is the Thames and Elizabeth entertained Leicester at
Greenwich House, near Greenwich reach (see line 275).

Elizabeth and Leicester – the Virgin Queen and the political
courtier *par excellence* – are no lovers but astute power-players,
employing 'the love game' (mere flirtation) for their own ends,
knowing that everything de Quadra sees will go straight back to
Philip of Spain. Matthiessen comments: 'although mention of
Elizabeth and Leicester brings an illusion of glamour, closer
thought reveals that the stale pretence of their relationship left it
essentially as empty as that between the typist and the clerk'.

ll. 286–9: a wind in the right quarter for carrying the sound of
bells the four or five miles down-river from the Tower of London
to Greenwich.

l. 289: when Eliot was working in the City, the air was smoke-
ridden and the buildings grimy. But in *The Dial* (August 1921),
he remarked that the lucky coincidence of fine weather and a
coal strike revealed 'for the first time towers and steeples of an
uncontaminated white'. The historical reference is probably to
the ancillary towers of the Tower of London, built of white Caen
stone in 1078 by William the Conqueror.

l. 290–303: Eliot's version of the song (see note to line 266) – a
sort of phonetic wailing – comes nowhere in the opera. Some-
thing similar is, however, found in Wagner's *Das Rheingold*;
and the allusion may be deliberate, given the gold of lines 282–3.
And see Dadaism note to lines 399–401.

l. 293 Highbury: Hayward: 'Highbury (North East London), in
the suburb of Islington, is a gloomy suburb of the petite bour-
geoisie.'

Richmond, Kew: two riverside districts, on the Thames west
of London, both spots favoured by Queen Elizabeth. Eliot refers
us to Dante, *Purgatorio* v, 133, quoting 'Ricorditi di me, che son
la Pia;/Siena mi fe', disfecemi Maremma' ('Remember me, who
am La Pia; Siena made me, Maremma unmade me'). (This is the
translation used in Eliot's 'Dante', 1929.) La Pia, the Lady of

Siena (a town in central Italy), is addressing Dante in Purgatory, where she is among those who failed to repent their sins before death. She is said to have been murdered at Maremma, pushed out of a castle window on her husband's orders.

l. 296 Moorgate: Hayward comments that Moorgate is 'at the heart of the financial district of the City. The "Thames Daughter" who sang this "complainte" was probably a typist in one of the great buildings of this area. When T. S. Eliot worked in a City bank, he took the tube to Moorgate station.'

l. 300 Margate Sands: Eliot stayed at Cliftonville, Margate, a seaside resort (traditionally a favourite of cockney day-trippers from London) on the Thames estuary from 12 October to 12 November, on doctor's orders, recovering from stress. This was a last-minute arrangement, breaking his plans (dating from the spring) to visit Paris at this time to see Pound and Joyce. Eliot had been told by a 'nerve specialist', 'the most celebrated specialist in London' (as Eliot put it), to 'go straight away for three months complete rest and change'. At Margate, he assembled the first three parts of *The Waste Land*.

ll. 300–303: cf. Ariel's Song in *The Tempest* I, ii, leading Ferdinand to Miranda: 'Come unto these yellow sands,/And then take hands'. Line 48 quotes from Ariel's next song.

l. 301 connect: cf. 'Only connect!', the epigraph to E. M. Forster's *Howard's End* (1910), a key phrase in ch. 22 of the novel, where the words are repeated three times: 'Only connect the prose and the passion ... Live in fragments no longer.' Eliot admired Forster's writing and invited him to contribute to *The Criterion*.

l. 302 Nothing: carries a Shakespearian resonance from *King Lear*, the exchange of 'Nothings' between Cordelia and Lear in the opening scene.

ll. 304–5: cf. ' "They are simple people – and I want nothing, you know" ' (Conrad, 'Heart of Darkness').

l. 304 My people: like line 259, this phrase carries Biblical overtones, as in Psalm L, 7, when God calls 'Hear, O my people, and I will speak; O Israel, and I will testify against thee: I am God, even thy God.'

l. 307: Eliot refers us to his source, the *Confessions* (iii, 1) of St Augustine (345–430): 'to Carthage then I came, where a caul-dron of unholy loves sang all about mine ears'. St Augustine is here writing of the sensual temptations by which he was assailed in his youth. Williamson: 'With this great representative docu-ment of Western asceticism is placed its fellow from the East, the Fire Sermon whose import is implicit in the repetition of the single word "burning".'

Carthage, an ancient city on the North coast of Africa, near Tunis, was notorious as a city of lust and indulgence.

l. 308: the meticulous wording of Eliot's note (he refers to *Bud-dhism in Translation* (correctly, *Translations*), 1896) reflects the importance he attached to this Buddhist element in the poem. For Christ's Sermon on the Mount, in which he explained to the people the nature of the Kingdom of Heaven, see Matthew v–vii.

In the Fire Sermon the Buddha tells his followers that every-thing is on fire: 'forms are on fire ... impressions received by the eye are on fire; and whatever sensation, pleasant, unpleasant, or indifferent, originates in dependence on impressions received by the eye, that also is on fire.' 'And with what are these on fire? With the fire of passion, say I, with the fire of hatred, with the fire of infatuation; with birth, old age, death, sorrow, lament-ation, misery, grief, and despair are they on fire ...'

Stephenson explains that beyond the 'burning' comes a weariness with things of the world and bodily experience. At the end of the Sermon the minds of the monks 'became free from attachment to the world ...' In 1919, Eliot wrote 'The method – the analogy, and the repetition – is the same as that once used by a greater master of the sermon than either Donne or Andrewes or Latimer: it is the method of the Fire-Sermon preached by the Buddha.'

l. 309: Eliot refers us to his source, the *Confessions* of St Augustine: 'I entangle my steps with these outward beauties, but Thou pluckest me out, O Lord, Thou pluckest me out!' Eliot remarks on his purposeful use of the Buddha and the Christian saint, 'representatives of eastern and western asceticism', as the 'culmination' of this section of the poem.

The significance of St Augustine's words is brought out in God's challenge to Satan: 'is not this a brand plucked out of the fire?' (Zechariah iii, 2). The 'brand' is the High Priest Joshua, once a non-believer, now a follower of the Messiah.

Eliot may also have had in mind *The Story of My Heart* (1883), the autobiography of the naturalist Richard Jefferies (1848–87), which he read at Harvard. Chapters 5 and 6, telling of his experiences in the City of London, in particular the Thames at London Bridge, include a litany around 'burning': 'Burning . . . burning . . . the sun burned in the sky'; 'Burning on, the great sun stood in the sky . . . Burning on steadfast, and ever present as my thought'; 'Burning in the sky, I can never forget the sun' plus more 'burning/burned' passages. Here too Jefferies refers to classical and Sanskrit literature and concludes, just as Eliot seems to, that no cultural system can account for the life he sees around him.

In the Buddhist tradition the image of fire carries both the pain of worldly experience and the process of purification. As Kearns points out, 'The point of the sermon lay not only in its metaphysical doctrine, but in its practical effect as a kind of active, communal meditation', accompanied by an 'emptying of personal identity' and a freeing from outside 'attachment': 'The end of Part III enacts this "emptying" in the Buddhist sense in its very syntax and typography, which abolish, by a kind of counting-out process, first the object, "me", and then the subject, "Lord", to leave only the gerund "burning".'

IV DEATH BY WATER

Composition: Parts IV and V were written while Eliot was at Dr Vittoz's sanatorium in Lausanne from mid-November to late December 1921. Part IV is a close adaptation of the last seven lines of a French poem by Eliot, 'Dans le Restaurant', written May–June 1918:

Phlebas, le Phénicien, pendant quinze jours noyé,

Oubliait les cris des mouettes et la houle de Cornouaille,
Et les profits et les pertes, et la cargaison d'étain:
Un courant de sous-mer l'emporta très loin,
Le repassant aux étapes de sa vie antérieure.
Figurez-vous donc, c'était un sort pénible;
Cependant, ce fut jadis un bel homme, de haute taille.

(Phlebas the Phoenician, a fortnight drowned, forgot the cry of gulls and the swell of the Cornish seas, and the profit and the loss, and the cargo of tin. An undersea current carried him far, took him back through the ages of his past. Imagine it – a terrible end for a man once so handsome and tall.)

Images and ideas for 'Dans le Restaurant' and its new version in 'Death by Water' may have been fed in from the Hades section in *Ulysses*. For example, the two elements in line 316, 'Picked his bones in whispers', may have been inspired by an observation at the cemetery, 'Gentle sweet air blew around the bared heads in a whisper. Whisper'; and the sight of a rat crawling around a crypt sets off this play of imagination in Bloom:

> One of those chaps would make short work of a fellow. Pick the bones clean no matter who it was. Ordinary meat for them. A corpse is meat gone bad. Well and what's cheese? Corpse of milk. I read in that *Voyages in China* that the Chinese say a white man smells like a corpse. Cremation better. Priests dead against it. Devilling for the other firm. Wholesale burners and Dutch oven dealers. Time of the plague. Quicklime fever pits to eat them. Lethal chamber. Ashes to ashes. Or bury at sea. Where is that Parsee tower of silence? Eaten by birds. Earth, fire, water. Drowning they say is the pleasantest. See your whole life in a flash.

Indeed, Eliot's account of death by water catches Bloom's reflection that 'Drowning' is the 'pleasantest' way of death. A further sense of the relationship between *Ulysses* and this Part is conveyed in Pound's comment: 'Bloom on life, death, resurrection, immortality' (*The Future*, May 1918).

According to Jessie Weston, each year at Alexandria an effigy of the head of the god was thrown into the sea as a symbol of the death of the powers of nature. The head was carried by the current to Byblos. It was then retrieved and worshipped as a symbol of the god reborn. Another powerful tradition of a life-bringing death-by-water is contained in the Christian sacrament of baptism: 'Know ye not that so many of us as were baptized into Jesus Christ were baptized into his death? Therefore we are buried with him by baptism into death' (Romans vi, 3–4).

Frazer treats the Phoenicians in Part IV of *The Golden Bough*. In Book xiv of the *Odyssey*, Homer tells the story of a Phoenician trader who is drowned.

The name Phlebas, together with some of his attributes, may have been suggested to Eliot by Plato's major dialogue on pleasure, *Philebas*.

Hayward: 'Phlebas, the drowned god of the fertility cults. Also the merchant. Cf. *Ash-Wednesday*' (Section VI, lines 188–90 are quoted). In these associations, Hayward is taking up Eliot's own references to 'The Phoenician Sailor and the Merchant' and 'Death by Water' in his note to line 46 and in lines 47–8 of the poem itself. Hayward also said that this section belongs to an evocation of Eliot's own experiences of sailing off the New England coast (see page 35).

Title: in line 55 'Fear death by water' is one of the injunctions Madame Sosostris reads from her Tarot pack.

l. 312: 'Dans le Restaurant' in turn may have been suggested to Eliot by a passage in the *Life and Death of Jason* (1867) by William Morris (1834–96). In Book IV, the song of Orpheus to the Argonauts refers to a Phoenician sailor as a victim of the sea. At this time Eliot was familiar with the poem and quoted from Book IV in his essay 'Andrew Marvell' (1921).

ll. 315–16: these lines take up the image of 'sea-change' in Ariel's song in *The Tempest* (see note to line 48).

l. 317: cf. the description of Asia in *Prometheus Unbound* (1820) by Shelley: 'passed Age's icy caves,/And Manhood's dark and tossing waves,/And Youth's smooth ocean'.

l. 319: i.e. all mankind, a note frequently struck in the New Testament: 'Is he the God of the Jews only? is he not also of the Gentiles? Yes, of the Gentiles also' (Romans, iii, 29); 'For by one Spirit are we all baptized into one body, whether we be Jews or Gentiles' (1 Corinthians, xii, 13). The association with the Phoenician, and with 'the profit and loss' of line 314, may have come from the 'Nestor' episode in *Ulysses*: 'A merchant, Stephen said, is one who buys cheap and sells dear, jew or gentile, is he not?'

l. 320 wheel: nominally, the ship's directional wheel. But Eliot may also have had in mind the wheel of fate, cf. 'The wheel is come full circle' (*King Lear*, v, 3, 176); and beyond this the Buddhist concept of *karma*, the unvarying and inevitable process of cause and effect which constitutes our individual fate or destiny in our successive states of existence. That this Buddhist concept was in Eliot's mind we know from a cancelled section of *The Waste Land*, with the line (twice repeated) 'London, your people is bound upon the wheel!' cf. Laforgue: 'O vous qui m'écoutez, rentrez chacun chez vous' ('Oh you who hear me, all of you, return to your homes'), 'Simple Agonie'.

l. 321: cf. Dante, *Inferno* xxvi, Ulysses' exhortation to his companions to make the final voyage: 'Considerate la vostra semenza:/fatti non foste a vier come bruti,/ma per sequir virtute e conoscenza' (Consider your nature, you were not made to live like beasts, but to pursue virtue and knowledge). This was one of the episodes, Eliot said, that 'impress themselves most at the first reading'. In 'Dante' (1926), he discussed it at length, quoting these very lines. Eliot's translation is given here. In *Philebas*, Socrates comments on the condition of self-ignorance: 'people who think themselves taller and more handsome and physically finer ... than they really are'.

v   WHAT THE THUNDER SAID

In his Introduction to *The 'Pensées' of Pascal* (1931) Eliot wrote: 'it is a commonplace that some forms of illness are extremely favourable, not only to religious illumination, but to artistic and literary composition. A piece of writing meditated, apparently without progress, for months or years, may suddenly take shape and word; and in this state long passages may be produced which require little or no retouch.' Eliot said that he was here describing his own experience of writing Part V.

Eliot wrote to Bertrand Russell (15 October 1923) that he was glad Russell liked *The Waste Land*, 'and especially Part V. which in my opinion is not only the best part, but the only part that justifies the whole, at all'.

In 1948, Eliot said that following Pound's criticism of the draft, he made 'some revisions and chiefly a great many excisions' but that 'the final section of the poem remained exactly as I first wrote it.' At the top of this final section Pound noted 'OK from here on I think'.

Howarth: 'There are two outstanding passages in which he explicitly incorporates memories of his reading in Sanskrit literature: the final section of *The Waste Land* with its red glimpses of Indian landscape, its myth of the thunder god releasing the pent-up rivers, and its three interpretations of the thunder as three complementary commandments or keys to life; and the middle section of "The Dry Salvages" . . .' (p. 202).

Title: The 'Thunder' is the voice of God in his fearful aspect (see note to lines 399–401).

Eliot notes that in the first part, lines 322–94, three themes are employed. First, the story told in Luke xxiv, 13–31 of the two disciples travelling on the road to Emmaus (a village some distance from Jerusalem) on the day of Christ's resurrection. He joins them but remains unrecognized until he blesses their evening meal. Meanwhile, the disciples talk over the recent events – the trial, the crucifixion and so on – referred to in more detail in the notes to lines 322–65.

The second theme specified by Eliot is the approach to the Chapel Perilous. This is the final stage of the Grail quest. The Knight is tested by the illusion of nothingness. This theme is interwoven with the Emmaus story from lines 331–94.

The third theme is the decay of Eastern Europe in the modern world, referred to in detail in the notes to lines 366–76.

l. 322: John xviii reports the arrest of Christ in the garden of Gethsemane: Judas, the chief priests and 'a band of men and officers ... cometh thither with lanterns and torches and weapons'. Hayward: 'The association of Jesus in the Garden of Gethsemane with the old hanged god of the legend'.

ll. 322–8: these lines refer to the course of events from the betrayal and arrest of Christ, after the night of agonized prayer in the garden of Gethsemane, until the moment of his death.

ll. 322–30: Matthiessen:

> The opening of the final section in particular furnished an example of the way Eliot is portraying the equivalence of different experiences by linking together various myths [quotes lines 322–30]. Reminiscence here is not only of the final scenes in the life of Christ and of the gnawing bafflement of his disciples before his appearance at Emmaus. The vigil of silence and the agony of spiritual struggle are not limited to one garden; they belong to the perilous quest of Parsival or Galahad as well. The 'shouting and the crying' re-echo not only from the mob that thronged Jerusalem at the time of the Crucifixion, but also, as is made clearer in ensuing lines, from the 'hordes swarming over endless plains' in revolt in contemporary Russia. In the 'thunder of spring over distant mountains' there is likewise a hint of the vegetation myths, of the approaching rebirth of the parched dead land through the life-giving rain. Thus he who 'is now dead' is not Christ alone, but the slain Vegetation God; he is Adonis and Osiris and Orpheus. And with the line, 'We who were living are now dying,' the link is made back to the realm of death in life of the opening section, the realm which focuses all the elements of the poem and resounds through all its lines, the waste land of contemporary existence, likewise waiting for salvation, salvation that can come only through sacrifice, as is revealed in the final apocalyptic command reverberating through 'What the Thunder Said': 'Give, Sympathize, Control.'

Williamson: 'This specific identification of Jesus with the gods of the mystery cults is not merely a synthesis elicited from the modern study of comparative religion, but the key to the connection between the Fertility Ritual and the Grail Romance. And although the sect of early Christian Gnostics which emphasised this identification was discountenanced as heretical, their teaching enhances the greatness of the Crucified One.'

l. 326: Christ was taken under arrest to the palace of the High Priest where he was publicly interrogated, before being taken to Pilate, the Roman Governor, in the Hall of Judgement.

l. 327: at the death of Christ the earth shook (see Matthew xxvii, 51).

ll. 331–58: in August 1923, Eliot wrote to the novelist Ford Madox Ford: 'There are, I think, about 30 *good* lines in *The Waste Land*. Can you find them? The rest is ephemeral.' Apparently, Ford was unable to come up with the right answer, for two months later, Eliot answered his own question: 'As for the lines I mention, you need not scratch your head over them. They are the 29 lines of the water-dripping song in the last part.'

ll. 331–6: the Biblical counter-image behind these lines is probably that of God's instruction to Moses, to relieve the thirst of the Israelites, having led them through the desert: take 'thy rod ... and thou shalt smite the rock, and there shall come water out of it, that the people may drink' (Exodus xvii, 5–6).

ll. 344–5: Hayward: 'Asiatic faces (Tibetan). The scene moves from Palestine to Central Asia.'

l. 346 If ... rock: this is printed as two lines, but the line-numbering of the text, followed in these notes, counts the words as a single line.

l. 353 cicada: sometimes called the harvest-fly and possibly known to Eliot as the American locust; 'singing', in line 354, because the male makes a shrill chirping sound. Eliot would have encountered the word in the *Poems* of Alan Seeger which he reviewed in the *Egoist* (December, 1917).

l. 354: cf. 'the grass singing under the wind' in *Kim* (1901) by Rudyard Kipling, a story set in India, in the Himalayas, with a similar emphasis upon dust, dryness, water and the importance of the quest.

l. 357: Eliot's elaborate note needs to be read with more than a pinch of salt (see Introduction, pages 27–8). Eliot said that as a boy he 'had been an eager bird-watcher' and that he 'knew most of the resident and migratory birds of New England'. The 'water-dripping song' is in Chapman's *Handbook* and Eliot parodies Chapman's procedure in representing bird-song onomatopoeically, the 'customary note' of the hermit-thrush being 'a low chuck'. The idea of giving in full the comically long Latin name (with its scatological first element) for the hermit-thrush may have come to Eliot from Edward Lear's 'Nonsense Botany', in which Lear illustrated such flowers as the 'Manypeeplia upsidownia'.

The singing of the hermit-thrush is in 'When Lilacs Last' by Whitman (see note to line 2).

Some commentators remark that the repetition of the water sound follows the use in the Vedas of mantras and magic formulae to bring the rains.

l. 359: Hayward: 'The return of God'.

ll. 360–65: Eliot notes that these lines were stimulated by the account (in ch. 10 of *South*, 1919, by Sir Ernest Shackleton) of an Antarctic expedition on which the exhausted explorers were haunted by the delusion that there was one more person with them than could be counted. Eliot may also have had in mind Section 14 of 'When Lilacs Last' (see note to line 2), where Whitman contemplates death and the soldiers who died in the American Civil War: 'Then with the knowledge of death as walking one side of me,/And the thought of death close-walking the other side of me,/And I in the middle, as with companions...'

l. 363 wrapt: wrapped. Why is Eliot using an archaic or poetic form? If it is to effect an allusion, its source has yet to be identified.

ll. 366–76: behind these lines sound the Old Testament Lamentations of Jeremiah bewailing the fate of Jerusalem (line 374), characterized as a 'widow', a city brought low (as are the other

cities named in lines 374–5, all centres of culture or civilization),
its 'strong holds' 'brought' 'down to the ground' for its 'trans-
gressions', its people 'rejected by God' 'gone into captivity' or
'pursued' into 'the mountains' and 'the wilderness'. The echoes
from *South* continue. Shackleton writes of the mirages of the
polar landscape, casting the illusion of 'white and golden cities'
and floating above them, 'wavering violet and creamy lines of
still more remote berg and pack'. 'Everything wears an aspect of
unreality'. 'We seems to be drifting helplessly in a strange world
of unreality' (as in line 376).

l. 366: see the account of Jesus's crucifixion in Luke xxiii, 27–8:
'And there followed him a great company of people, and of
women, which also bewailed and lamented him. But Jesus turn-
ing unto them said, Daughters of Jerusalem, weep not for me,
but weep for yourselves, and for your children.'

l. 368 hooded: cf. Wordsworth's poem 'The French Army in
Russia, 1812–13': 'Humanity, delighting to behold/A fond
reflection of her own decay,/Hath painted Winter like a traveller
old,/Propped on a staff, and, through the sullen day,/In hooded
mantle, limping o'er the plain,/' (and see 'plains', line 369).

hordes: meaning an unorganized, as distinct from an
organized tribe, an anthropological/historical distinction which
Eliot was familiar with. Matthiessen remarks that they are 'in
revolt in contemporary Russia'.

ll. 368–9: Eliot refers us to *Blick ins Chaos* (1920) (*A Glimpse
into Chaos*) by Hermann Hesse (1872–1962), and quotes a
passage from the German text, referring to the Russian Revolu-
tion and other upheavals in Europe: 'Already half of Europe,
already at least half of Eastern Europe, on the way to Chaos,
drives drunkenly in spiritual frenzy along the edge of the abyss,
sings drunkenly, as though singing hymns, as Dmitri Karamazov
sang in *The Brothers Karamazov*. The offended bourgeois
laughs at the songs; the saint and the seer hear them with tears.'
In this specific context, the 'Murmur' (line 367) would be the
voice of Mother Russia lamenting the Bolshevik Revolution of
1917. *Blick ins Chaos* was published in Bern and Eliot came
across it while he was attending Dr Vittoz's clinic in December

1921. Subsequently, he wrote to Hesse, seeking a contribution for the first issue of *The Criterion*, for which he was the founding editor. Eliot told Hesse that in his book he found 'a seriousness the like of which has not yet occurred in England' (letter of 13 March 1922).

ll. 371–6: Bertrand Russell recalled that he had once told Eliot of a nightmare in which he had a vision of London as an unreal city, its inhabitants like hallucinations, its bridges collapsing, its buildings passing into a mist – all of which, Russell said, Eliot put into the poem.

l. 377: the hair was both a symbol of fertility and an object of sacrifice to the fertility gods. Hayward: 'One of the "Daughters of Music" (cf. *Ecclesiastes* 12)'; (see xii, 4: 'And the doors shall be shut in the streets, when the sound of the grinding is low, and he shall rise up at the voice of the bird, and all the daughters of musick shall be brought low').

ll. 377–84: Conrad Aiken reported having seen this passage long before *The Waste Land* (see Appendix, pages 258–9).

l. 378: Kipling may stand behind this image. In 'Rudyard Kipling', Eliot asks the reader to 'Compare the description of the agony in *In the Same Boat* . . .: "Suppose you were a violin string – vibrating – and someone put his finger on you" with the image of the "banjo string drawn tight" for the breaking wave in *The Finest Story in the World*.' Eliot is here discussing the further reaches of Kipling's imagination, in penetrating 'deeper and darker caverns' of experience: 'external events which have exact nightmare correspondence to some spiritual terror' (a remark which could attach to this part of *The Waste Land*).

ll. 379–84: medieval versions of the Grail legend tell of the horrors with which the Chapel Perilous was filled to test the Knight's courage, and of the nightmare visions, including bats with baby faces, that assail him on his approach. According to Eliot some of the details here were inspired by a painting of the school of Hieronymus Bosch, the fifteenth-century Dutch artist. Some of his best-known works are mysterious, often grotesque and horrifying visions of Hell, its devils, temptations and torments.

l. 381: despite Eliot's insistence that he had never read *Dracula*
(1897), the Gothic thriller by Bram Stoker, critics have persis-
ted in identifying that work as the source of the 'crawled head
downward' image. (Stoker has the imprisoned Jonathan Harker
see a man 'crawl down the castle wall' in the moonlight, 'face
down, with his cloak spreading out around him like great
wings', ch. 3.)

ll. 382–3: the church bells of London (cf. line 67); and accord-
ing to Jessie Weston a bell was rung at the Chapel Perilous to
signify that the Knight had survived his ordeal.

l. 384: in the language of the Old Testament the empty wells
and cisterns would signify the drying up of faith and the
worship of false gods, cf. the words of God to his prophet
Jeremiah: 'For my people have committed two evils; they have
forsaken me the fountain of living waters, and hewed them out
cisterns, broken cisterns, that can hold no water' (Jeremiah ii,
13); and the words of Solomon to his people: 'Drink waters out
of thine own cisterns, and running waters out of thine own
well' (Proverbs v, 15).

ll. 385–94: Hayward: 'See *From Ritual to Romance*: the jour-
ney to the Chapel Perilous, an initiation ceremony. The
macabre furnishings of the mythical chapel were designed to
test the courage of the initiate. The cemetery is associated with
the Chapel Perilous in some versions of the Grail Legend.'

l. 388: this is the Chapel Perilous of medieval legend, sur-
rounded by horrors to deter the seeker. Cf. 'Than Sir Galahad
com to a mountayne where he founde a chapell passynge olde,
and found therein nobody, for all was desolate. And there he
... harde a voyce ...' (Malory, *Morte d'Arthur*).

Williamson: 'At the goal of the Quest all the forces of evil
gather to make one last effort to deter the Knight.'

l. 391 rooftree: the main ridge beam in the construction of the
roof.

ll. 391–2: Eliot may be drawing upon two traditions of the
crowing cock. Firstly, the story told in the Gospels: that as
Christ foretold, his disciple Peter denied acquaintance with him
when Christ was under arrest before his trial; this happened

three times, and when a cock had crowed twice, Peter broke down in tears at his own shame and cowardice. In this context, the crowing of the cock is seen as part of the ritual preceding the death of Christ, salvation for mankind.

The second tradition is that of the cock as 'trumpet of the morn', a signal to ghosts and spirits that as darkness fades they must return to their homes, as the Ghost of Hamlet's father disappears at its call in *Hamlet* 1, i. The chapel is now empty of nightmares and apparitions.

l. 392: this is the French rendering of the English 'Cock-a-doodle-do'. Eliot referred to the French cock-crow in *The Athenaeum*, 25 July 1919, writing about the verse-play *Chanticleer* (1910) by Edmond Rostand. It was a hit in Paris in the winter of 1910 and came to Boston in 1911.

l. 395 Ganga: the familiar and affectionate name used in India for the sacred River Ganges. Hayward: 'A reference to ancient aryan fertility beliefs'.

l. 397 Himavant: a holy mountain in the Himalaya range.

ll. 399–401: Eliot refers us to the source of the Indian legend of the Thunder in the sacred book *Brihadaranyaka-Upanishad* v, 2. Three groups – gods, men, demons – approach the creator Prajapti and each in turn asks him to speak. To each group he answers 'DA'. Each group interprets this reply differently: the gods understand it as Damyata, 'Control yourselves'; the men, as Datta, 'Give alms'; the demons, as Dayadhvam, 'Be compassionate'. Eliot's departure from the order of the legend, in placing Damyata last, has given rise to much interpretative speculation. (In his notes, Eliot incorrectly cites v, 1, a mistake that probably occurred when he was referring to Deussen's edition (1921), which he mentions: on Deussen page 489, the reference he provides, the running head erroneously gives v, 1. Incidentally, the 'translation' is into German.)

Eliot departs from the order of the legend. Eliot's attention was first drawn to these words in May 1912 by Charles Lanman, his Sanskrit teacher at Harvard, who gave him a copy of Phansikar's 1906 edition of *The Twenty-Eight Upanishads* in Sanskrit. Among the passages listed for Eliot's attention, Lanman assisted his pupil with the explanation 'Da-da-da = *damyata datta da-yadhvam*'.

('Two years spent in the study of Sanskrit under Charles Lanman, and a year in the mazes of Patanjali's metaphysics under the guidance of James Woods, left me in a state of enlightened mystification' (*After Strange Gods*, 1934).)

But the repeated 'DA' also carried a contemporary reference spelt out by Sami Rosenstock (1896–1963), writing under the name of Tristan Tzara, in the manifesto of Dadaism, an anarchistic, anti-bourgeois, anti-art movement which set out to scandalize and subvert. It originated in the 1916 and faded about 1922. Its message is caught in such lines as 'DADA; abolition de la mémoire:/DADA; abolition de l'archéologie:/ DADA; abolition des prophètes/'. Eliot knew Tzara's work and reviewed his *Vingt-cinq poèmes* (1918) in the *Egoist* in July 1919; and would have heard much of the Dadaists from Pound and Joyce who mixed with them in Paris. The *Dada Almanac*, published in Berlin in June 1920, contained phonetic wailings not unlike the wailings Eliot gives to the Rhine Maidens in lines 290–1.

l. 401 Datta: give.

l. 403 surrender: cf. Eliot's use of the word in describing the experience of the poet, i.e. himself, in 'Tradition and the Individual Talent', 1917: 'What happens is a continual surrender of himself as he is at the moment to something which is more valuable. The progress of an artist is a continual self-sacrifice, a continual extinction of personality.'

l. 407: Eliot refers us to *The White Devil* v, vi, by John Webster, the speech of Flamineo warning against the inconstancy of women:

> ... they'll re-marry

> Ere the worm pierce your winding-sheet, ere the spider
> Make a thin curtain for your epitaphs.

l. 408 seals: to close a room or document case etc., to be opened by a lawyer only at the owner's death.

l. 411 Dayadhvam: Eliot translates this as 'sympathize'; other translations, including Stephenson, prefer 'be compassionate'.

Eliot refers us to Dante, *Inferno* xxxiii, 46, quoting the words of Ugolino della Gherardesca, a thirteenth-century Italian noble, as he recalls his imprisonment in a tower with his two sons and two grandsons, where they starved to death: 'ed io sentii chiavar l'uscio di sotto/all'orribile torre' ('and below I heard the door of the horrible tower being nailed up'). Dante's 'chiavar' means this, rather than 'locked', from 'chiave'. But lines 411–14 use this erroneous translation, which Eliot may have followed from the parallel Italian–English text in the Temple Classics edition of Dante, which he often used. This would explain the reference to the 'key' turning 'once only', for the notes in the Temple Classics edition explain that 'the keys of the prison' (rather than the tower) 'were thrown into the river and the captives left to starve'.

Beyond these references may also stand an echo of the nursery rhyme 'London Bridge is falling down' (see note to line 426). Later in the song come the lines 'Take the key and lock her up ... my fair lady'.

In his 'London Letter' in *The Dial*, June 1921, Eliot refers to this passage from Dante, likening his own working days at a City office of Lloyds Bank to Ugolino's imprisonment. In 'Dante' (1929), Eliot cited this episode as being 'among those which impress themselves most at a first reading'.

Eliot also quotes from *Appearance and Reality* (1893) by the philosopher F. H. Bradley (1846–1924), which he purchased at Harvard in June 1913. His Harvard doctoral thesis (completed April 1916) was published as *Knowledge and Experience in the Philosophy of F. H. Bradley*, in 1964. Eliot went to Merton College, Oxford, Bradley's college, in October 1914, to study the philosophy of Bradley under Harold Joachim. By then Bradley was a recluse at Merton, rarely seen, and Eliot never met him. But the impact of Bradley's writing remained with him and his 'personality as manifested in his works – affected me profoundly' ('To Criticize the Critic', 1961).

l. 416 Coriolanus: the title-hero of Shakespeare's play, 'broken' because pride and selfish integrity brought about his death to the shouts of the mob he despised.

l. 418 Damyata: Eliot translates this as 'control'; other translations prefer 'restrain/subdue yourselves' (Stephenson, the latter). Eliot's translation may reflect the theories of Dr Vittoz (see note to line 180): that his patients could be trained to control their brain waves, not in order to stifle suppressed memories and desires but to achieve a balanced freedom from them. The way to this control was through 'paroles, nettes et lumineuses' (words, simple and luminous), healing through their very clarity, and the three ideas he gave Eliot to work with were 'calm', 'energy' and 'control' (*Treatment of Neurasthenia by Means of Brain Control*, French 1913, English 1921). This prescription may also be reflected in Eliot's use of DA at lines 400, 410 and 417.

ll. 418–19: Eliot was himself 'expert' with a sailboat from childhood holidays on the Massachusetts or Maine coast, see Howarth (pages 114–23), and later, when he was also an oarsman at Harvard and afterwards at Oxford.

ll. 418–22: Hayward: 'In his youth, T. S. Eliot was a keen and experienced yachtsman: the biographical fact is not unconnected with the sea imagery he likes to use.' Matthiessen: 'how often a sudden release of the spirit is expressed through sea-imagery which, with its exact notation of gulls and granite rocks and the details of sailing, seems always to spring from his own boyhood experience of the New England coast'.

l. 422 controlling hands: immediately, as in line 419, of the boatsman. But a practical aspect of Dr Vittoz's treatment was placing his hand on his patient's forehead, a gesture both diagnostic and therapeutic, a step on the way to control (see note to line 418).

ll. 423–33: the medley of languages displayed in these final lines is a stylistic device commonly found in late Latin poetry, e.g. Ausonius c. AD 310–90 and employed by Dante himself, whose cantos are varied with Latin and Provençal verses and Hebraic rhymes.

l. 424: Eliot refers us to the chapter on the Fisher King in *From Ritual to Romance*.

l. 425: cf. the words of the prophet Isaiah to King Hezekiah, a sick man whose kingdom lies waste under Assyrian conquest: 'Thus saith the Lord, Set thine house in order: for thou shalt die; and not live' (Isaiah xxxviii, 1). Hezekiah prays for mercy and God answers him, promising to deliver his country from the Assyrians and granting him a further fifteen years of life.

Compare also, 'Set my love in order, O thou who lovest me' ('Ordina quest' amore O tu che m' ami'), a prayer of the Italian poet Jacopone da Todi (1230–1306), placed by Dante at the head of the *Purgatorio*.

A further layer of allusion may be to the *Antigone* by Sophocles. In the play's opening scene, Ismene expresses her fears for Antigone's life. Antigone rejects these and adds scornfully: 'Set your own life in order.'

l. 426: 'London Bridge is falling down, falling down,/London Bridge is falling down,/My fair lady', the refrain of a nursery rhyme. Until 1750 London's only bridge over the Thames, by the eighteenth century it was in a ruinous state and the nursery rhyme declares how it can be set right.

l. 427: Eliot refers us to his source in Dante, *Purgatorio* xxvi, 145–8: ' "Ara vos prec, per aquella valor/que vos guida al som de l'escalina,/sovegna vos a temps de ma dolor."/Poi s'ascose nel foco che gli affina' (' "And so I pray you, by that Virtue which leads you to the topmost of the stair – be mindful in due time of my pain." Then dived he back into the fire which refines them.'). As he climbs the Mount of Purgatory, Dante is addressed by Arnaut Daniel, the twelfth-century troubadour, speaking here in his native Provençal, now suffering the punishment of the lustful in the cleansing fires of Purgatory: Eliot commented on these lines: 'The souls in purgatory suffer because they wish to suffer, for purgation . . . in their suffering is hope' ('Dante').

Williamson: 'Historically, in introducing Arnaut Daniel, greatest of the Troubadours, friend of Richard Cœur de Lion, it evokes that magnificent Provençal civilisation and the singers who bequeathed the Romance legends to the modern world. Symbolically it gives, at last, a Christian interpretation to the element of fire, and at the same time epitomises the poem by reminding us of the penitential suffering of the Lustful.'

This passage from Dante was important to Eliot and he quoted from it on several occasions. His third volume of poetry, published in London in 1920, was entitled *Ara Vos Prec*. In October 1919, Eliot wrote to John Rodker, the publisher: 'It has just occurred to me that the title ARA VUS PREC would do. For it is non-committal about the newness of the contents, and unintelligible to most people'. VUS should be VOS. But not knowing Provençal, Eliot was misled by a misprint in the Italian edition of Dante which he had carried with him since 1911. When the mistake was noticed there was only time to correct the book's label. 'Sovegna vos' occurs in 'Exequy', a discarded poem in *The Waste Land* manuscript, which became Section IV of *Ash-Wednesday*; and Section III originally appeared as a separate poem with the title 'Som de L'Escalina'.

Eliot's attention may have been drawn to these lines by Pound, who noted that 'Arnaut speaks, not in Italian, but in his own tongue; an honour paid to no one else in the *Commedia*' and wrote of the 'superb verses of Arnaut Daniel in his Provençal tongue'.

l. 428 Quando . . . chelidon: 'When shall I be like the swallow?', a line which Eliot refers to its source in an anonymous pre-Christian Latin poem, 'Pervigilium Veneris' ('The Vigil of Venus'). In the Latin original the line continues 'and my voice no longer silent'. Having told the story of Tereus and Philomela in the preceding stanza, the poet laments that his song is unheard and asks when the spring will return to give it voice, like the swallow: his classical analogy is with the violation of Philomela and the song of the bird, the story of Tereus and Philomela having been retold in the preceding stanza. Williamson: The poem is 'the link between classical and mediæval literature, "the earliest known poem belonging in spirit to the literature of the Middle Ages." Its continual refrain "To-morrow shall be love for the loveless and for the lover to-morrow shall be love," the atmosphere of mysterious excitement which preludes the re-awakening of life, makes it of all spring songs the loveliest.' Eliot also refers to the story of Procne (see note to line 99), touched upon at the close of the hymn, who was turned into a swallow. Eliot may have first come across 'Pervigilium Veneris' in *The Spirit of Romance* by Ezra Pound (1910), where Pound explains the poem for the feast of Venus Genetrix, surviving in May Day, in celebration of summer and fertility.

'O Swallow, Swallow' opens the Prince's song in Section IV of Tennyson's *The Princess*. He appeals to the bird to be the messenger of his love.

l. 429: 'The Prince of Aquitaine, of the ruined tower', a line which Eliot refers to its source in the sonnet 'El Desdichado' ('The Disinherited') by Gérard de Nerval (1808–55). The poet speaks of himself as the disinherited prince, heir to the tradition of the French troubadour poets who were associated with the castles of Aquitaine in south-western France. The 'most sinister card' (Williamson) in the Tarot pack is the tower struck by lightning, symbolizing a lost tradition.

l. 430: the words from Dante in line 427 are a case in point, since they come from a short passage, one of 'these fragments', to which Eliot returned many times; 'fragments' may come from *Howard's End* (see note to line 301).

l. 431: Eliot refers us to his source in *The Spanish Tragedy* by Thomas Kyd (?1557–95), subtitled *Hieronymo is Mad Againe*. Hieronymo is driven mad by the murder of his son. Asked to write a court entertainment he replies, 'Why then Ile fit you!' ('fit', oblige), a double-edged agreement, for in doing so he arranges that his son's murderers are themselves killed in his little play, which was made up from fragments of poetry in 'sundry languages' (exactly as here in *The Waste Land*).

l. 432: Give. Sympathize. Control.

l. 433: Eliot's note tells us that this Sanskrit word so repeated signifies 'The peace which passeth understanding', and serves as the formal ending to the Upanishads, the poetic dialogues and commentary which follow the Vedas, the ancient Hindu scriptures. Eliot's interpretation derives from the words of Paul to the early Christians: 'And the Peace of God, which passeth all understanding, shall keep your hearts and minds through Christ Jesus' (Philippians iv, 7).

In Hindu tradition, 'shantih' is a mantra (a word of great religious and psychological power), a closing prayer employed as a formal ending to Hindu Scriptures and religious rites, and a Sanskrit term for the goal of meditative truth.

Kearns (1987) points out that in the formal ending to an Upanishad, the full wording is 'Om shantih shantih shantih'. The syllable 'Om' conveys 'the logos' or word of revealed truth. In this light, Eliot ends the poem declining to strike a conclusive note of total and final illumination (see Kearns, pages 228–9).

THE HOLLOW MEN

On *The Waste Land:* 'I find this poem as far behind me as Prufrock now: my present ideas are very different.'
Letter to Gilbert Seldes, Managing Editor of *The Dial*,
12 November 1922

'As for "The Waste Land", that is a thing of the past so far as I am concerned and I am now feeling toward a new form and style.'
Letter to Richard Aldington, 15 November 1922

'. . . the work I have in mind, which is more ambitious than anything I have ever done yet'.
Letter to John Quinn, 26 April 1923

The Hollow Men

Origins date from 1921.
For full details of composition and publication (1925)
see Appendix

Prefatory Note: As late as October 1925, a month before the poem's publication, Eliot had grave doubts about 'The Hollow Men', writing anxiously to Pound: 'Is it too bad to print? If not, can anything be done to it? Can it be cleaned up in any way? I feel I want something of about this length (I–V) to end the volume [*Poems 1909–1925*] as post-Waste.' But there is no record that Pound answered Eliot's uncertainties about the poem. 'The Hollow Men' is an extraordinarily difficult poem to annotate. Its language and imagery are disarmingly simple. There are no problems of historical reference or translation. But it is highly allusive, allusive almost to the point of obscurity, and the identification of Eliot's sources cannot be made without some degree of interpretation. My method has been to consider one by one the four major sources or areas of reference, and then to provide an item-by-item identification and interpretative commentary in the detailed notes to the poem.

The four major sources or areas of reference are the historical account of the Gunpowder Plot; the assassination of Caesar as presented in Shakespeare's *Julius Caesar*; the three parts of Dante's *Divina Commedia*; and Conrad's story, 'Heart of Darkness' (see Introduction, page 22).

In addition, Robert Crawford suggests that Eliot also draws upon the kingdoms of the dead in anthropologists' accounts of West African wandering spirits. 'The landscape is very much a country of the mind, drawing on many of the ideas found in the pages of the anthropologists whom he catalogued as folklore experts in 1924.' These I have not detailed and readers should consult *The Savage and the City in the Work of T. S. Eliot.*

Eliot's use of the first two sources is straightforward, and particular points of reference are detailed in the notes of the poem. At this stage, however, it may be useful for readers to have general facts before them.

(*i*) *The Gunpowder Plot:* In the Epigraph, Eliot refers to the present-day celebration of the plot's failure; and he closes the poem with another, more tragic allusion.

The plot had its origin in the resentment of the English Catholics under James I. After the death of Elizabeth, they had hoped for a more liberal regime. But, instead, they found themselves under the threat of suppression. A group of extremist Catholics was brought together by Robert Catesby, a brave man with a dominating personality. Their plan was to seize power by killing King James and all his ministers at the State Opening of Parliament, thus leaving the country without a king and government.

But Francis Tresham, one of the conspirators, inadvertently betrayed the plot when he wrote to his brother-in-law, Lord Monteagle, warning him to keep away from the Houses of Parliament on the day of the State Opening, 5 November 1605. Monteagle informed the Lord Chancellor of this warning, and in turn the King was told. Catesby got wind of this but decided nevertheless to attempt the mass assassination. Thus, on the night of 4 November, Guy Fawkes was arrested in the cellars of the House of Lords where he stood guard over nearly two tons of gunpowder. After days of torture he broke down and revealed the names of the other conspirators. Those who had not fled the country were executed.

The circumstances of the plot seem to be referred to in line 10 ('dry cellar'), line 16 ('violent souls'), and in the operation of the Shadow in Section V, whatever it is in human affairs or within human beings that prevents fulfilment and success. The failure of the plot sounds clearly in the final lines, a macabre-comic chorus. Indeed the world of the King, his Lords and his Commons did not end with an explosive 'bang' that day, whereas for

Guy Fawkes and his fellow conspirators there was the 'whimper' of betrayal and death.

(*ii*) *Julius Caesar:* This, like the Gunpowder Plot, is a conspiracy of men who resort to violence and who are blinded by their cause. Shakespeare's play is alluded to indirectly in the poem's title and specifically in lines 72–90 (Brutus's soliloquy is quoted fully in the notes). Brutus, a leading Roman citizen, is approached by Cassius who is gathering a group to assassinate Julius Caesar, the head of the Roman state. Cassius is motivated by ambition, envy and personal malice. But he persuades Brutus that Caesar is himself an ambitious tyrant who will destroy the tradition of Roman republicanism.

Cassius plays upon Brutus's vanity, his self-importance as the head of a leading Roman family, famed for its championing of the public good, and upon his sense of personal honour, which blinds him to the possibility that the plot is evil. In terms of the dramatic action, Brutus, the man who would lay claim to the highest motives, is shown up as the hollowest of them all, the most deceived and self-deceiving.

(*iii*) Eliot's use of Dante is more indirect and much more important. The three books of the *Divina Commedia* compose an allegorical dream-vision in which Dante himself is conducted through the hell of punishment and of lost souls (in the *Inferno*), the Purgatory of suffering towards redemption (*Purgatorio*), and Paradise, a higher, perfect world of beauty, light and music (*Paradiso*). Putting the matter very arbitrarily, it can be said that the condition of the hollow men is that of the lost souls in Hell. They are the inhabitants of 'death's dream kingdom' gathered at their last meeting-place beside a 'tumid river' (lines 57–60). In Dante, this corresponds to the scene beside the River Acheron (*Inferno* iii) where the spirits of the damned wait to be ferried across to Hell. There is also another group, which seems to correspond more precisely to Eliot's hollow men. These are the shades which have never been spiritually alive, never experienced good or evil, having lived narrowly for themselves. They are rejected by both Heaven and Hell, and are condemned to stay eternally by the river. Eliot seems to be referring to their condition in lines 11–12. In *The Waste Land* (see note to line 63) Eliot associates them with the crowds crossing London Bridge. In this respect, the hollow men are not narrowly the conspirators; they are all mankind (an interpretation supported by Eliot's use of 'Heart of Darkness').

Eliot refers to a second kingdom, 'death's other kingdom'. If 'death's dream kingdom' is related to the fallen, sinful world of the *Inferno* and *Purgatorio*, this second kingdom is related to the *Paradiso*, and the aspect of this perfect world which Dante glimpses in the closing books of the *Purgatorio*. Here we read of Dante's arrival at the summit of the Mount of Purgatory, at the top of which is the Earthly Paradise, the Garden of Eden where he meets Beatrice, formerly his beloved on earth, now a figure of blessedness, spiritual beauty, and revelation. Section II of Eliot's poem is concerned with the courage and self-scrutiny which are needed even to catch a glimpse of that vision.

There is a third kingdom, 'death's twilight kingdom' (lines 38, 65). This seems to be a transitional stage between the 'dream' and the 'other' kingdoms. In Dante, it corresponds with the poet's progress towards Beatrice in the Earthly Paradise. He has first to pass through the River Lethe, which flows in shadow, then through the River Eunoë; the first river washes away all memory of sin, the second restores the memory of righteousness. It is a stage at which Dante is humbled and shamed by the memory of his sins and unfaithfulness to Beatrice. In the scheme of Eliot's poem, this 'twilight kingdom' is the condition in which man has to face the truth about himself and life, as Kurtz does (see note *iv*, below). The fourth kingdom is the kingdom of God, which can be spoken of only in broken words (see line 77).

(*iv*) It is quite impossible to convey in summary notes the complexity of the relationship between 'The Hollow Men' and 'Heart of Darkness'. Next to Dante, Conrad's story is possibly the most important single literary experience in Eliot's poetry from 'Prufrock' onwards. He once described it as an outstanding instance of the literary evocation of evil, a tale 'of horror'. Conrad's story is full of hollow men – empty of faith, of personality, of moral strength, of humanity. Marlow tells of his

journey into a nightmare kingdom of death, the heart of dark-
ness in the forests of the Congo, where he feels himself to have
'stepped into the gloomy circle of some Inferno' and sees around
him figures 'in all the attitudes of pain, abandonment, and
despair' (a scene which could come straight from Dante). There
is a constant and emphatic imagery of eyes (matched in Eliot), of
whispers, of shades and shadows, of twilight greyness, of form-
lessness and impalpability, of inertia, paralysis, unfulfilment and
aimlessness. In a native village beside a river, an 'infernal
stream', at the heart of the jungle Marlow comes to Kurtz, 'the
hollow sham', the man who came from Europe full of an empty,
rhetorical idealism, which collapsed under the force of the sav-
age, barbaric 'darkness'. Yet there is a civilized 'darkness' too.
Speaking of London, Marlow remarks, 'And this also has been
one of the dark places of the earth.'

Conrad's affirmation is that all men are hollow, all fated to
endure the condition that Eliot figures so allusively in 'The
Hollow Men', and all fated to be blind to their condition; all,
excepting those few, and Kurtz himself is one, who are able,
eventually, to glimpse and face this horrifying truth. This is the
force of Eliot's 'We' in the opening lines; it is the 'We' of all
mankind, save for 'Those who have crossed/With direct eyes'
(lines 13–14) like Kurtz, whose dying 'stare' remains to haunt
Marlow: 'his stare ... wide enough to embrace the whole uni-
verse, piercing enough to penetrate all the hearts that beat in the
darkness ... that wide and immense stare embracing, condemn-
ing, loathing all the universe'. This is the stare with which Kurtz
meets the vision of ultimate truth, in a 'supreme moment of
complete knowledge', greeting it with his final cry – 'The horror!
The horror!', the words that signified so much to Eliot that he
originally planned to use them as the epigraph to *The Waste
Land*. Hugh Kenner (1959) comments that in life Kurtz was 'a
person of unfailing eloquence. His words, like those in an Eliot
poem, "were common everyday words – the familiar vague
sounds exchanged on every working day of life. But what of
that? They had behind them, to my mind, the terrific suggest-
iveness of words heard in dreams".'

Readers should be aware that the significance of these areas of reference has been put in question by Ronald Bush. His argument runs thus: that Eliot 'layered the narratives of Guy Fawkes and *Heart of Darkness* over his drama of salvation', seeking 'to overlay the formal and ethical shapeliness of a clear narrative pattern onto material he was afraid had too little shape' – exactly as he had done with *The Waste Land*, with the late addition of its 'controlling myth (the Grail legend)' and the poem's myth title. 'And once again', in 'The Hollow Men', 'he sent readers hunting through history and literature to reconstruct the skeletons of stories that at best suggestively mirror the action that is *there* on the page.' Professor Bush's conclusions are based upon an analysis of the process by which Eliot selected and arranged the sections which came to make up the final version of the poem. Interested readers should consult chapter 6 of Bush (1984).

Epigraph to section: the words are spoken by a servant in 'Heart of Darkness', reporting Kurtz's death. Howarth: 'meaning that the figure of evil has disappeared from life, and thus all values have disappeared'.

Title: In answer to a scholarly suggestion Eliot explained in 1935 that he had made up this title by combining that of 'The Hollow Land', a romance by William Morris (1834–96), with 'The Broken Men', a poem by Kipling. This sounds suspiciously like one of Possum's false trails. But on an early typescript of Section III Eliot jotted down these two titles, with the names of their authors, alongside 'The Hollow Men'; and he said in 1959 that he 'could never have thought of this title but for Kipling's poem'.

The phrase 'hollow men' occurs in *Julius Caesar* IV, ii, where it is used by Brutus when he learns that his former ally and fellow conspirator Cassius is now behaving in a less friendly way towards him. Brutus reflects:

> But hollow men, like horses hot at hand,
> Make gallant show and promise of their mettle;
> But when they should endure the bloody spur,
> They fall their crests, and, like deceitful jades,
> Sink in the trial.

'Heart of Darkness' also contributes to the poem's title. Kurtz is described as a 'hollow sham', 'hollow at the core', and the theme of hollowness runs through the story.

Composition: Eliot gave the original typescript of Part I – then a poem on its own – to Lady Ottoline Morrell prior to 1922. Although it was then untitled, it carried the epigraph 'A penny for the Old Guy' and may well have been written around Guy Fawkes Day in November 1921, when Eliot was working on *The Waste Land.* At that time, local detail was entering his poetry, visibly in 'Margate Sands', line 300, written while Eliot was actually staying at Margate; and the Guy Fawkes epigraph may share that same biographical proximity. (For another possible connection with *The Waste Land*, see page 162, note to line 126.)

During this period Eliot was on sick-leave from the bank, having suffered a breakdown. The experience of being a 'hollow' man, in particular of suffering the depressive condition described in lines 11–12, accords closely with what is known of Eliot's own psychological affliction, 'aboulie'.

The poet and critic Herbert Read – with whom (from 1917 onwards) Eliot discussed the drafts and proofs of his poetry, inviting Read's criticism – described 'The Hollow Men' as 'the most significant of Eliot's poems, from a confessional point of view'.

Such an acutely autobiographical poem, on the painful subject of his own illness, would have made a pointedly meaningful gift to Ottoline Morrell, since it was she who had suggested to Eliot that he consult the Lausanne psychotherapist, Dr Vittoz, as he did in mid-November 1921 (see pages 166–7, note to line 182). Eliot treated Lady Ottoline as a confidante and had previously sought her opinion of his poetry in manuscript.

Eliot never explained what the hollow men of the poem signified to him. But the paradoxical force of their negative lifelessness is hinted at in his remarks on the minor comic characters in the plays of Marston: 'And yet something is conveyed, after a time, by the very emptiness and irrelevance of this empty and irrelevant gabble; there is a kind of significant lifelessness in this shadow-show' ('John Marston', 1934). Further light is thrown upon the hollow men, particularly those speaking lines 15–18, in Eliot's essay on 'Baudelaire' (1930):

> So far as we are human, what we do must be either evil or good; so far as we do evil or good, we are human; and it is better, in a paradoxical way, to do evil than to do nothing: at least, we exist. It is true to say that the glory of man is his capacity for salvation; it is also true to say that his glory is his capacity for damnation. The worst that can be said of most of our malefactors, from statesmen to thieves, is that they are not men enough to be damned.

Epigraph to poem: A version (Eliot's mishearing, or deliberate in the addition of 'Old'?) of the children's cry – 'A penny for the Guy?' when begging money to buy fireworks for the celebration of Guy Fawkes Day, November the Fifth. The Guy itself is a home-made effigy, made of old clothes stuffed with paper, straw and old rags. It has to be on display if the children are to collect any money. On the evening of Guy Fawkes Day the Guy is burned on top of a bonfire, while fireworks are let off.

ll. 1–4: the reference to 'the hollow ... stuffed men' combines allusions to Guy Fawkes, to *Julius Caesar* and to 'Heart of Darkness'. The first two sources are explained in the notes above. In 'Heart of Darkness', Marlow sees himself as a 'pretence' and sees other people in similar terms: one man a 'papier-mâché Mephistopheles', another a 'harlequin', 'in motley, as though he had absconded from a troupe of mimes ...

His very existence was improbable, inexplicable'; and Kurtz, the central figure, is seen as a 'hollow sham'.

l. 2: according to Valerie Eliot, the poet had in mind the marionette in Stravinsky's *Petrouchka* (1911).

l. 4 straw: straw-stuffed effigies are associated with harvest rituals celebrating the death of the fertility god or Fisher King (see *The Golden Bough*).

l. 6: 'whispers' are an instrument of fate in 'Heart of Darkness': it was the wilderness, the jungle that Kurtz exploited, as a trader, that 'had whispered to him things about himself which he did not know . . . and the whisper had proved irresistibly fascinating. It echoed loudly within him because he was hollow at the core.' And the whisper of Kurtz's last words sounds a year after his death, when Marlow is begged to repeat them by Kurtz's fiancée.

ll. 11–12: this condition of unfulfilment is matched in the spiritual state of the shades described in the *Inferno* iii (see above, pages 204–5) and in 'Heart of Darkness' by the members of the Eldorado Exploring Expedition: 'Their talk was . . . the talk of sordid buccaneers: it was reckless without hardihood, greedy without audacity, and cruel without courage . . . To tear treasure out of the bowels of the land was their desire, with no more moral purpose at the back of it than there is in burglars breaking into a safe.'

A second passage in 'Heart of Darkness' seems also to have been in Eliot's mind, Marlow's account of his fight against death:

> It is the most unexciting contest you can imagine. It takes place in an impalpable greyness, with nothing underfoot, with nothing around, without spectators, without clamour, without glory . . . in a sickly atmosphere of tepid scepticism, without much belief in your own right, and still less in that of your adversary . . . a vision of greyness without form,

from which he emerges to find life 'like a passage through some inconceivable world that had no hope in it and no desire'. This experience is also relevant to lines 72–90.

ll. 13–15: the hollow men are reflecting on those who have passed from their world (or moral and spiritual state), 'death's dream kingdom' to 'death's other kingdom', a higher world, for those who are capable of looking with 'direct eyes'.

In the last cantos of the *Purgatorio* we read how Dante crosses from the Purgatorial world, passing through the two rivers (referred to above, see pages 204–5) to approach the higher world of Beatrice. Until he is freed from shame and sin, he is unable to meet her gaze. In 'Heart of Darkness' Kurtz passes from life to death with a fixed 'stare' (referred to above, see page 206).

l. 15 Remember: cf. the opening lines of the Guy Fawkes Day begging song: 'Please to remember/The Fifth of November,/ Gunpowder, treason and plot'.

l. 19: Beatrice tells Dante how she came to him in his dreams to call him back to the path of virtue.

ll. 19–22: the image of 'eyes' that cannot be faced is important both in Dante and Conrad.

In Dante, the significant eyes are those of Beatrice: Dante is shamed and reproved by them; they recall to him his love for Beatrice during her life on earth and his subsequent infidelity; their divine beauty has a piercing brightness; and at their meeting in the Earthly Paradise he is like a small child, unable to meet her gaze.

In 'Heart of Darkness', Marlow encounters the force of eyes and glances wherever he goes – reproachful, fearful, intense; and the glance of Kurtz's fiancée, 'guileless, profound, confident, and trustful', yet, ironically, in all its qualities, dangerous, as it drives him into a 'hollowness' (see note to line 37–8).

ll. 20–22: these lines can be interpreted as meaning that the eyes of line 19 are not encountered in 'death's dream kingdom'; in that kingdom, instead of eyes one sees the images of lines 23–8.

ll. 23–8: this seems to be a vision of 'death's other kingdom', glimpsed from afar and brokenly. The details seem to originate in *Purgatorio* xxvii-xxix, in the description of the Earthly Paradise: the birds and the breeze are singing in the trees, there is the sound of chanting and a light glows under the boughs. The star, here a 'fading star', is used by Dante as an image of God or of Mary.

l. 23: the graveyard memorial for a premature death.

l. 24: The Sacred Dance by W. O. E. Oesterley, reviewed by Eliot on its publication in 1923, mentions a savage who was awe-struck when 'a tree, swayed by the wind, moved'.

ll. 31–2: the notion of 'deliberate disguises' is important in 'Heart of Darkness' (see note to lines 1–4).

In the following lines, this idea relates to 'The Propitiation of Vermin by Farmers', in *The Golden Bough*, where Frazer discusses dressing in animal skins for ritual purposes and making divine effigies from straw, the origins of the scarecrow and the country custom of hanging up the bodies of vermin or birds that damage the crops in order to scare off any other of the same species.

Eliot's imagery may also derive from *From Ritual to Romance* (pp. 92–5), where Jessie Weston discusses the 'staves' of the Morris Dancers, whose members include the 'Clown' in 'a costume of animal skin, or cap of skin'. She sees the Morris Dancers as a survival of early Vegetation ceremonies.

l. 35: in the *Inferno* the spirits are blown by the wind. In 'Heart of Darkness' there is a similar image in Marlow's account of a native who was killed only because he left open a shutter that should have been kept closed: 'He had no restraint, no restraint – just like Kurtz – a tree swayed by the wind.'

ll. 37–8: there is such a feared meeting in both Dante and Conrad. In *Purgatorio* xxx, Dante at last meets Beatrice. It is a fearful meeting for him, since it faces him with a divine beauty which reminds him of all his sins and failings. The River Lethe, which he has to cross to meet her, flows in 'everlasting shadow' (xxvii, 31–3).

In 'Heart of Darkness', there is the meeting between Marlow and Kurtz's fiancée, where he hands her the letters and picture left by the dead man. It is literally a 'twilight' meeting (see the quotation in the note to lines 61–2). Dusk is falling. This symbolizes Marlow's moral twilight. He had intended to tell her the bitter truth about Kurtz's life and death. But under the compulsion of her utter trust in Kurtz's goodness, he covers up, and falsifies the man's last words, reporting that he died with her name on his lips. This white lie is Marlow's own shameful submission to the 'heart of darkness', a darkness, so Conrad's story declares, whose twilight shadow is cast across the world.

ll. 39–44: these lines probably belong to the material discarded from *The Waste Land*. The 'stone images' (line 41) and the 'broken stone' (line 51) are connected with idolatrous worship (see *The Waste Land*, note to line 22); cf. 'the worship of stones is a degradation of a higher form of worship', F. B. Jevons, *An Introduction to the History of Religion* (1896), a work which Eliot studied in detail at Harvard.

l. 47: cf. Marlow's words, 'We live, as we dream – alone.'

ll. 49–51: in 'Heart of Darkness' this corresponds to the pathetic trust that Kurtz's fiancée has in his nobility, his truth, his love for her. In point of fact, Kurtz sank from faithfulness to her to the worship of pagan forces.

ll. 50–51: cf. 'Lips only sing when they cannot kiss', 'Art' by James Thomson (1834–82) (Eliot cited this line in *The Use of Poetry*; and Juliet's comment on religious people: 'lips that they must use in prayer' rather than in kissing (*Romeo and Juliet* I, v), an orthodox view, echoing the prayer from Psalm 51: 'Lord, open thou my lips; and my mouth shall shew forth thy praise', words which form part of the Anglican liturgy; and found in *Purgatorio* xxiii, ii: 'Labia mea domine'.

ll. 52–6: the hollow valley is a province of 'death's dream kingdom'. In 'Heart of Darkness' it is the excavated valley, full of derelict objects and hopeless native labourers, that Marlow comes to on his way to the interior of the Congo: 'it seemed to me I had stepped into the gloomy circle of some Inferno ... Black shapes crouched, lay, sat between the trees, leaning against the trunks, clinging to the earth, half coming out, half effaced within the dim light, in all the attitudes of pain, abandonment, and despair.'

l. 56: Eliot may be playing upon the contrast with the whole and highly effective 'new jaw bone of an ass' (Judges xv, 15–19) with which Samson slew a thousand Philistines.

Remembering that this poem began from the residue of *The Waste Land*, we have also to take account of an anthropological layer of reference to *The Golden Bough*, in particular to the two volumes treating *Adonis, Attis, Osiris* (which Eliot said he had 'used especially' in *The Waste Land*). In volume 2, we read of an African people, the Baganda, who believe that the spirit of the dead clings to the jaw-bone; the jaw-bone of their king is fashioned into an effigy and placed in a temple.

ll. 57–60: the association of these lines with Dante, and with the conspiracy situation in the Gunpowder Plot and *Julius Caesar*, is discussed on pages 203 ff. The motif of conspiracy and plotting is also dominant in 'Heart of Darkness'. At the head office of the trading company on whose behalf he travels to the Congo, Marlow promised not to disclose any trade secrets: 'It was just as though I had been let into some conspiracy.' Later, at one of the trading stations, he finds the twenty or so white employees passing the time 'by backbiting and intriguing against each other in a foolish kind of way. There was an air of plotting about that station, but nothing came of it, of course. It was as unreal as everything else . . .' And Kurtz is described as a man who 'would have been a splendid leader of an extreme party'.

l. 60 tumid river: in Dante, this corresponds with the River Acheron flowing around Hell. In 'Heart of Darkness', Marlow recollects the river up which he sailed to the 'heart of darkness' in the Congo as 'the infernal stream, the stream of darkness'. 'Tumid' usually means unhealthily swollen.

ll. 61–2: in Dante, the reappearance of the eyes signifies Dante's meeting with Beatrice, a moment of 'hope' (line 66). In 'Heart of Darkness', Marlow's meeting with Kurtz's fiancée is invested by Conrad with a tone and feeling which is momentous and spiritually significant, with a similar emphasis upon a woman's eyes: 'The room seemed to have grown darker, as if all the sad light of the cloudy evening had taken refuge on her forehead. This fair hair, this pale visage, this pure brow, seemed surrounded by an ashy halo from which the dark eyes looked out at me. Their glance was guileless, profound, confident, and trustful.'

ll. 63–4: in the *Paradiso* xxx, the rose is Dante's vision of the highest level of Heaven, in which Mary and the saints form the

many petals (Italian 'foglia' is petal). In xxxi, the 'single star' is
Dante's vision of God. In xxxii and elsewhere, the 'rose' is
Dante's vision of Mary. Eliot is not trying to establish an exact
correspondence; but the general terms of reference are clear.

l. 65: the significance of 'death's twilight kingdom', as a condi-
tion of spiritual power, seems to be brought out in the passage
from Conrad quoted for lines 61–2; although we should not
ignore the bitter irony: the purity and strength of the fiancée's
virtue is the very thing that drives Marlow to his own 'hol-
lowness' in lying to her.

ll. 68–71: a parody of the children's song-game, with its origin in
a fertility dance: 'Here we go round the mulberry bush,/The
mulberry bush, the mulberry bush,/Here we go round the mul-
berry bush/On a cold and frosty morning.'

The 'prickly pear' is a cactus that flourishes in the desert.

Five a.m. is the traditional hour of Christ's resurrection.

There seems to be an anthropological explanation for Eliot's
use of a children's song here. In a 1923 review, he quoted from
Frazer: 'how often with the decay of old faiths the serious rites
and pageants ... [primitive religious dances] have degenerated
into the sports of children'. In this context, the old fertility dance
has become a modern *in*fertility dance.

ll.72–90: cf.

> Between the acting of a dreadful thing
> And the first motion, all the interim is
> Like a phantasma, or a hideous dream:
> The genius and the mortal instruments
> Are then in council; and the state of man,
> Like to a little kingdom, suffers then
> The nature of an insurrection.
>
>   (*Julius Caesar* II, i, see note ii, page 204)

But there may have been a more immediate allusion. Eliot
contributed an Introduction to Valéry's *Le Serpent* (1924), in
which he quoted several separate lines from 'Le Cimetière marin'
('The Cemetery by the Sea') ('to my mind one of Valéry's finest
poems') including 'Entre le vide et l'évènement pur' ('Between

the void and its pure issue'). He commented that this line 'suggests so strongly though accidentally Brutus's "Between the acting ..."', continuing the quotation to 'a hideous dream'.

Eliot regarded 'Le Cimetière marin' as an expression of Valéry's melancholy scepticism which he attributed to 'the agony of creation ... the mind constantly mocks and dissuades, and urges that the creative activity is vain'. The three central stanzas of Section V are very close to Valéry in their phrasal structure and emphatic rhythm; also in the theme contrasting 'idea' and 'reality'.

l. 76: Eliot accepted the suggestion, made in 1935, that this line was derived by him from 'Non sum qualis eram' ('I am not now as once I was'), the best-known poem by Ernest Dowson (1867–1900), in which there are the phrases 'Then fell thy shadow' and 'Then falls thy shadow'. Eliot commented that 'This derivation had not occurred to my mind, but I believe it to be correct, because the lines ... have always run in my head.' Shadows, literal and figurative, always symbolic, are cast throughout 'Heart of Darkness'. The boat on which Marlow travels upstream to Kurtz moves in shadows, once into a fog, through which is heard a cry 'as of infinite desolation' which turns into a shrieking but whose source and meaning they never know; men die with shadows across their faces; 'pain' is a shadow, feeding on Kurtz like a beast 'satiated and calm'; Marlow's knowledge of Kurtz's involvement with savage rites and ceremonies is a 'nightmare' secret, a 'shadow' which he keeps to himself, to deal with alone; Kurtz himself, drawn to these rites, appears to Marlow as a 'Shadow – that wandering and tormented thing'; and at the very end of the story, after Marlow's tale is finished, as the unnamed narrator describes the scene before him, we see that it is a shadow over all mankind: 'the tranquil waterway leading to the uttermost ends of the earth flowed sombre under an overcast sky – seemed to lead into the heart of an immense darkness'.

l. 77: 'For thine is the kingdom, the power, and the glory', from the Lord's Prayer, words which originally occur in 1 Chronicles xxix, 11, and in 15 there is a reference to the 'shadow': 'our days on the earth are as a shadow'.

l. 83: the fact that Eliot italicized these words suggests that we are to regard them as a quotation (as with lines 77 and 91); they occur in *An Outcast of the Islands* (1896) by Joseph Conrad, where a broken man is to be punished by being kept alive rather than killed.

ll. 86–7: in terms of Aristotelian philosophy, matter has only potency until form gives it existence.

ll. 88–9: in Platonic philosophy, the essence is the inapprehensible ideal, which finds material expression in its descent to the lower, material plane of reality.

ll. 95–8: a parody, combining a line from the children's song 'Here we go round the mulberry bush' – 'This is the way we clap our hands' – with a distortion of the phrase 'world without end' from the prayer: 'Glory be to the Father, and to the Son, and to the Holy Ghost, as it was in the beginning, is now, and ever shall be, world without end. Amen.'

l. 98: Not with a bang: cf. 'it all ends, not with a bang, not with some casual incident, but in sustained reflection . . .', in George Santayana's account of the *Divine Comedy*, in *Three Philosophical Poets* (1910). Santayana (1863–1952) was lecturing on Dante at Harvard during Eliot's student days.

whimper: Eliot may have had in mind two lines from 'Danny Deever' (1892) by Rudyard Kipling, a poem he knew by heart at the age of ten. Deever, a British soldier, is executed in front of his regiment for killing another comrade:

> 'What's that that whimpers over'ead?' said Files-on-Parade,
> 'It's Danny's soul that's passin' now,' the Colour-Sergeant said.

Eliot referred to this 'remarkable' poem in his Introduction to *A Choice of Kipling's Verse* (1941), quoting these lines and commenting that Kipling's choice of the word 'whimpers' is 'exactly right'.

The 'whimper' may also combine an allusive reference to Dante, suggesting the cry of a baby, the new-born leaving one world to enter another, just as at the end of the *Purgatorio* Dante is leaving the sinful, fallen world in the presence of Beatrice in

the Earthly Paradise. In xxx, 43ff. and xxxi, 64ff, he stands
before her, shamed and conscience-stricken, repentant and
silent, like a child before a stern mother.

ASH-WEDNESDAY

The first edition was dedicated 'To My Wife', Vivien Eliot, reunited to the poet after their separation of 1926–8. These words were removed by Eliot in the later 1930s when he prepared *Collected Poems 1909–35* (1936).

'between the usual subjects of poetry and 'devotional' verse there is a very important field still very unexplored by modern poets – the experience of man in search of God, and trying to explain to himself his intenser human feelings in terms of the divine goal. I have tried to do something of that in "Ash Wednesday".'

Letter to his confessor, William Force Stead, 9 August 1930

'If a poem of mine entitled *Ash-Wednesday* ever goes into a second edition, I have thought of prefixing to it the lines of Byron from *Don Juan*:

> Some have accused me of a strange design
> Against the creed and morals of this land,
> And trace it in this poem, every line.
> I don't pretend that I quite understand
> My own meaning when I would be *very* fine;
> But the fact is that I have nothing planned
> Except perhaps to be a moment merry . . .'

The Use of Poetry and the Use of Criticism (1933)

The Byron passage was important to Eliot. Twenty years earlier, he had quoted the last four lines in a letter to Conrad Aiken (16 November 1914), explaining that although he was dissatisfied with the poetry he was then writing, he felt that 'such matters' were beyond his control and had 'no dependence upon our planning', comments which relate appropriately to Part V of *The Waste Land*.

Ash-Wednesday

For details of composition and publication (1930) see Appendix

In June 1930, Eliot wrote to a close friend that this poem 'is really a first attempt at a sketchy application of the *Vita Nuova* to modern life', explaining that the *VN* was of great help in the struggle to discipline feeling.

In 'Dante' (1929), in the section given to the *Vita Nuova*, Eliot wrote: '*Acceptance* is more important than anything that can be called belief. There is almost a definite moment of acceptance at which the New Life begins.'

The other presence is that of Lancelot Andrewes (see page 71, note to 'Gerontion', lines 18–19), whose Ash-Wednesday Sermons, both in their language and their method, seem to play an important part in Eliot's diction and handling of language in this poem. We know from 'Lancelot Andrewes', which appeared in September 1926, how closely Eliot had studied the sermons and some of his comments there help us to see the connections between Andrewes's prose and his own poetry: 'Andrewes takes a word and derives the world from it; squeezing and squeezing the word until it yields a full juice of meaning which we should never have supposed any word to possess.' This exegetical method can be seen, for example, in the Sermon for Ash Wednesday 1619, with its attention to the single word 'turn', taken from Joel ii, 12–13, the text for the Sermon: 'Therefore also now, saith the Lord, turn ye even to me with all your heart, and with fasting and with weeping, and with mourning: And rend your heart, and not your garments, and turn unto the Lord your God: for he is gracious and merciful, slow to anger, and of great kindness, and repenteth him of the evil.' The text for the

1602 Ash-Wednesday Sermon is Jeremiah viii, 4–7, which opens 'Moreover thou shalt say unto Him, Thus saith the Lord; Shall they fall, and not arise? shall he turn away, and not return?'

These texts help us to understand the religious context in which Eliot searches the idea of turning again; and in 'Lancelot Andrewes' Eliot points to aspects of the preacher's method that are directly reflected in the accretive style of his poem: 'And then, after this succession of short sentences – no one is more master of the short sentence than Andrewes – in which the effort is to find the exact meaning and make that meaning live, he slightly but sufficiently alters the rhythm in proceeding more at large ... this extraordinary prose, which appears to repeat, to stand still, but is nevertheless proceeding in the most deliberate manner ...'

Beyond the religious context, we know that the poem also has a biographical reference back into Eliot's childhood. On a manuscript of 'Because I do not hope to turn again', Eliot wrote the title 'All aboard for Natchez, Cairo and St Louis'. This is the title of a popular song; and St Louis, Missouri, was his birthplace and childhood home. I. A. Richards recalled that in the early 1920s this was a favourite record of Eliot's.

'Tom's autobiography' was the comment of another close friend having read the poem on its completion.

J. P. Riquelme finds specific evocations of Wordsworth's 'Immortality' Ode throughout the poem.

Prefatory Note: Readers may find it helpful to refer to the Appendix which gives details of the indicative Dantean titles which Eliot originally provided for the sections of the poem.

Title: In the Christian calendar this is the first day of Lent, a period of forty days' penance and fasting to commemorate the forty days Christ spent fasting in the wilderness, where he was tempted by Satan and triumphed over him (see Matthew iv, 1–11; Luke iv, 1–13). It is a period when the Christian repents for his past sins and turns away from the world towards God.

In the Church ceremony for Ash Wednesday, the priest marks

the foreheads of the laity with ashes in the form of a cross, saying these words: 'Remember, O man, that thou art dust, and unto dust thou shalt return', a version of God's words to Adam (Genesis iii, 19).

I

When Part I was first published, as a separate poem, it carried 'Perch'io Non Spero' as its title (see note to line 1).

l. 1: a translation of 'Perch'io non spero di tornar già mai', the opening line of 'Ballata, written in exile at Saranza' by the Provençal poet Guido Cavalcanti (1255–1300). (A line Eliot may first have seen in Pound's Introduction to *Cavalcanti Poems* (1912, revised 1920), where he described it as 'that matchless and poignant ballad' (no. xi) or in 'The Serious Artist', an essay by Ezra Pound which appeared in *The Egoist* in 1913, where Pound describes it as possessing a 'poignancy' of 'phrasing', 'that passionate simplicity which is beyond the precisions of the intellect'.) The poet is heart-broken and exiled, expecting never again to see his lady and thinking of death. And besides this theme of worldly loss and resignation, there is also the spiritual act of turning to God, seen in its penitential aspect, as in Joel ii, 12–13: '... turn ye even to me with all your heart, and with fasting, and with weeping, and with mourning: And rend your heart, and not your garments, and turn unto the Lord your God.' And again in Lamentations v, 21: 'Turn thou us unto thee, O Lord, and we shall be turned.' This was a favourite text of Lancelot Andrewes; another was Jeremiah 8, in which there recurs the idea of turning and returning. Andrewes's sermon for Ash Wednesday 1609 touched on this wording ('turn away', 'turn again'); and he preached another 'turn' and 'return' sermon on Ash Wednesday 1619. All these would have been familiar to Eliot through his study of Andrewes.

l. 4: a version of a line from Shakespeare's Sonnet xxix, 'Desiring this man's art and that man's scope.' The poet describes his troubled state of mind when he is alone and outcast, a bitter, discontented sadness which is transformed to joy at the thought of his beloved.

l. 6 agèd eagle: from Psalm ciii, 5, 'so that thy youth is renewed like the eagle's'. In medieval Christian allegory the eagle in its old age is able to renew its youth in the light of the sun and in the waters of a fountain; this signifies an access of spiritual life through a turning to God and through baptism.

In the *Inferno* iv, the unbaptized poets of the classical world (Homer *et alii*) are described as 'those lords of highest song, which, like an eagle, soars above the rest'.

l. 10 infirm glory: Eliot may have picked up this striking phrase from *Night and Day* (1919), a novel by Virginia Woolf, where it refers, half ironically, to the state of those, now elderly, who were once famous: 'all the poets, all the novelists, all the beautiful women and distinguished men'. Also cf. Shakespeare's memorable line, 'The uncertain glory of an April day' (*Two Gentlemen of Verona*, I, iii).

ll. 14–15: this is the Biblical imagery for spiritual sustenance.

l. 26: cf. Psalm vi, 2: 'Have mercy upon me, O Lord', one of the Psalms for Ash Wednesday, an entreaty which sounds throughout the Bible.

l. 32: cf. 'When thou hast done, thou hast not done', lines 5 and 11 of 'A Hymne to God the Father' by Donne. The allusion to Donne's double-punning line is significant, since the 'Hymne', like this part of *Ash-Wednesday* (beginning at line 26), is a prayer to God pleading for forgiveness for sin. Moreover, Section I of *Ash-Wednesday*, with its slow and studied word-to-word movement, is a further reminder of the special verbal emphasis of Donne's 'Hymne'.

l. 33: Eliot seems to be touching on the Biblical story of the eviction from the Garden of Eden and the original sin then laid on mankind for the 'transgression' of Adam and Eve (see Genesis iii). In any event, 'the judgement', as it is phrased here, echoes 'the judgment is God's' (Deuteronomy i, 17).

l. 35 vans: can simply mean wings. But in the light of the next two lines, Eliot seems to be using the word in a more specialized sense, for a type of fan formerly used in winnowing to separate the chaff from the grain of the wheat.

l. 39: cf. Psalm xlvi, 10: 'Be still and know that I am God.' Also cf. 'all the troubles of man come from his not knowing how to sit still', i.e. his inability to achieve tranquillity, in the *Pensées* of Blaise Pascal (1623–62), a work that Eliot knew well, providing the Introduction to an edition in 1931. According to the Spanish mystic, St John of the Cross (1542–91), this was the passive way for the soul to prepare for God.

ll. 40–41: the close of the Roman Catholic prayer, the 'Hail Mary', asking the Blessed Virgin Mary to intercede and give spiritual aid on behalf of sinful mankind.

II

On its first publication, as a separate poem, in *Saturday Review of Literature* (10 December 1927), this section was entitled 'Salutation'. One reference is to the salutation Beatrice makes to Dante in the *Vita Nuova* iii: the poet is greeted by the Lady 'with a salutation of such virtue that I thought then to see the world of blessedness', and he is deeply affected in the three principal sources of life: the heart, the brain and the liver. When the poet's equilibrium is upset, his confidence shattered, the energies of growth are released. This is linked with the story of the dry bones in Ezekiel (see note to lines 43–7) and to the account by Revd Nathaniel Wanley (1634–80) of the bizarre notion of the partial resurrection of legs and arms on Good Friday (see lines 45–7), quoted by Eliot in *The Times Literary Supplement*, 31 December 1925.

l. 42 Lady: distinguished in lines 49 and 51 from the Virgin Mary, this may be Dante's Beatrice, an attendant of Mary in Paradise and his helper on the path to salvation.

leopards: leopards are named as God's agents of destruction in Jeremiah v, 6 and Hosea xiii, 7. The entire line is much speculated about. When, in 1929, Eliot was asked what it meant, he simply answered 'I mean' and then recited the line without comment. Some light is thrown on this statement by a passage in 'Dante', where Eliot writes that he does 'not recommend, in first reading the first canto of the *Inferno*, worrying about the identity of the Leopard, the Lion, or the She-Wolf. It is really better, at the start, not to know or care what they do mean.' In point of fact, in the *Inferno*, the Leopard can be understood as worldly pleasure.

However, at a public reading of the poem in 1932, Eliot said that the three leopards are 'the world, the flesh and the devil' (see The Litany in *The Book of Common Prayer*: '*Good Lord, deliver us*. From fornication, and all other dreadful sin; and from all the deceits of the world, the flesh and the devil'). T. S. Matthews suggests, *Great Tom* (1973), that in telling this to his audience of women college students, Eliot was up to one of his sly jokes.

juniper-tree: cf. the Biblical story of Elijah. Jezebel threatened him with death. He went into the wilderness and under the shade of a juniper-tree prayed that God would take his life. Instead, God sent him food (see 1 Kings xix, 1–8).

Also see the fairy-tale by the brothers Grimm, 'The Juniper-Tree', which tells how the bones of a murdered child are brought back to life under the tree. Eliot performs a uniting of bones in line 92.

ll. 42–50: see headnote, page 225.

ll. 46–7: cf. the vision of Ezekiel, in which God predicts the spiritual regeneration of the Israelites, his chosen people: 'And he said unto me, Son of man, can these bones live? ... he said unto me, Prophesy upon these bones and say unto them, O ye dry bones, hear the voice of the Lord' (see Ezekiel xxxvii, 1–10).

l. 48 chirping: according to the French anthropologist Lucien Lévy-Bruhl (1857–1939), whose works Eliot studied, primitive man understood the chirping of crickets as an appeal for rain.

l. 52 dissembled: a rare meaning is dismembered; but also carrying a hint of its more common sense of feigned or pretended.

l. 53: in direct contradiction to the Biblical suggestion that we offer alms in order to be remembered favourably by God, as in Acts x, 4: 'Thy prayers and thine alms are come up for a memorial before God.' Shakespeare plays with this idea in *Troilus and Cressida* III, iii: 'Time hath, my lord, a wallet at his back,/Wherein he puts alms for oblivion.' There is a destructive force to the Shakespearian 'oblivion' in *Richard III*, III, vii: 'In the swallowing gulf/Of dark forgetfulness and deep oblivion'. All this seems to be gathered in Eliot's use of the word here.

l. 54: the gourd does have a fruit. But Eliot seems to be alluding to Jonah iv, 6–8: God, having planted a gourd to protect Jonah from the sun, sets a worm to attack and destroy it, leaving him at the mercy of the sun and the wind. This image of fruitlessness and erosion accords with the earlier statements in this and the previous line, for the 'desert', an image of sterility, has no offspring or 'posterity' and 'deeds' proffered to 'oblivion' are lost to history and human record.

ll. 62–4: cf. Ezekiel xxxvii, 9, in the valley of bones: 'Prophesy unto the wind, prophesy, son of man, and say to the wind, Thus saith the Lord God; Come from the four winds, O breath, and breathe upon those slain, that they may live.'

l. 64 bones sang: see Psalm li (sung on Ash Wednesday): 'Make me to hear joy and gladness; that the bones which thou has broken may rejoice.' Also line 89.

l. 65 the burden of the grasshopper: this is a reference to Ecclesiastes xii, 5: 'the grasshopper shall be a burden' (a plague) which combines punningly, with 'burden', the refrain or chorus of a song or message.

ll. 66–88: these lines imitate the Roman Catholic Litany to the Blessed Virgin Mary, a form of solemn public supplication. The sequence of contraries that Eliot constructs here may be inspired by the essential paradox contained in the idea of Mary as Virgin and Mother.

l. 69 Rose: Mary is referred to as a rose in the Litany. And see St Bernard's prayer to the Virgin: 'The Rose wherein the Word divine made itself flesh'.

ll. 72: these contrary qualities are seen in Isaiah, xxxv, 1: 'The wilderness and the solitary place shall be glad for them; and the desert shall rejoice, and blossom as the rose.'

l. 77: according to William Empson, with whom Eliot discussed his poetry, Eliot was referring here to his own experience of marriage.

l. 91: cf. Genesis iii, 8: in the Garden of Eden, having eaten the apple, Adam and Eve 'heard the voice of the Lord God walking in the garden in the cool of the day' and hid themselves from him.

ll. 93–5: cf. 'This is the land which ye shall divide by lot unto the tribes of Israel for inheritance, and these are their portions, saith the Lord God' (Ezekiel xlviii, 29), God's instructions to the prophet in his vision. In xxxvii, 15–22, God instructs Ezekiel to unite the divided tribes of Joseph and Judah.

III

This section was first published as a separate poem in *Commerce*, Autumn 1929, entitled 'Som de L'Escalina' (see note to *The Waste Land*, line 427).

Matthiessen: 'each turning of the stair presents a distinct stage of spiritual struggle' and he connects Eliot's 'stair' with the three main divisions of Dante's hill of Purgatory:

> At the foot of the hill were those whose sin had been the greatest, who had been guilty of love distorted, those who had loved evil things instead of God, those whose self-absorbed pride had shut them off from Him. Higher up were those whose love of God had been defective; higher still, the least gravely sinful, whose who had loved excessively things which should take only a secondary place in the affections, among them the sensual and lustful. (A hint of the correspondence between these particular qualities of excess and Eliot's third stair is underscored by the image describing the window itself 'bellied like the fig's fruit'.) Such a reminder that the stages of the soul which Eliot is depicting correspond also to a completely developed pattern of philosophic and religious thought would remove the experience from anything purely

personal, and would thus enable it to possess a more universal significance.

ll. 96, 102, 107: Eliot may be recalling the 'turns' that occur in Lancelot Andrewes's sermon 'Of Repentance', preached on Ash Wednesday 1619: two 'turns' are necessary to conversion, one that looks forward to God, one that looks back on to one's own past sins.

The 'turns' may also be related to the Dantean staircase image carried in the title (see headnote, page 228).

l. 99: cf. Dante's experience as he awakens in the Third Circle of the Inferno, in the place for the Gluttonous, amongst their punishments the ground that gives off a foul smell ('pute la terra che questo riceve', vi, 12).

ll. 100–101: cf. Eliot's description of the demon faced by Pascal, 'the demon of doubt which is inseparable from the spirit of belief', in his Introduction to *Pensées*.

l. 108 slotted window: it is not clear precisely what kind of window is meant here. According to Stephenson, it is a slit-window used for shooting arrows from a stronghold.

ll. 117–19: these fragments are taken from Matthew viii, 8: 'Lord, I am not worthy that thou shouldest come under my roof, but speak the word only, and my servant shall be healed.' These are the words of the centurion at Capernaum, one of whose servants was ill. He asked Christ to cure him, crediting him with the power to do this at a distance, without needing to visit the sick man at his house. Christ pointed to the centurion's trust in him as a supreme act of faith.

The first part of the sentence is spoken by the priest, as an act of humility, just before he takes the sacrament.

IV

In this section Eliot makes extensive general reference to the final cantos of the *Purgatorio*, where Dante reaches the summit of the Mount of Purgatory, enters the Earthly Paradise and sees

Beatrice, his beloved on earth, now a figure of divine beauty, reminding him of his sinful past. This source is described more fully in the notes to 'The Hollow Men', see especially page 205.

l. 120 violet: the liturgical colour for penitence and intercession.

l. 123: the liturgical colours of the Blessed Virgin Mary.

l. 125 eternal dolour: a direct translation of 'Eterno Dolore', according to Dante, in the *Inferno*, the inscription above the gate of hell, 'dolour' meaning pain.

ll. 127–8: these lines echo a line from Baudelaire: 'Makes the rocks pour forth water and the desert flourish', an echo which is more evident in the phrasing and rhythm of the original French: 'Fait couler le rocher et fleurir le désert' (from 'Bohémiens en voyage'). In this poem, 'The Travelling Gipsies', it is the goddess of the earth, Cybele, who eases the journey of the gipsies.

l. 128 larkspur: the delphinium.

l. 130: be mindful. From the words of Arnaut Daniel to Dante, praying him to remember, when he returns to Earth, Daniel's suffering for his lust (see note to line 427 of *The Waste Land*).

l. 134: according to a note by Hayward, this line is a specific allusion to *Paradiso* xxx, 51, in which 'fascinto' is usually translated as 'swathed'. Hence 'sheathed' departs from the allusion source.

ll. 137–8 Redeem/The time: Eliot is using a phrase usually associated with the wise and proper use of one's life for Christian purposes, as St Paul employed it in his Epistles: 'Walk in wisdom toward them that are without, redeeming the time' (Colossians iv, 5); 'See then that ye walk circumspectly, not as fools but as wise, Redeeming the time, because the days are evil' (Ephesians v, 15–16). In both these Epistles, St Paul is advising early Christian communities on their duty towards God and men.

The modern significance of this phrase for Eliot can be seen in his essay 'Thoughts after Lambeth' (1931): 'redeeming the time, so that the Faith may be preserved alive through the dark ages before us; to renew and rebuild civilization, and save the World from suicide'.

ll. 139–40: in *Purgatorio* xxix, Dante sees the Divine Pageant, in which Beatrice is drawn by a griffon in a triumphal chariot. Eliot associates the 'pageantry' of that scene with 'the world of what I call the *high dream*, and the modern world seems capable only of the *low dream*' ('Dante'). See also the Epistle for Ash Wednesday, Joel ii, 28: amongst God's promises is that 'your old men shall dream dreams, your young men shall see visions'.

l. 140: unicorns/hearse: these are echoes of 'Senlin', a poem by Conrad Aiken, published in 1918, in which the 'unicorns' appear, also a 'hearse' drawn by white horses. Senlin wonders, '"Is it my childhood there", he asks,/"Sealed in a hearse and hurrying by?"' Aiken Dantefied is how the passage has been described. Eliot referred to 'Senlin' in 1919, in a review of Conrad Aiken's work.

l. 141 veiled: Beatrice is veiled before Dante is permitted to see the divine beauty of her face (*Purgatorio* xxx, 31); also see lines 168, 172, 177 below.

l. 142 yews: critics have sought a symbolic interpretation. Eliot averred to the contrary. When John Hayward suggested such a symbolic meaning (in April 1930), Eliot replied that 'Perhaps the yew does not mean so much as you suppose. It happened to occur in two or three dreams – one was a dream of "the boarhound between the yew trees"; and that's all I know about it.' This dream fed the line in 'Animula': 'Pray for Floret, by the boarhound slain between the yew trees.'

ll. 142–3: Priapus, a Greek god of fertility, was usually honoured with statues in gardens and orchards, although the reference to the 'flute' would suggest Pan with his pipes, the Greek god of shepherds and huntsmen.

ll. 144, 147: Dante draws attention to the singing of the birds and to the song of the wind in the trees as he enters the Garden of Eden, *Purgatorio* xxviii.

l. 148: Matthiessen relates the source of this line to 'the turning movement' of the whole poem:

> The line itself is a phrase from the prayer, 'Salve Regina', which follows the celebration of the Catholic Mass. The immediate context is: 'To thee do we send up our sighs mourning and weeping in this valley of tears; turn, then, most gracious advocate, thine eyes of mercy towards us; and after this our exile, show unto us the blessed fruit of thy womb, Jesus.' If the

reader is also aware of that context, the line in the poem not only points away from the vision back to life, but also from life once more back to the vision, and thus re-emphasizes the turning movement upon which so much of the entire poem is built.

V

ll. 149–57: the word/Word/world/World configuration in this verse paragraph draws upon the verbal imagery developed in the Nativity Sermon preached by Lancelot Andrewes in 1618 (see page 71, note to lines 18–19). In particular both Andrewes and Eliot use 'Word' in its original Greek sense of 'logos', as in John i, 1: 'In the beginning was the Word, and the Word was with God, and the Word was God.'

l. 153: 'The Word without a word' is a phrase in Andrewes, referring to the 'miracle', '*Verbum infans*', the wordless Word incarnate in the infant Jesus.

ll. 156–7: the 'world-whirled' homophone is probably copied from the pun-etymology of stanza 34 of *Orchestra* by Sir John Davies (1565–1618): 'Behold the world, how it is whirled round!/And for it is so whirled, is named so.'

Cf. Dante, the concluding lines of the *Divine Comedy*: 'But already my desire and will were turned, like a wheel that spins evenly, by the Love which moves the sun and the other stars.'

l. 158: from Micah vi, 3. The Lord cries to the people, reproaching them for their departure from the ways of virtue and faith. These words have been taken into the liturgy of the Church. In the Roman Catholic mass for Good Friday, the day of the crucifixion, these words are part of the Reproaches, a liturgy in which Christ on the cross speaks to the people: 'O my people, what have I done unto thee? Or in what have I grieved thee? Because I brought thee out of the land of Egypt, thou hast prepared a cross for thy Saviour.'

VI

l. 180: Eliot reverses the usual Christian concept of public denial and private recognition or acceptance, see Matthew xxvi, 34–5, where Jesus prophesies to Peter that 'thou shalt deny me thrice', and duly he does (70–74), 'before them all', in swearing 'I know not the man.'

ll. 188–90: Hayward connects these lines with 'Death by Water', Section IV of *The Waste Land* (see his note to line 312). Possibly this part of *Ash-Wednesday* was among the materials left over from *The Waste Land.*

l. 191 (Bless me father): 'Bless me, father, for I have sinned' are the opening words of the penitent to the priest in the sacrament of confession.

ll. 191–203: Matthiesen: 'Exact description of memories of the varied loveliness of the New England coast' where Eliot spent childhood holidays.

l. 192 wide window: a notable feature of the Eliot holiday house overlooking the harbour and the sea beyond, at Gloucester, Cape Ann, Massachusetts, with granite rocks between the house and the shore.

l. 193: cf. 'And white sails flying on the yellow sea', from 'Elaine' (1859), one of the *Idylls of the King* by Tennyson; 'white sails' would fill the harbour at Gloucester, a centre for yachting.

l. 196 lilac: according to Hargrove, still growing in the grounds of the Eliot house.

l. 197 quickens: comes to life; in the Bible, it is a spiritual quickening.

l. 198 golden-rod: a long-stemmed bright yellow flower (hence its name) native to North America and abundant along the rocky coast of Cape Ann. *This American World*, 1928, by Edgar Angel Mowrer, carries a Preface by Eliot in which he recalls the 'golden-rod' of New England and 'the red granite' of Massachusetts (see line 192). There may also be a second area of reference to the Biblical image of the 'rod' as an instrument of rule and discipline, as in the 'rod of iron' in Revelation ii, 27; xii, 5; and xix, 15. This idea fits with line 197.

l. 202: false and delusive dreams pass out of the ivory gate of the underworld on their way to earth (see Virgil, *Aeneid* vi).

l. 208 other yew: because it is a tree of immortality as well as death.

l. 214: the words of Piccarda (see page 101, note to line 24 of 'A Cooking Egg') to Dante, *Paradiso* iii, 85–7: 'Our peace is His will, His will is our peace. It is the sea towards which moves all that it creates and all that nature makes.' 'When Dante says *la sua voluntade è nostra pace* it is great poetry, and there is a great philosophy behind it' ('Shakespeare and the Stoicism of Seneca', 1927); 'the statement of Dante seems to me *literally true*. And I confess that it has more beauty for me now, when my own experience has deepened its meaning, than it did when I first read it' ('Dante', 1929). Eliot quotes the words in his 'Dante' essay, translating them as 'His will is our peace', with the comment that these are 'words which even those who know no Dante know'.

ll. 216–17: in one of the forms of the Roman Catholic Litany Mary is addressed as 'Stella Maris' ('Star of the Sea').

l. 218: 'Suffer me not to be separated from thee' is a line from the Roman Catholic hymn 'Soul of Christ'.

l. 219: in the Roman Catholic mass, this is the response to the words of the priest, 'Hear my prayer, O Lord.' The sentence as a whole comes from Psalm cii, 1.

ARIEL POEMS

'I thought my poetry was over after "The Hollow Men" ...
writing the Ariel poems released the stream and led directly to
"Ash Wednesday".'

The New York Times, 29 November 1953

The earliest step towards this release came in 1927 when Geof-
frey Faber invited Eliot to contribute to 'The Ariel Poems', a
series of illustrated Christmas greetings pamphlets priced at one
shilling. The result was Eliot's first commissioned poem, 'Jour-
ney of the Magi', published in August 1927. It was followed in
September 1928 by 'A Song for Simeon', 'Animula' in October
1929 and 'Marina' in September 1930.

Eliot may have been stimulated by this commission to write
for a wide audience, a circumstance which seems to be reflected
in the relative accessibility of this and the other Ariel poems. In
the event, they did not sell as well as hoped. While the 'Magi'
was printed in 5,000 copies, the print-run dropped successively
for each of the later poems: 'Simeon' 3,500, 'Animula' 3,000
and 'Marina' 2,000.

Journey of the Magi

Published August 1927

An important influence in the writing of this poem was the first section of the French poem *Anabase* (1924) by St-John Perse, which Eliot began to translate in 1926. He completed the first draft in January 1927 and in 1930 it was published as *Anabasis*. In 1949, writing (in French) to Jean Paulhan, Eliot explained that Perse's 'influence is seen in several of the poems that I wrote after having completed the translation: the influence of images and also perhaps of rhythm. Students of my later works will perhaps find that this influence always persists.' Here, the influence is seen coming from Perse's descriptions of deserts, camel caravans, marches and the servant girls of line 10.

A detailed analysis is given by Richard Abel, 'The Influence of St-John Perse on T. S. Eliot', *Contemporary Literature*, xiv, no. 2 (1973), pp. 213–39.

The Magi: the three wise men who came from the east to honour the new-born Jesus. Their story is told in Matthew ii, 1–12. Later tradition identified them as three kings – Balthazar (King of Chaldea), Caspar (the Ethiopian King of Tarshish) and Melchior (King of Nubia).

In the final section of the poem Eliot seems to be exploiting the associations of the word 'magi' with the priestly class of magicians in Ancient Persia.

Vickery (1973) points out the influence of Frazer in Eliot's account of the natural and vegetation cycles which embody the god's dying and revival, as seen in the stories of Attis, Adonis, Osiris and Dionysus, and now in the birth of Jesus.

ll. 1–5: adapted from a Nativity Sermon preached before James I by Lancelot Andrewes on Christmas Day 1622: 'A cold coming they had of it at this time of the year, just the worst time of the year to take a journey, and specially a long journey in. The ways deep, the weather sharp, the days short, the sun farthest off, *in solstitio brumali,* "the very dead of winter".' Eliot cites these lines in his 'Lancelot Andrewes' essay (1926) as one of those 'flashing phrases' which 'never desert the memory', and Eliot's text is given here, not Andrewes's original, which differs in several small details. Immediately before this passage, Andrewes reviews the hardships of the journey, details of which Eliot uses in lines 6–20: 'This was nothing pleasant, for through deserts, all the way waste and desolate. Nor easy neither; for over the rocks and crags of both Arabias, specially Petraea their journey lay ... Exceeding dangerous, as lying through the midst of the "black tents of Kedar", a nation of thieves and cut-throats; to pass over the hills of robbers ... It was no summer progress.'

Eliot seems to have cast Andrewes's wording in the relaxed and idiomatic conversational flow of the 'Exile's Letter' (*Cathay,* 1915) by Pound, one of the poems Eliot included in the *Selected Poems* (1928). See, for example: 'And what with broken wheels and so on, I won't say it wasn't hard going,/Over roads twisted like sheep's guts./And I was still going, late in the year, in the cutting wind from the North ..., And the vermilioned girls getting drunk about sunset ...'

ll. 21–8: Eliot said that certain images were charged for him with a personal yet inexplicable meaning. Giving some examples, he mentioned 'six ruffians seen through an open window playing cards at night at a small French railway junction where there was a water-mill'. He commented that 'such memories may have a symbolic value ... for they come to represent the depths of feeling into which we cannot peer' (*The Use of Poetry,* 1933).

l. 24: there were three crosses on Calvary, those of Christ and the two 'malefactors' (see Luke xxiii, 32–3).

l. 25 white horse: in Revelation vi, 2 and xix, 11–14, Christ the conqueror rides on a white horse.

l. 27: a glancing allusion to the Biblical accounts of the betrayal of Christ for 30 pieces of silver and the soldiers dicing for the robes of Christ at the crucifixion (see, for example, Matthew xxvi, 14–15; xxvii, 35).

ll. 32 to end: the tone of mystified acceptance in which the magus speaks may have been suggested to Eliot by a passage in Andrewes's sermon where the rhetorical question is posed – what did the magi find?: 'No sight to comfort them, nor a word for which they any whit the wiser; nothing worth their travel . . . Well, they will take Him as they find Him, and all this notwithstanding, worship Him for all that.'

ll. 33–4: cf. 'Secondly, set down this', in Andrewes's sermon.

ll. 33–5: these lines set the dramatic situation. The magus is reminiscing for the benefit of a listener who is to make a record of these events and experiences. Eliot may have taken the idea for this situation from 'The Adoration of the Magi', a prose piece by Yeats, then recently republished in a volume which Yeats entitled *Mythologies* (1925). He tells how three old men sat by his fireside and told their story. They insisted that he 'take notes' so that he 'might have the exact words'.

Further, the very specific details and the broken utterances of Eliot's magus may be stylistic devices suggested by Yeats's account: 'Now one talked and now another, and they often interrupted one another, with a desire like that of countrymen, when they tell a story, to leave no detail untold' (p. 308).

ll. 35–6: Andrewes compares the magi with the Queen of Sheba coming from afar to see Solomon in all his glory: 'Weigh what she found, and what these here – as poor and unlikely a birth as could be, ever to prove a King, or any great matter. No sight to comfort them, nor a word for which they any whit the wiser; nothing worth their travel . . .'

ll. 36–8: this interplay of 'birth' and 'death' may have been suggested by 'The Fourth Magus', a short story by R. B. Cunninghame Graham, which was first published in the magazine *Hope* in 1910 and reprinted in Duckworth's *Readers' Library* in 1915. The fourth magus is Nicanor. On the road to Bethlehem he hears of Christ on the cross: 'It is now time to rest. Fate has deprived me of the joy of being present at the birth of him the star announced; I can at least be present at his death ... and birth and death are not so very different, after all.'

l. 41 the old dispensation: the 'new' dispensation is the reign of Christianity; see Paul's address to the early Christians, in which he speaks of 'the dispensation of the Grace of God' and his 'knowledge in the mystery of Christ' (Ephesians iii, 2–4).

A Song for Simeon

Published September 1928

Simeon: the story of Simeon is told in Luke ii, 25–35. He is an old and devout Jew, living in Jerusalem, awaiting the coming of the Messiah. The Holy Ghost reveals to him that he is not to die until he has seen Christ, and guides him to the temple, where the new-born Jesus has been brought by Joseph and Mary for the circumcision. Simeon takes Jesus in his arms, his destiny now fulfilled: 'Lord, now lettest thou thy servant depart in peace, according to thy word: For mine eyes have seen thy salvation, Which thou hast prepared before the face of all people; A light to lighten the Gentiles, and the glory of thy people Israel.'

Simeon also prophesies to Mary the suffering to come: 'Behold, this child is set for the fall and rising again of many in Israel; and for a sign which shall be spoken against; (Yea, a sword shall pierce through thy own soul also), that the thoughts of many hearts may be revealed.' These words look forward darkly to the sufferings of Christ and the persecution of the early Christians, to which Eliot refers in line 13 onwards.

In the Anglican Book of Common Prayer, the words from Luke ii, 29 onwards ('Lord, now lettest thou thy servant depart in peace . . .') constitute what is called (in The Order for Evening Prayer) the 'Nunc Dimittis (or the Song of Simeon)' – hence the poem's title. From the manuscript, it appears that Eliot introduced the sequence 'Grant us thy peace . . . Grant us thy peace . . . According to thy word . . . Grant me thy peace . . . Having seen thy salvation' at a late stage, when the poem was already far advanced.

There may be a family tribute in Eliot's choice of this subject:

his grandfather, Revd. William Greenleaf Eliot, wrote a 'Nunc Dimittis' poem, with the same theme and taking over some of the same Biblical phrasing, in celebration of his seventy-sixth birthday, on 5 August 1886.

l. 1 Lord: Eliot opens the poem with the first word of Simeon's entreaty to God (quoted above).

Roman hyacinths: Roman, because Judaea was then under Roman rule; 'blooming in bowls', because the Roman variety is a special type of flower suitable for forced indoor cultivation.

l. 8: a liturgical form of appeal for God's blessing.

l. 14: see second note below to line 19.

ll. 14–16: these lines combine a variety of Biblical prophecies and the imagery of grief, hiding and pursuit. Isaiah liii, 3: 'despised and rejected of men; a man of sorrows, and acquainted with grief'; and Jesus foretells of 'the beginnings of sorrows' to be suffered before the second coming (Matthew xxiv, 8 and Mark xiii, 8).

Jeremiah complains to God that he has forsaken his chosen people and that 'the mountain of Zion . . . is desolate, the foxes walk upon it' (Lamentations v, 17). In Leviticus, the goat is the 'scapegoat', cast into the 'wilderness' (xvi, 22). The animal imagery is also found in Matthew viii, 20: 'The foxes have holes, and the birds of the air have nests; but the Son of man hath not where to lay his head.'

l. 17 scourges: Christ was later scourged at the order of Pilate, the Roman governor.

lamentation: Luke xxxiii, 27–9 tells of the crowd of women, bewailing and lamenting, that followed Christ out of Jerusalem on the way to the crucifixion.

l. 19 stations: the Stations of the Cross is a Roman Catholic devotion conducted before a series of fourteen images or pictures representing the sequence of events from the time that Christ was sentenced to death, to the placing of his corpse in the sepulchre.

the mountain of desolation: Calvary, where the crucifixion took place. Eliot seems to have made up this phrase from Mark xiii, 14, in a passage where Christ is forewarning the disciples of the persecution yet to be faced: 'But when ye shall see the abomination of desolation ... then let them that be in Judaea flee to the mountains.'

l. 20: the Gospels record that Christ died at 'the ninth hour'.

ll. 22–31: Williamson describes this section of the poem as 'its Prayer of the Threshold'.

l. 22: Eliot's association of the 'Infant' and the 'unspeaking and unspoken Word' suggests that he has in mind John i, 1 and the image developed by Lancelot Andrewes on the baby Jesus: '*Verbum infans*, the Word without a word; the eternal Word not able to speak a word'. (See page 71, note to lines 18–19 of 'Gerontion'.)

l. 23 Israel's: Israel was the community promised by God to the Israelites, his chosen people, where they could live in freedom after their years of wandering and captivity.

ll. 27–8: a version of Simeon's prophetic warning to Mary (see headnote on Simeon); he is referring to the suffering Mary will have to endure at the sight of her son's torment and death.

ll. 32–3: an adaptation of Simeon's words (see headnote on Simeon).

Animula

Published October 1929

Title: Latin, meaning a little soul. Eliot seems to have in mind the most notable use of the word, in the poem addressed by the Roman Emperor Hadrian (AD 76–138) to his soul, with the first line 'Animula vagula blandula' ('Little soul – fleeting away and charming'). A more immediate source, however, may be *Marius the Epicurean* (1885) by Walter Pater, brought to Eliot's notice at this time. It is a philosophical romance set in ancient Rome. Chapter 8 is entitled 'Animula Vagula', invoking Hadrian's poem. It tells how Marius's soul sets out on the journey from pagan infancy towards Christian maturity. Marius was in Eliot's mind at this time. In September 1930 there appeared in *The Bookman* 'Arnold and Pater', where Eliot remarks that 'To the end, Marius remains only a half-wakened soul'; and concludes the essay, 'Pater represents more positively than Coleridge of whom he wrote the words, "that inexhaustable discontent, languor and home-sickness . . . the chords of which ring all through our modern literature".'

l. 1: this line Eliot has derived from a passage in Dante, *Purgatorio* xvi, 85–8, where the poet is discussing the nature of the human soul and its need for discipline: 'From the hands of Him who loves her before she is, there issues like a little child that plays, with weeping and laughter, the simple soul, that knows nothing except that, come from the hands of a glad creator, she turns willingly to everything that delights her. First she tastes the flavour of a trifling good; then is beguiled, and pursues it, if neither guide nor check withhold her. Therefore laws were needed as a curb; a ruler was needed, who should at least see afar the tower of the true City.' (The translation is that given by Eliot in the 'Dante' essay, published in September 1929, which he was writing at the same time as this poem).

Eliot also quoted the Italian original of *Purgatorio*, xvi, 85–7, a different translation, at the close of 'Sir John Davies' (1926) as an illustration that Dante was, in comparison with Davies (1565–1618), 'a vastly greater poet' and his philosophy 'infinitely more substantial and subtle'.

l. 19 'is and seems': a concept taken from the philosopher F. H. Bradley (see *The Waste Land*, note to line 411): the distinction is between appearance ('seems') and reality ('is'). In itself reality is an awareness of the gap between the actual and the ideal, giving rise to the notions of obligation, duty, and ethical value contained in the philosophical term 'imperatives', those considerations that move us to act morally.

l. 23 Encyclopaedia Britannica: the 'British Encyclopaedia', the largest and, by tradition, the most authoritative encyclopaedia in English. For Eliot, however, the *EB* held negative associations. At this time, he was working on the papers of his friend, the essayist Charles Whibley, and would have recently read Whibley's description of the *EB* (in 1903) as 'the worst possible enemy of true Learning' (for its encapsulation of knowledge). In *Charles Whibley, A Memoir* (1932) Eliot writes of 'a debased Encyclopaedia Britannica'. This view of the *EB* relates to the theme of discipline in the Dante passage referred to at the opening to the poem.

l. 31 viaticum: the last sacrament of communion given to the dying, from the Latin meaning travelling money or provisions for the journey. Eliot seems to be referring to this etymological meaning in the idea of living on, spiritually, after the last sacrament.

ll. 32–3 Guiterriez, Boudin: in answer to Stephenson's inquiry Eliot said that these two men 'represent different types of career, the successful person of the machine age and someone who was killed in the last war' (meaning the First World War). The first name is probably Eliot's mistake for the Spanish surname Gutierrez.

For the source of the second name, several suggestions have been made. It may be a misremembering or deliberate variation of the French anarchist Martial Bourdin, killed by a bomb at Greenwich Observatory in 1894; or Eliot may have taken the name Boudin from Joyce's *Ulysses*; or from the French slang for explosive, from the word which usually refers to a sausage-shaped blood pudding.

l. 36 Floret: Eliot also commented on this name to Stephenson, saying that the figure is 'so entirely imaginary' that 'no identification' is to be made. But he added that the name Floret 'may suggest not wholly irrelevantly to some minds certain folklore memories'. This rather cryptic remark may be Eliot's way of saying that some readers might be reminded of two figures of Greek legend, Actaeon the hunter, who was torn to death by his own hounds, or Adonis, the beautiful youth who was killed by a wild boar, as was the god Attis in the ancient vegetation cults. Eliot once dreamt of a 'boarhound between the yew trees' (see note to *Ash-Wednesday*, line 142).

l. 37: Eliot gives the final line of the Roman Catholic prayer, the 'Hail Mary', changing the last word, 'death'.

Marina

Written July 1930; published September 1930

Marina: the daughter of Pericles in *Pericles, Prince of Tyre* by Shakespeare. Her name is associated with the sea (Latin *mare*, adjective *marinus, marina*). In the play, we hear how she was born at sea, as a baby lost to her father, believed by him to be dead, and is in womanhood restored to him seemingly miraculously. Eliot considered this to be one of the great moments in literature, as we learn from his remarks in a lecture given in 1937: 'To my mind the finest of all the "recognition scenes" is Act v, i of that very great play *Pericles*. It is a perfect example of the "ultra-dramatic", a dramatic action of beings who are more than human ... or rather, seen in a light more than that of day.' At the climax of the scene, Pericles' words are 'Down on thy knees, thank the holy gods as loud/As thunder threatens us: this is Marina'.

For Eliot's further exposition of the 'theme' of *Marina* and the connection of the Epigraph, see the extracts from two letters given below.

Epigraph: 'What is this place, what country, what region of the world?' These are the words of Hercules as he returns to sanity, about to discover that in his madness he has killed his wife and children; from the play *Hercules Furens* (line 1138) by Seneca (died AD 65).

In a letter dated 9 May 1930, accompanying the copy of the manuscript presented to Magdalene College, Cambridge, Eliot explained, 'I intend a crisscross between Pericles finding alive, and Hercules finding dead – the two extremes of the recognition

scene – but I thought that if I labelled the quotation it might lead
readers astray rather than direct them. It is only an accident that
I know Seneca better than I know Euripides.' i.e. Eliot chose his
epigraph from Seneca rather than from Euripides' *Mad Heracles*,
in which there is a similar 'recognition' scene.

In July 1930, Eliot also wrote about the poem to E. McKnight
Kauffer, who provided the drawings with the poem, published as
an Ariel pamphlet in September:

> I dont know whether it is any good at all. The theme is
> paternity; with a crisscross between the text and the quota-
> tion. The theme is a comment on the Recognition Motive in
> Shakespeare's later plays, and particularly of course the recog-
> nition of Pericles. The quotation is from 'Hercules Furens,'
> where Hercules, having killed his children in a fit of madness
> induced by an angry god, comes to without remembering
> what he has done. (I didnt give the reference for fear it might
> be more distracting than helpful to the reader who did not
> grasp the exact point): the contrast of death and life in Her-
> cules and Pericles ... The scenery in which it is dressed up is
> Casco Bay, Maine. I am afraid no scenery except the Missis-
> sippi, the prairie and the North East Coast has ever made
> much impression on me.

Eliot refers twice to this part of *Hercules Furens*, with great
admiration, in 'Seneca in Elizabethan Translation' (1927).

Eliot made a typically ambiguous joke out of the sheer obscur-
ity of the epigraph when he told William Empson that 'all the
classical men were caught out' by it.

ll. 1–3: Eliot recorded on the manuscript of the poem that the
specific place he had in mind was Rogue Island, on the Maine
coast, in whose vicinity he had sailed (sometimes in fog) during
his years at Harvard. Hargrove tells us that it is a 'tiny island of
grey rock' (see the 'grey rocks' of line 1) with a pine grove at one
end, a persistent mist and the cry of gulls (see line 15). Similarly,
the details in lines 25–8 come from Eliot's own sailing experi-
ences off the New England coast (see Hayward on page 35).

ll. 1–5: the rhetorical question-form of the epigraph is echoed in this opening section; and again at lines 16 and 33.

l. 6 dog: for the dog as an image of menace and evil, see note to *The Waste Land*, line 74. Fighting dogs are prepared by sharpening their teeth.

ll. 17–18: cf. 'But are you flesh and blood?/Have you a working pulse?' (*Pericles* v, i), the wondering questions of Pericles as it begins to dawn upon him that Marina may, by some miracle, be his daughter, alive. Eliot seems to be combining this allusion with verbal echoes of the scene in Shakespeare's *Macbeth* (i, iii): on the Heath the First Witch greets Banquo as 'Lesser than Macbeth, and greater'; and the Second Witch, 'Not so happy, yet much happier.' Banquo, like Eliot's Pericles, questions the nature of what he sees.

l. 17 to end: the train of thought and imagery, involving the 'face, less clear and clearer', the knowing and 'unknowing', childhood and age, seem to draw upon associations in 1 Corinthians xiii, where Paul reflects upon the meaning of his life and on the passage from the simplicity and innocence of childhood to the state of manhood: 'For now we see through a glass, darkly; but then face to face: now I know in part; but then shall I know even as also I am known' (verse 12).

l. 28 garboard strake: a single breadth of planking next to the keel. cf. one of the discarded lines from *The Waste Land*: 'And then the garboard-strake began to leak.' Eliot may be recalling *The Pioneers* (1823) by Fenimore Cooper, where there is reference to the 'garboard streak' (see page 50, note to line 10 of 'Prufrock').

CHORUSES FROM 'THE ROCK'

'The invitation to write the words ... came at a moment [September 1933] when I seemed to myself to have exhausted my meagre poetic gifts, and to have nothing more to say. To be, at such a moment, commissioned to write something which, good or bad, must be delivered by a certain date, may have the effect that vigorous cranking sometimes has upon a motor car when the battery is run down. The task was clearly laid out: I had only to write the words of prose dialogue for scenes of the usual historical pageant pattern, for which I had been given a scenario.'

'The Three Voices of Poetry', 1953

'We must find a new form of verse which shall be as satisfactory a vehicle for us as blank verse was for the Elizabethans.'

'A Dialogue on Dramatic Poetry', 1928

'The most useful poetry, socially, would be one which could cut across all the present stratifications of public taste – stratifications which are perhaps a sign of social disintegration. The ideal medium for poetry ... and the most direct means of social "usefulness" for poetry, is the theatre.'

The Use of Poetry, 1933

Choruses from 'The Rock'

Written October 1933–March 1934;
Performed Sadler's Wells Theatre,
London 28 May – 9 June 1934; Published 1934

The Rock: A Pageant Play, accompanied by music and dancing, was written in support of the Forty-Five Churches Fund of the Diocese of London, a fund devoted to the preservation of existing churches and for church-building in new housing areas in London north of the Thames.

In a Prefatory Note (dated April 1934) to the published text, Eliot wrote 'I cannot consider myself the author of the "play", but only of the words which are printed here.' He explained that the scenario was the work of E. Martin Browne, 'under whose direction I wrote the choruses and dialogues'.

The play tells of the coming of Christianity, with the conversion of Saxon London by Mellitus in 605, and some later highpoints, including the vision of Rahere in the twelfth century and Wren's St Paul's. These historical moments are linked to actual church-building in London in 1934.

Title: According to Eliot, 'The Rock' (who speaks as a character in the play) is not 'St Peter pure and simple' (see the words of Christ to St Peter: 'thou art Peter, and upon this rock I will build my church', Matthew xvi, 18) but also Christ himself ('And that Rock was Christ', 1 Corinthians x, 4). The 'rock' metaphor is explained in 2 Samuel xxii, 2–3: 'The Lord is my rock, and my fortress, and my deliverer; The God of my rock; in him will I trust.'

At the time, Eliot wrote to a friend: 'I am trying to combine the simplicity and immediate intelligibility necessary for dramatic verse with concentration under the inspiration of, chiefly, Isaiah and Ezekiel.' Indeed, much of the verse is deeply grounded in the Bible – in its language, imagery and rhythms – and in general the notes attend only to specific references. The second area of reference is to life in contemporary London, and explanatory notes are provided.

A further dimension is indicated in Eliot's letter to a friend, May 1934: 'The only really interesting thing about the "Rock" (28th inst) will be to see how the public responds to the political allusions in it. But I fear a dull and lethargic audience for that sort of thing.'

Eliot heard the 'voice' of the Chorus not as a 'dramatic voice' but 'myself addressing – indeed haranguing – an audience ... Its members were speaking *for me*, not uttering words that really represented any supposed character of their own.' He noted that 'the more voices you have in your choir, the simpler and more direct the vocabulary, the syntax, and the content of your lines must be'.

I

This section opens the play. To quote the full text, 'The scene is an open place, with an irregular rocky hill in the middle. The Chorus, seven male and ten female figures, are discovered. They speak as the voice of the Church of God.'

ll. 1, 2: constellations of stars.

l. 11 Word: cf. 'In the beginning was the Word, and the Word was with God, and the Word was God' (John i, 1).

l. 18 Dust: cf. the words of God to Satan in the Garden of Eden: 'upon thy belly shalt thou go, and dust shalt thou eat all the days of thy life'; and God's words to Adam, 'for dust thou art, and unto dust shalt thou return' (Genesis iii, 14, 19).

l. 19 the timekept City: the business area of London, governed by time, as the office workers come in the morning and leave at night and as the clocks of the many City churches sound the hours (aspects of the City which enter *The Waste Land* at lines 61–8).

l. 20: Eliot plays upon two meanings: foreign merchant ships on the River Thames; the flow of money in and out of the City, then the world's great financial centre, for the support of business overseas.

l. 22 chop-houses: the traditional City restaurants, serving good quick lunches for businessmen.

l. 29: Hindhead in Surrey is a beauty-spot within easy motoring distance of London, as is Maidenhead, a small town beside the Thames west of London.

l. 49: to tread the grapes, the ancient method of getting juice for wine, is a Biblical metaphor for doing the work of the Lord, often the work of the God of wrath, as in Isaiah lxiii, 3: 'I have trodden the winepress alone; and of the people there was none with me; for I will tread them in my anger, and trample them in my fury.'

l. 57: an echo of many Biblical injunctions to serve God willingly, to become perfect in one's determination to serve God.

ll. 58–9: cf. 'Take therefore no thought for the morrow' (Matthew vi, 34). The Biblical metaphor instructs man to live a Christian life without regard to its rewards or punishments.

l. 72 tube-train: a train on London's underground railway, trains which are frequently packed tight with passengers.

l. 94: cf. 'no man hath hired us', the words of the unemployed labourers to the master of the vineyard (Matthew xx, 7).

ll. 102, 105 In this land: with this phrase God promises to the prophet Jeremiah a place where the faithful will prosper (Jeremiah xxxii, 41, 43). Eliot parodies both the Biblical sentiments and the cadence of their statement.

l. 108 'The Times': then England's most formally respectable daily newspaper, whose obituaries of the great are still world-renowned.

ll. 115–16: cf. 'For the bed is shorter than that a man can stretch himself on it: and the covering narrower than that he can wrap himself in it' (Isaiah xxviii, 20).

l. 120 without haste: cf. 'he that believeth shall not make haste' (Isaiah xxviii, 16).

II

The scene is London in Saxon times, following the singing of the Builders.

l. 3 cornerstone: an image found in the Old and New Testaments. Its force is well brought out in Isaiah xxviii, 16: 'Therefore thus saith the Lord God, Behold, I lay in Zion for a foundation a stone, a tried stone, a precious corner stone, a sure foundation.'

l. 7 the Spirit . . . on the face of the waters: 'And the Spirit of God moved upon the face of the waters' (Genesis i, 2) as he prepared to create light in the darkness and void before the creation of the world. The comparison, which follows, with the tortoise, may refer to a Hindu creation myth, in which the world itself is on the tortoise's back.

l. 8 love our neighbour: one of the tenets of Christianity, as in, 'Thou shalt love thy neighbour as thyself' (Matthew xix, 19).

l. 13 citizenship: cf. 'Now therefore ye are no more strangers and foreigners, but fellow citizens with the saints, and of the household of God' (Ephesians ii, 19).

l. 16 Whipsnade: a zoo near London.

l. 22: the British and Foreign Bible Society translated the Bible into many languages.

ll. 36–7 prosperity . . . adversity: cf. 'both in prosperity and adversity' in the Anglican Book of Common Prayer.

l. 37 Temple: used in the Bible to signify the Church of God.

l. 44 ribbon roads: roads so called because of the ribbon-like lines of houses built on either side, a phenomenon of the 1920s and 1930s, especially around London.

III

Later in the same scene.

ll. 1–19: the style of this section echoes the way in which the Old Testament prophets record the words of God, coming to them in dreams and visions.

l. 15 race reports: newspaper reports of horse and greyhound races provided for betting.

l. 20 East: the East End of London, a dockland area then filled with slums.

ll. 31–6: Eliot is characterizing the prosperous middle-class suburbs of London, the flower-gardens and the tennis-courts.

ll. 37–8: cf. 'Except the Lord build the house, they labour in vain that build it: except the Lord keep the city, the watchman waketh but in vain' (Psalm cxxvii, 1).

l. 41: cavies, guinea pigs; *marmots,* rodents of the squirrel family.

l. 44 Thy House: archaically phrased and capitalized in the traditional form of reference to the Church of God, both spiritual and in its worldly structure.

l. 65: Eliot is playing upon the association of the stars with human fortune in astrology, the ancient art of prophecy; but today men seek another, financial fortune on the stock exchange, in ordinary (Eliot's 'common') or preference shares.

VII

Part II (Section VII). This follows the Preacher's prophecy that 'God will come'.

The structure of this section is derived from the Biblical account of the creation in Genesis.

l. 1: cf. 'In the beginning God created the heaven and the earth. And the earth was without form, and void; and darkness was upon the face of the deep' (Genesis i, 1–2). 'I beheld the earth, and lo, it was waste and void' (Jeremiah iv, 23).

l. 7: 'And the spirit of God moved upon the face of the waters' (Genesis i, 2).

l. 9 Higher Religions: those spiritually informed, as distinct from the primitive, pagan religions.

l. 10 Good and Evil: this was the knowledge with which Satan tempted Eve, to be gained by eating of the fruit from 'the tree of the knowledge of good and evil' which God had forbidden Adam to eat from, under pain of death (see Genesis ii–iii).

l. 15 Prayer wheels: used in Tibetan Buddhism.

l. 18 moment: the birth of Christ.

l. 22 Passion: the period of the crucifixion is known as Passion Week, from the agony in the garden, the arrest, the trial and scourging, to the resurrection.

Sacrifice: the death of Christ seen as God's sacrifice of his only son on behalf of mankind.

l. 29 Race: ideology of racial superiority, currently Hitler's championing of the German (Aryan) super-race over (primarily) the Jewish under-race.

Dialectic: uncapitalized, dialectic is the investigation of truth by critical, rational discussion; capitalized, it probably refers to the worship of an ideology, most likely Marxist socialism in which dialectic or dialectical materialism is a primal concept.

IX

ll. 1–15: as in Section III, lines 1–18, Eliot is echoing the form of address employed by God in speaking to his prophets.

l. 3 House of Sorrow: cf. 'It is better to go to the house of mourning than to go to the house of feasting: for that is the end of all men; and the living will lay it to his heart' (Ecclesiastes vii, 2).

l. 15 communion of saints: a phrase from the Apostles' Creed, in which the Christian makes a declaration of his credo, the tenets of his faith.

l. 25: a version of the traditional grace spoken before meals: 'Bless, O Lord, this food (*or* these gifts) to our use and us to thy service; for Jesus Christ's sake, Amen.'

l. 44: cf. 'O World invisible, we view thee', the opening line to 'The Kingdom of God', a devotional poem by Francis Thompson (1859–1907).

X

The final chorus of the play. Set in 1704, it follows the building of Wren's St Paul's Cathedral in the City of London.

l. 3 light ... hill: cf. 'Ye are the light of the world. A city that is set on an hill cannot be hid' (Matthew v. 14).

l. 7 the great snake: the Devil, combining his Biblical character of snake (see Genesis iii) and sea-monster (Job xli, 1).

l. 17: see note to IX, line 44.

l. 32: the altar lights are candles. When the sacrament is on the altar, then a sanctuary light is displayed as well.

ll. 37–8: in the final canto of Dante's *Paradiso* is a line which may have stimulated Eliot's 'submarine' image: 'che fe' Nettuno ammirar l'ombra d'Argo' ('which made Neptune wonder at the shadow of the Argo (passing over him)'). This is the translation used by Eliot in 'Dante' (1929) where he discusses the passage in which this line stands: 'Nowhere in poetry has experience so remote from ordinary experience been expressed so concretely, by a masterly use of that imagery of *light* [T.S.E.'s italics] which is the form of certain types of mystical experience.' Of the line itself, he remarks that he does not know 'anywhere in poetry more authentic sign of greatness than the power of association' here effected. Possibly, this was the achievement which Eliot was himself striving to emulate in this, his most considerable poetic contemplation of 'light'.

l. 51: cf.: 'we give thanks to thee for thy great glory' (Book of Common Prayer).

Appendix

The Composition of *The Waste Land*, 'The Hollow Men' and *Ash-Wednesday*

In approaching these three works, it may be helpful to remember that they were, in fact, assembled from individual poems or fragments of verse that Eliot had already published on their own, or kept by him in manuscript for several years (just as, Eliot said, 'Prufrock' was made up of 'several fragments', as was the sequence of 'Preludes'); and it was not until relatively late that he saw how these bits and pieces fitted together to make the poems we know today as single entities. In this light, we can see that the overall structure of these longer poems was a secondary matter which arose only after the individual sections were written. Eliot was then faced with the task of choice and arrangement, a course which can be followed through the bibliographical details set out here.

The earliest of the three, *The Waste Land*, published in October 1922, was part written and assembled during the previous twenty months, drawing upon materials dating from years earlier. Eliot had harboured the ambition to write a long poem since 1916–17. But he was weighed down by his wife's ill health, the 'great tragedy' of the war and his own personal situation. In November 1919, he was hoping 'to get started on a poem I have in mind' and on 18 December he told his mother that it was his New Year's resolution 'to write a long poem I have had on my mind for a long time', an ambition which eluded him through 1920 and much of 1921. In May of that year he was complaining that his 'private anxieties', his work at the bank, and the 'lack of *continuous* time ... breaks the concentration required for turning out a poem of any length'. But, by then, his 'long poem' was 'in mind' and 'partly on paper'. Among the material 'on paper' was what eventually became Section I; in July 1919, he had thought of offering this for publication as an independent poem (see *Composition*, page 138).

Following a breakdown, four weeks' enforced rest at Margate in October and November 1921 finally set the poem in motion. It was here that Eliot assembled the fragments of many years into some kind of sequence, of which he left a copy with Pound in Paris, on his way to Dr Vittoz's sanatorium in Switzerland. The remainder was added at Lausanne during the next month and Pound, over the course of several weeks, and with much discussion and correspondence with Eliot, was then able to perform his 'caesarean Operation', reducing the 'sprawling, chaotic poem' as Eliot later described it (although it was really an aggregation of drafts) 'to about half its size'. Pound suggested that material should be pruned; he indicated detailed verbal changes (reproduced in Valerie Eliot's edition); and in all this it seems that Eliot followed his friend's advice. More than that, Pound helped Eliot towards an understanding of the poem's unity. In January 1922 Eliot advised *The Dial* that it was a poem in 'four parts' which could be spread over 'four issues' of the magazine. Eliot was uncertain about Section IV, which he was ready to omit. But Pound was firm on this point (and helpfully interpretative): 'I DO advise keeping Phlebas. In fact I more'n advise. Phlebas is an integral part of the poem; the card pack introduces him, the drowned phoen. sailor, and he is needed ABSolootly where he is. Must stay in.' (The bizarre spelling is Pound's own personal style of emphasis, what Eliot called his 'Yankee dialect'). In the event, Eliot retained Phlebas.

Eliot's uncertainty is worth remarking on, for Section IV of *The Waste Land* was not, at the time, an original and new piece of verse; it was an English version (with some changes) of the last seven lines of 'Dans le Restaurant', a French poem he had written in 1918. And this is not the only part of *The Waste Land* to have been derived from earlier material. When Eliot showed the published version to his friend and fellow poet Conrad

Aiken, Aiken found himself reading a work some of which had been known to him since at least as far back as 1914. He recollected, years later: '. . . I had long been familiar with such passages as "A woman drew her long black hair out tight", which I had seen as poems, or part-poems in themselves. And now saw inserted into *The Waste Land* as into a mosaic' – an accurate recollection, as these lines are in Eliot's writing of about 1914 or even earlier. Aiken drew upon his private knowledge in reviewing *The Waste Land* in *New Republic* in February 1923. Knowing perfectly well that the work was an assembly of pieces written at different times, some of which Eliot had sent him for criticism, he commented disingenuously, 'One might assume that it originally consisted of a number of separate poems which have been telescoped – given a kind of forced unity . . . not perhaps all written at one time or with one aim, to which a spurious but happy sequence has been given.' We can consider the force of these remarks alongside Pound's comment, made in March 1922, that *The Waste Land* was 'a sequence of poems'. Eliot seems to have shared this view, with his proposal that the poem be spread over four issues of *The Dial*; and as late as September 1922 he suggested printing it in two instalments (Parts I and II in October 1922, Parts III, IV, V in January 1923) in *The Criterion*. As Donald Gallup put it, 'It was only Pound's "howling to high heaven that this was an outrage" that kept the poem from being split in this fashion in its original periodical appearances.' Subsequently, Eliot was staunch in defending its unity. In July 1923, when L. A. G. Strong asked him if he could include part of the poem in an anthology, Eliot replied that '*The Waste Land* is intended to form a whole, and I should not care to have anyone read *parts* of it . . .' That indeed was his intention. But the actual experience of assembling its component parts must have been fresh in his mind when, in the same year, in 'The Function of Criticism', he described the 'frightful toil' of composition, 'the labour of sifting, combining, constructing, expurging, correcting, testing . . .'

The composite nature of the other two poems was pointed out by Eliot himself. *Ash-Wednesday*, like 'The Hollow Men', 'originated out of separate poems ... Then gradually I came to see it as a sequence. That's one way in which my mind does seem to have worked throughout the years poetically – doing things separately and then seeing the possibility of fusing them together, altering them, and making a kind of whole of them.' These remarks, given at an interview in 1959, accord with the publishing history of 'The Hollow Men'. The poem, as we know it today, was first published in November 1925 in the volume *Poems 1909–1925*. But by then four of the five sections had already appeared in print: Section I (dated November 1924) in the periodical *Commerce*, Winter 1924, under the title 'Poème'; Sections II and IV in a group entitled 'Three Poems' in *The Criterion*, January 1925; Section III as one of 'Doris's Dream Songs' (1924). A version of 'The Hollow Men' (Sections I, II, and IV) was published in *The Dial*, March 1925. Later in the year came the final version, incorporating the already published Section III and the hitherto unpublished Section V. The process of assembling this poem may have been difficult for Eliot, since at least one section had its origins in materials left over from *The Waste Land*. The typescript of Part I (in the Eliot collection at the University of Texas) bears a note by Rayner Heppenstall: 'A typescript of Eliot's, given by him to Ottoline Morrell, and by her to me – about 1922.' Other *Waste Land* materials were used in *Marina* and *The Dry Salvages* (and we might note that, according to Eliot, *Burnt Norton* 'began with bits that had to be cut out of *Murder in the Cathedral*'); and *Sweeney Agonistes*, too, seems to have been a by-product of *The Waste Land*, and connected to 'The Hollow Men' also through the character of Doris, remembering that Section III first appeared as one of 'Doris's Dream Songs'.

It was the task of arranging the components of 'The Hollow Men' that seems to have caused particular difficulty. Eliot tried out several different combinations, drawing upon seven sections, before arriving at his final selection of five and establishing the order in which they now stand. But Eliot was also uncertain about the poem's unity. Whereas in July 1923 he had refused L. A. G. Strong's request for a section from *The Waste Land*, in

June 1925, when Strong made a similar request to anthologize Part I of 'The Hollow Men', Eliot agreed. So his sense of the wholeness of 'The Hollow Men' must have come late in the day. Likewise his confidence in the poem, as we can see in the questions he put to Pound when he sent him a copy late in October: 'Is it too bad to print? If not, can anything be done to it? Can it be cleaned up in any way? I feel I want something about this length (I–V) to end the volume [*Poems 1909–1925*] as post-Waste.'

The publishing history of *Ash-Wednesday* is similar. When the six sections were published together under the single title in 1930, three had been published before, as single, independent poems. Section II appeared in the *Saturday Review of Literature*, December 1927, under the title 'Salutation'; Section I in *Commerce*, Spring 1928, with the title 'Perch'io Non Spero'; and Section III in *Commerce*, Autumn 1929, entitled 'Som de L'Escalina'. Sections IV, V and VI, previously unpublished, were then added to complete the sequence.

The titles of the *Ash-Wednesday* sections, as separately published, provide some useful pointers. 'Salutation' (Section II), in its ordinary sense, is an apt title; but beyond the word's normal meaning Eliot had in mind a specific Dantean salutation, that in *Vita Nuova* iii, where the poet is greeted by the Lady 'with a salutation of such virtue that I thought then to see the world of blessedness'. The title 'Perch'io Non Spero' (Section I) is the opening words to a poem by Cavalcanti (see note to line 1), and Eliot used these words for his own first line, 'Because I do not hope'. 'Som de L'Escalina' (Section III) are the words addressed to Dante as he climbs the third section of stairway on the Mount of Purgatory, at the top of which – 'the topmost of the stair' is the Garden of Eden. The speaker is the Provençal poet Arnaut Daniel, consigned to Purgatory for lustfulness. The relevance of the Dante source (given in full on page 196, note to *The Waste Land*, line 427) is apparent in Eliot's references in this poem to the 'stair' and to sensual distractions, in lines 106–15.

The complete *Ash-Wednesday* was eventually published with

the sections numbered, not titled. But up to the last moment Eliot had retained a system of titles. These were noted by his friend and publisher Leonard Woolf, who saw a typescript. Sections I and III carried the titles they bore as separate poems. Section II had a different title – 'Jausen lo Jorn' – a phrase spoken by Arnaut Daniel in the same speech from which Eliot had taken the title for Section III; it is italicized here: 'And I see *with joy the day* for which I hope, before me.' (Eliot could have seen the words 'jauzen lo jorn' in Pound's 'Elizabethan Classicists', *Egoist*, November 1917). This change of title suggests that Eliot wanted to draw attention to the purgatorial aspect of the section. Section IV was headed 'Vestita di Color di Fiamma' ('clad in the colour of flame'), a phrase which occurs in the description of Beatrice (*Purgatorio* xxx, 33) at the Divine Pageant. This helps to identify the spiritual nature of the Lady in Eliot's poem and suggests the basis for the details in line 140. Section V was entitled 'La Sua Volontade' ('His Will'), taken from the line 'la sua volontade è nostra pace' ('His will is our peace') (*Paradiso* iii, 85; see page 234, note to line 214).

Why Eliot decided to strip the poem of these titles is an open question. He may have felt that the specific reference of these quotation-titles was unduly limiting and that the sequence would be better understood as a unit without the Dantean reminders. Whatever the reason, Eliot removed these literary sign-posts, so opening the poem to wider and freer interpretation (recent critics have taken the opportunity to suggest a strongly autobiographical dimension).

Given all this, we can understand why the connections between the separate sections of these three poems are not always easy to trace. There are thematic and associational links, and recurrent imagery. But the way in which these join the sections to form a single, coherent poem is not always clear. Indeed, we may well ask what kind of coherence and unity we are to look for. It is unlikely to be an intellectual scheme. As early as 1926 I. A. Richards took up this question, what he saw as 'the most characteristic feature of Mr Eliot's technique', describing his poetry as a 'music of ideas': 'like the musician's phrases', the ideas 'are arranged, not that they may tell us something, but that their effects in us may combine into a coherent whole of feeling and attitude ... They are there to be responded to, not to be pondered or worked out.' Richards ended his account with the observation that in *The Waste Land* and 'The Hollow Men' (*Ash-Wednesday* was then not yet published) 'the pretence of a continuous thread of associations is dropped'.

Writing of *Anabasis* (1930) by St-John Perse, a poem which he had translated (see headnote, page 236), Eliot commented that 'There is a logic of the imagination as well as a logic of concepts.' This holds true of his own poetry; and it is through the 'music of ideas' and the 'logic of the imagination' that the unity of these poems is likely to be discovered, an act of understanding that we have to take for ourselves and in which this *Guide* plays no further part.

Select Bibliography

Also see Sources, pages 39–41, for comments on Greene, Hastings, Hayward, Howarth, Jordan, Matthiessen, Stephenson and Williamson.

Ackroyd, Peter, *T. S. Eliot*, 1984

Brooks, Cleanth, *Modern Poetry and the Tradition*, 1948

Bush, Ronald, *The Genesis of Ezra Pound's Cantos*, 1976

Bush, Ronald, *T. S. Eliot: A Study in Character and Style*, 1984

Bush, Ronald, *T. S. Eliot: The Modernist in History*, 1991

Crawford, Robert, *The Savage and the City in the Work of T. S. Eliot*, 1987

Cuddy, Lois A., 'Eliot's Classicism: A Study in Allusional Method and Design', *T. S. Eliot Annual No. 1*, ed. Shyamal Bagchee, 1990

D'Ambrosio, Vinnie, *Eliot Possessed: T. S. Eliot and Fitzgerald's Rubaiyat*, 1989

Drew, Elizabeth, *T. S. Eliot, the Design of his Poetry*, 1949

Eliot, Valerie, *The Waste Land: a facsimile and transcript*, 1971

Eliot, Valerie, *The Letters of T. S. Eliot: Volume I 1898–1922*, 1988

Empson, William, *Argufying: Essays on Literature and Culture*, 1988, ed. John Haffenden

Frye, Northrop, *T. S. Eliot*, 1963

Gallup, Donald, *T. S. Eliot: A Bibliography*, rev. edition, 1969

Gardner, Helen, *The Art of T. S. Eliot*, 1949

Gardner, Helen, *The Composition of Four Quartets*, 1978

Gordon, Lyndall, *Eliot's Early Years*, 1977

Gordon, Lyndall, *Eliot's New Life*, 1988

Gray, Piers, *T. S. Eliot's Intellectual and Poetic Development 1909–1922*, 1982

Greene, E. J. H., *T. S. Eliot et la France*, Paris, 1951

Hargrove, Nancy Duval, *Landscape as Symbol in the Poetry of T. S. Eliot*, 1978

Hastings, Michael, *Tom and Viv*, 1984, new Introduction 1992

Hayward, John, notes in Leyris

Howarth, Herbert, *Notes on Some Figures Behind T. S. Eliot*, 1964.

Particularly valuable since Howarth corresponded with Eliot in the preparation of this book.

Jain, Manju, *T. S. Eliot and American Philosophy: The Harvard Years*, 1992

Jordan, Heather Bryant, *Notes and Queries*, December 1990

Kearns, Cleo McNelly, *T. S. Eliot and Indic Traditions: A Study of Poetry and Belief*, 1987

Kenner, Hugh, *The Invisible Poet: T. S. Eliot*, 1959

Kenner, Hugh, *The Pound Era*, 1971

Langbaum, Robert, *The Mysteries of Identity: A Theme in Modern Literature*, 1977

Leyris, Pierre, *Poèmes 1910–1930*, Paris, 1947

Litz, Walton, ed., *Eliot in His Time*, 1973

Manganiello, Dominic, *T. S. Eliot and Dante*, 1989

Matthiessen, F. O., and Barber, C. L., *The Achievement of T. S. Eliot: an essay on the nature of poetry*, 1935, enlarged edition 1958. This work has particular authority. Matthiessen was at Harvard when Eliot came in 1932–3 as Charles Eliot Norton Professor and he acknowledged 'the great benefit of conversation' with the poet during that period.

Mayer, John T., *T. S. Eliot's Silent Voices*, 1989. Especially valuable for its account of a manuscript notebook, containing poems as yet unpublished, which Eliot entitled 'The Complete Poems of T. S. Eliot', with the sub-title, added later, 'Inventions of the March Hare'.

Melchiori, Giorgi, *The Tightrope Walkers*, 1956

Moody, A. D., *Thomas Stearns Eliot, Poet*, 1979

Olney, James, ed., *T. S. Eliot: Essays from the 'Southern Review'*, 1988

Praz, Mario, 'T. S. Eliot and Dante', *Southern Review*, II, 4, 1937

Richards, I. A., *Principles of Literary Criticism*, second edition 1926, with Appendix B on Eliot's Poetry

Ricks, Christopher, *T. S. Eliot and Prejudice*, 1988

Riquelme, John Paul, *Harmony of Dissonances*, 1991

Robey, Kinley E., *Critical Essays on T. S. Eliot: The Sweeney Motif*, 1985

Sackton, A., *The T. S. Eliot Collection of the University of Texas at Austin*, 1975

Schwarz, Robert L, *Broken Images: A Study of The Waste Land*, 1988

Sigg, Eric, *The American T. S. Eliot: A Study of the Early Writings*, 1989

Smith, Grover, *T. S. Eliot's Poetry and Plays: a study in sources and meaning*, 1956, second edition 1974

Smith, Grover, *The Waste Land*, 1983

Stead, C. K., *The New Poetic: Yeats to Eliot*, 1964

Stephenson, Ethel M., *T. S. Eliot and the Lay Reader*, 1944

Sultan, Stanley, *Eliot, Joyce and Company*, 1987

Surette, Leon, *The Birth of Modernism: Ezra Pound, T. S. Eliot, W. B. Yeats and the Occult*, 1993

Tate, Allan, ed., *T. S. Eliot: The Man and his Work*, 1960

Tobin, D. N., *The Presence of the Past: T. S. Eliot's Victorian Inheritance*, 1983

Unger, Leonard, *T. S. Eliot: Movements and Patterns*, 1966

Vickery, John B., *The Literary Impact of The Golden Bough*, 1973

Ward, David, *T. S. Eliot Between Two Worlds*, 1973

Williamson, George, *A Reader's Guide to T. S. Eliot: a poem-by-poem analysis*, revised edition 1955

Williamson, H. R., *The Poetry of T. S. Eliot*, 1932

Symbolist Movement in Literature

light + rain — revivify